A JEWISH FAMILY IN GERMANY TODAY

Y. MICHAL BODEMANN

A Jewish Family in Germany Today

AN INTIMATE PORTRAIT

Duke University Press   Durham & London

2005

© 2005 Duke University Press

All rights reserved

Printed in the United States of America on acid-free paper ∞

Designed by C. H. Westmoreland

Typeset in Sabon by Keystone Typesetting, Inc.

Library of Congress Cataloging-in-Publication Data appear

on the last printed page of this book.

FOR THOMAS AND BEATE

At times, a breeze blows by,

delighting the heart and the mind. You do not know

what it is or why; it cannot be grasped. Similarly, when

the sefirah of Nothingness is aroused, it radiates and

sparkles and cannot be grasped at all.

— Zohar

Contents

Acknowledgments

My thanks are due to all the Kalmans, a remarkable and extraordinary family, for their openness and generosity, for taking me into their lives and spending so much time with me over the years, usually on more than one or two occasions. Without Dina, of course, this project could never even have begun, and Esther in particular arranged access to the other members of her family; I wish I could thank all the Kalmans more directly and by name. They have given me a great deal personally as well, and I hope they will find my rendition of their voices satisfactory.

The Social Science and Humanities Research Council of Canada provided much financial support, and numerous friends and colleagues have listened to my stories and travails and provided advice. Among these I would like to mention Steven Aschheim, Uri Ben-Eliezer, Michael Brenner, Avi Cordova, Natalie Zemon Davis, Norma Drimmer, Avishai Ehrlich, Micha Frajman, Haim Hazan, Dagmar Herzog, Hanna Herzog, Dana Hollander, Adriana Kemp, Anita Kugler, Ruth Mandel, Olga and Ernst Mannheimer, Gulie Ne'eman Arad, Jeffrey Peck, Diana Pinto, Ellen Presser, Minka Pradelski, Anson Rabinbach, Rachel Salamander, Frank Stern, Hella Stern, and Moshe Zuckermann. Among those who read and commented on the manuscript are Robin Griller and Denis Wall, my students in Toronto, and Jack Zipes, Sander Gilman, and Fredric Jameson; their help was invaluable, and the latter two played a pivotal and decisive role as the manuscript evolved — my deepest gratitude to them. M. and M. O., in loco parentis for so many years, taught me much of what I have come to know on the subject; their affection and kindness will never be forgotten. In recent years, Gökçeçiçek Yurdakul has not spared helpful criticism, love, and support when I needed it most.

Carla Rösler did an expert job with most of the interview transcriptions, and J. Reynolds Smith and Kate Lothman at Duke University Press gave me splendid counsel on how to turn a manuscript into this book.

A JEWISH FAMILY IN GERMANY TODAY

The Kalman Family of Slawkusz, Poland

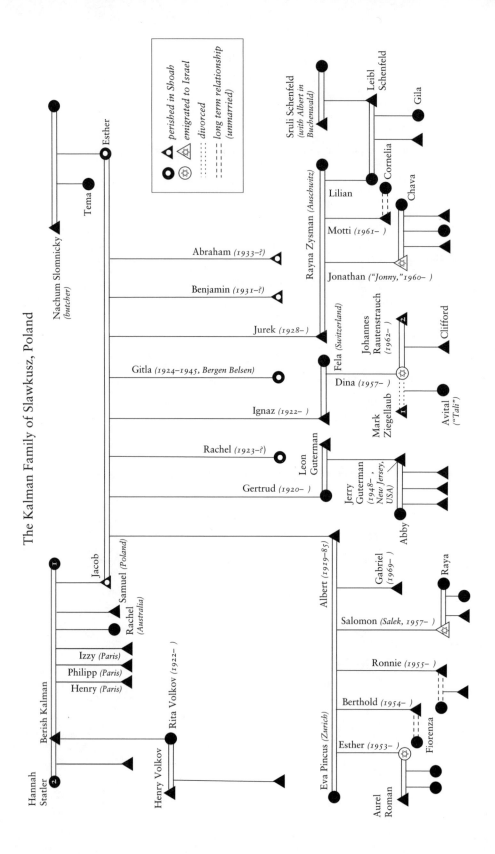

Introduction

This book tells the story of a Jewish family in Germany. It is a family of four siblings from Slawkusz in Polish Galizia who, out of a total of eight children, survived the Holocaust and the camps. In the Slawkusz Jewish community, the Kalmans[1] belonged to the respectable families and owned a fine house right in the main square. In the mid-nineteenth century, the Kalmans' ancestors were tradespeople, butchers on the grandfather's, and tailors on the grandmother's side. Toward the beginning of the twentieth century, we find them as store owners, with the state tobacco license on the grandfather's, and a leather goods store on the grandmother's side. Today, more distant cousins live in France, Canada, and Australia.

Why did they stay in the "land of Amalek," a foreign land to them with a foreign language, the land of the murderers of their wives or husbands, their parents, siblings, or children? The reasons ordinarily given invoke the early successes of some in the postwar West German economy, poor health that did not equip some for a strenuous life and climate in Palestine or in other countries, or the fact that they had met non-Jewish German spouses and were therefore prepared to stay. Other, psychological or psychoanalytic explanations include a desire for revenge on Germans, as in Rainer Werner Fassbinder's play *The City, Garbage and Death*, or affirming survival by direct confrontation with the German environment. In reality, their reasons for staying on are quite diffuse, weighted somewhat differently in each individual case. The most important reason for staying on was, ironically, their general intention to leave, staying in Germany just for another short period of time, the proverbial sitting on packed suitcases which makes the actual waiting for the right moment only easier.

One of the surviving four siblings who did leave Germany, Gertrud, had married a fellow survivor in the Displaced Persons' (DP) camp of Landsberg in Bavaria and left shortly thereafter with her husband for Brooklyn, New York. (The DPs were Jewish and non-Jewish refugees who at the end of World War II were left stranded mostly in the three occupied zones of western Germany.) Gertrud's three brothers, on the other hand, were stranded in southern Germany in the chaotic postwar years. These were the years of the Allied presence in the four occupied zones of Germany, with streams of refugees, DP camps of surviving Jews and non-Jews from Eastern Europe, the black market economy, West German currency reform, and the surviving Nazism in civil society in the newly founded Federal Republic.

Like so many others, the three Kalman brothers at first traded in a great variety of sought-after goods, closely associated with the U.S. forces in Bavaria. After some time, their various ventures evolved into a major kitchen appliances retail chain. From the early 1950s on, their business grew prodigiously.

The brothers married and had children, but they soon became entangled in protracted conflicts with each other. These conflicts appear to have gradually escalated in the mid-1960s. After many attempts at resolution, their problems with each other led to growing difficulties for the firm in the 1970s and brought about its downfall in 1984; Albert, one of the founding brothers, died a year later. In this sense, the firm was a child of the German economic miracle, rising with it and then disappearing later on. The conflicts among the brothers have left the family fractured to this day.

My account focuses primarily on the children of these four siblings who today live in Haifa, Jerusalem, and Tel Aviv and in cities in Germany and the United States. This post-war Jewish generation in Germany, to which the Kalman children belong, has begun to play an extraordinary role in the astonishing revival of Jewish life in Germany after the greatest Jewish disaster in modern times. This is a story that has largely been ignored by people in English-speaking countries. The story of the Kalmans will help us understand some of the issues and problems of Jewish life in contemporary Germany.

IN GERMANY AFTER THE SHOAH:
THE "MIRACLE" OF JEWISH REBIRTH

After 1945, only a few, perhaps between 5,000 and 10,000 of the old German Jews — a community of over 600,000 in 1933[2] — had survived or subsequently returned to Germany. Many of these had survived in mixed marriages and/or were highly assimilated in other ways. Victor Klemperer, a scholar of Romance languages, from a converted family and married to a Gentile, would fit that category, as would the writer Ralph Giordano, with a non-Jewish Italian father and a Jewish mother, classified by the Nazis as "Mischling," or of mixed race. The majority of Jews in postwar Germany, however, were Jews from Poland and elsewhere in Eastern Europe.

The story of the Kalmans, on the other hand, corresponds to the story of those 200,000 to 300,000 Jews stranded in Germany after the war, the so-called she'erit hapletah, or "remnant of the saved." The Kalmans' story is quite typical for those who arrived in Germany from the concentration camps or from hiding in the forests in Poland and the Ukraine. Like many other survivors, at least the more lucky ones, these surviving four siblings were reunited at the end of the war, and they belong to the minority of those 20,000 who, for various reasons, ended up staying in Germany.

There are a number of distinct periods that describe the Jewish existence in Germany after World War II. The first period runs from 1945 to about 1951. This is the time during which Jewish life in Germany came to be reconstituted piece by piece, with most of the 250,000 Jews stranded there at first gradually leaving, while another, far smaller number of Jews returned to Germany, not often with the intention of staying for long. It was a time in which Jewishness itself, turned into a racial category during Nazism, had to be newly, ethnoreligiously, defined — a major task for the postwar rabbinate, because often it was unclear who could be member of a congregation and who could not.

In the GDR — communist East Germany — most Jews who had returned were not at all interested in any traditionally Jewish, let alone religious, life. Most of them were socialist and secular and were hoping to build a democratic Germany and saw themselves as "antifascists." Only a small minority retained a religious orientation and were involved with the Jewish communities there. By 1952 and the time of the

Stalinist Slansky trials in most of Eastern Europe including the GDR, this community was decimated, losing much of its leadership when the anti-Semitic campaign forced many to flee the country. Those who remained were very largely a mere appendage of the party and the state.

In West Germany, a few years earlier, the Jewish community experienced a radical transformation as well. In what were then the western occupied zones, a political force field of allies surrounded the displaced Jews like a protective shield. It included the occupying powers, mostly the U.S. forces; American, international, and Jewish aid organizations, and also antifascist organizations such as the VVN (Union of Persecutees of the Nazi Regime). At that time, moreover, Jewry had a number of strong, charismatic leaders who represented the community quite effectively and who mediated between the disparate Jewish groups, especially the German Jews and those of Polish or other Eastern European background.

Within two or three years, this constellation was to change radically; first, by 1951, most of the DPs had left Germany for a new home in Palestine/Israel, the Americas, or Australia; with their departure, the Jewish and international aid organizations left Germany as well. Second, most of the Jewish leaders of the first hour in Germany had either emigrated or they had passed away, and with the Cold War rising on the horizon, antifascist groups with their strong contingent of communists and other antifascists became discredited, leaving the Jews in Germany with few if any German allies. And finally, now that West Germany was turned into an important Western ally directly at the Iron Curtain, the Americans in particular began to court the German government, abandoning much of their erstwhile role as guarantors of the Jews. Reduced to a very small group, Jews were left with two options: making overtures to German governments or withdrawing into their own little world, in isolation from the German environment.

In fact, during that second phase of Jewish life, from about 1951 to 1969, the Jews did both: the Jewish leadership threw itself at the shoulders of the German political authorities, while the rank and file withdrew into a cocoon, often with romantic fantasies about a life in Israel. The following two decades were nevertheless a time of administrative consolidation of the community and represented a disciplining process toward its members in what I describe as bureaucratic patronage. By that I mean that compliance was enforced by rewarding supporters of the leadership and penalizing dissidents and troublemakers. This took place in a context characterized by the persistence of Nazism in civil society, former Nazis in office, and Jewish functionaries' incessant and frustrating struggle over restitution payments.

The community began to change gradually during the 1960s, when West Germany took greater cognizance of crimes committed during Nazism. The decade opened with the Eichmann trial in Jerusalem; from 1963 onward, the Auschwitz trials took place in Frankfurt; apart from the drama in the courtroom, Germany's most important political and documentary theater developed in just these years: Martin Walser's *Eiche und Angora* (1962); Rolf Hochhuth's *The Deputy* (1963), Peter Weiss's *The Investigation* (1965), and Heinar Kipphart's *Joel Brand* (1965), among others. In these plays, however, German guilt was interpreted in universalistic terms, as crimes human beings commit against each other. Apart from that, the Six Day War in 1967 had an enormous impact on German attitudes toward Jews as well, and the end of the decade was marked by Willy Brandt's dramatic kneeling at the Warsaw Ghetto memorial. This, in turn, opened the way, a decade later, to the virtual explosion of memory after 1978.

The West Germans began to address the issue of the perpetrators and of German crimes against the Jews; later on, they turned from the perpetrators and began to address the victims, at least the Jewish ones. In this very period, especially during the 1970s, German Jewry in turn, in response to that new orientation toward the victims, passed into a third period, what I call the phase of representationism, of stagnating, atrophied institutional structures, combined with a great deal of demand on their representatives at public and state functions. Many young Jews at the time, however, rejected that type of life and left their parental homes for Israel. Ironically, then, while the community became weaker internally, its representatives were in ever greater demand. Jewish leaders' presence was sought after for local and national commemorative and other ceremonial political events, from Christian-Jewish dialogue in the annual "Brotherhood Week" in March all the way to accompanying German politicians on visits to Israel or the United States.

This period came to a close with the immigration of Jews from the former Soviet Union to Germany. That immigration began slowly at first, from the late 1970s onward, and turned into a tide after the Wende in 1989, the fall of the Berlin Wall. It opened the stage to a fourth period, which I will call the renascence period. This immigration, which quadrupled the size of German Jewry, set into motion the most incisive changes within the community since the late forties. The first of these is the massive influx itself. The pre-Wende influx brought Russian-speaking Jews, who arrived via a stay of a few years in Israel and had therefore become reacquainted with an "Israelized" version of Jewish culture. Those Russian Jews who came after 1989 arrived directly and as a rule therefore lacked that "Israeli" experience.

This new influx was greeted, at least at first, with less than full enthusiasm by the established community. The Jewish functionaries faced a huge new task, finding housing, schooling, and social assistance for the immigrants and also accommodating the newcomers within their own institutions in terms of synagogues, religious instruction, and cultural and social programs. There can be no question that this brought an infusion of new life. The old welfare machinery and bureaucracy, however, so characteristic of the community from its postwar beginnings, came to be reactivated as well.

Over the past fifteen years, most of the new Jewish immigrants have become settled in Germany and have taken control of their own affairs in the communities, often resisted by the previously existing hierarchies. Partly coincidental, partly catalyzed by the Russian influx, there have been other changes. In the times before the 1980s, the Einheitsgemeinden as parent organizations for the orthodox and sometimes liberal synagogues were, almost invariably, exclusive mens clubs, with regard to both synagogue life and community affairs. More recently, a new, educated generation of women has become highly visible in virtually all aspects of community life and especially in egalitarian forms of religious service. This has also given far greater prominence to the World Union for Progressive Judaism, which has returned to Germany with considerable presence.

The second important development in this regard is the emergence of a new generation of Jewish intellectuals, artists, and writers in Germany or writing in German, who in their outlook are markedly different from the transitional pre/post-Shoah generation epitomized by Wolfgang Hildesheimer, Paul Celan, Ilse Aichinger, and others. The younger ones — among them Jurek Becker, Barbara Honigmann, Maxim Biller, Salomon Korn, Esther Dischereit, and Michel Friedman — are, occasional protestations to the contrary, firmly embedded in German cultural life. Where someone like Rafael Seligmann asserts that he is a German Jew, acting as a columnist for several German papers, with frequent appearances on television, it is apparent that his place is in Germany, notwithstanding his particular Jewish and often distanced perspective; particular critical perspectives and perspectives from particular points of view, however, are not the purview of Jews alone and not a Jewish monopoly.

All these developments—Russian immigration, renascence of Jewish communal life, Jewish intellectuals finding their voice in Germany—express in one way or another what journalist Richard Chaim Schneider, in the title of one of his books on the new German Jewry, has called *Wir sind da*—We are here: a firm reassertion of Jewish life in Germany in full awareness of a terrible recent history. At the same time, while the influx of Jews after 1945 had created a community of (Holocaust) memory, the new Russian migration, often without the direct experience of the Shoah, might well represent a group without memory: a group with the experience of Russian anti-Semitism, but not of the Shoah itself—a group which sooner or later may overwhelm that "remnant of the saved," a remnant with memory. That by itself will have serious consequences for the national German discourse on Holocaust commemoration.

SOJOURNERS: THE JEWS WHO STAYED ON

Given their critical position in German Jewry, we return now to the Eastern European survivors, this group with memory who originally built the inner foundations of German Jewish life after the Holocaust in Germany. Those who remained in the land of Amalek.

In this sense, these Jews who stayed were no ordinary immigrants, no strangers who, in Georg Simmel's celebrated definition, "come today and stay tomorrow." They were, rather, sojourners, that is, strangers who came today and intended to leave tomorrow . . . but never did. This orientation of sojourning, congealed as a particular mentality, has shaped the behavior of this group and has produced its peculiar character. As they were not planning on settling down in Germany, or investing in elaborate, well-furnished homes to welcome and impress friends and neighbors, cultivating and investing in social relations with their environment which would need many years and much time to develop, they could focus their entire energy on two basic goals. The first was earning as much money as possible, in the shortest possible time, sometimes disregarding how disreputable some of their activities might have been in the eyes of their German environment. The black market at first, and gambling halls and night clubs later on, were among those activities. As will become apparent, the Kalman family did not enter into any of these disreputable activities.

One further characteristic objective of the DP community was to focus on easily transportable businesses, businesses that could be easily liquidated, as no one was planning to stay for an extended period of time. The objective had to be, therefore, to set up short-term, quick-return, higher-risk business ventures such as real estate and not ventures such as factories and agencies that needed to be built up over a longer period of time, with delayed rates of return. This pattern, however, at least in the later stages, does not fit the Kalmans, who ended up — possibly against their own designs — building a firm that was oriented toward long-term perspectives. It was, in fact, one of the few Jewish firms of this type; one other being that of Alexander Moksel, who set up a major meat-processing plant in southern Bavaria. Yet despite the atypicalness, the Kalmans still share with other former DPs a complete absorption in work, for they were entirely focused on the firm itself; stories invariably return to the ferocious, untiring working habits of the three brothers, especially in the early years. At the same time, they ignored the necessity — as became sorely apparent with the firm's demise — of cultivating relations with their German environment, especially the local political elite.

The Kalmans treated their own Jewish surroundings not very differently from their non-Jewish ones. Back in Poland, the Kalman family was steeped in Jewish tradition. The parents of the four siblings were still observant Jews of Hasidic background. In Germany, however, their religious commitment both inside and, even more so, outside the home diminished, and their commitment to their community and involvement with their congregations appears to have remained sporadic at best. This is entirely in keeping with the majority of Jews from the DP milieu, who, as a rule, were less religious than their parents and who saw not much use in building up local communities as they intended to leave Germany in the foreseeable future. As sojourners, they saw the communities they belonged to as temporary. Until the late 1980s and the massive influx of Russian Jews, this attitude found its expression in outwardly sterile communities and the typical one-man authoritarian leadership in most of the Gemeinden.

The second goal of these Jews was a total devotion to family, a characteristic of survivors living in Israel as well. Since they were not planning on "making it" in German society, they kept to themselves, minimizing contact with the German environment and remaining firmly anchored in their families. In the early years in particular, marriages and the birth rate were exceedingly high and contact with the outside world was limited to close circles of friends. Parents sent their children to Jewish winter and summer camps and preferably had them spend their free time after school with other Jewish children in the activities of the ZJD, the Zionist Youth organization in Germany.

While only some of the Kalman cousins became active in the ZJD, it is apparent that this organization had a profound influence on Jewish youth in Germany.[3] Whether the children were religious or not, the ZJD could serve as a common denominator for youth of a variety of persuasions, and it helped provide them with dignity, with rousing ideals and heroism, with an answer to the absurdities and the perceived degradations and shame of their and their parents' lives in Germany. This answer was to leave for Israel and a wholesome life without the agonizing contradictions encountered in Germany.

Not infrequently, then, some of these children eventually did what their parents were unable to accomplish: emigrate to Israel, "going on aliyah." Emigrating was an attractive option in particular in the 1950s and 1960s and diminished from the late 1970s onward. In the 1970s, a political climate developed in Germany that discovered the Holocaust as a public, national issue, made a new attempt at coming to grips with the Nazi past, and began to give greater recognition to the Jewish community in Germany itself. The case of the Kalmans supports this timeline. We see, for example, that four of the nine German-born cousins — Esther, Salek, Dina, and Jonny — left for Israel in the 1970s; only Salek returned to Germany soon, and, under somewhat more complex circumstances, left for Israel a second time, in 1989. By around that time, in 1988, Dina had returned to Germany from Israel after living there for eleven years, which leaves three of the altogether ten cousins in Israel today.

Those Jews of the younger generation, who chose to stay in Germany with their parents at that early time, far more than those born from the 1960s onward, can appropriately be described as transnationally oriented. Typically, they did not choose careers that would have tied them to Germany or to more intensive contact with Germans.

These careers include the fields of law, teaching, and social work — traditional Jewish occupations, but difficult to travel with. Of the nine German-born cousins of the Kalman families, for example, five chose business careers, one is a translator and interpreter, one a physician, and one a sculptor; one, Jonny, studied law in Israel and practices there. In Germany itself, not even one of the Kalmans decided to go into law, social work, or teaching.

As far as their family orientation is concerned, there are marked differences between those cousins living in Germany and those living in Israel and the United States. All four cousins living outside Germany are married and have children. Of the six cousins in Germany, however, only two are married and have children, a pattern that is not uncommon. It can be explained, on one hand, by the much higher value placed on family and children in both Israel and the United States than in Germany, and on the other by the reluctance to bring up children in Germany, the difficulty of finding a Jewish partner there, and the reluctance to marry a non-Jewish German.

Why have I focused on a Jewish family in Germany of Polish Jewish origin? The other groups that make up contemporary German Jewry are all significant in their own right. The descendants of the old German Jewry in Germany, albeit small in number, are of interest on account of their immediate relationship to their heritage and the prominent role of some of their intellectuals in German public life today.[4] The presence of Israelis in Germany is astonishing.[5] Last but not least, the Russian Jewish immigrants would be of interest — Germany, after Israel and the United States, has the third largest number of Russian Jews.[6] This latest migration in particular not only has quadrupled the size of the community but also has brought about, sociologically, its substantial transformation.

All these groups have, in fact, been written about in historical or sociological terms. What makes the "Polish" group particularly important, is that they, more than all the others, have shaped the inner foundations of the new German Jewry as it exists today. "Polish" is in quotation marks here because we have to speak, more accurately, about Jews from the milieu of the Displaced Persons camps, which also includes some Lithuanian, Czech, Hungarian, and Rumanian Jews. It is true, of course, that as a rule, in the early years especially, the leadership of Jewish Gemeinden (congregations) was largely in the hands of German Jews who had returned or survived somehow. Other German

Jews who returned, within or outside the formal Gemeinden, among them Max Horkheimer, Theodor Adorno, Wolfgang Hildesheimer, and Hilde Domin, faintly represented to Germans an imagined Jewish community of the past, irrevocably vanished. That was the glorious world of Albert Ballin, Sigmund Freud, and Henriette Herz, of Albert Einstein, of the Warburgs and the Feuchtwangers, of Max Liebermann, Rosa Luxemburg and other leaders of the labor movement, and numerous figures in academia and cultural life. The DP community alone, with few if any distinctive names, however, occupied the inner life, the old religious sites, and the religious calendar of these communities.

We can therefore speak of a division of labor: the minute German Jewish segment was in possession of the social and cultural capital with which they represented Jewry politically and culturally in Germany. They furnished legal expertise for example, Hendrik George van Dam, longtime secretary general of the newly founded Zentralrat der Juden in Deutschland (Central Council of Jews in Germany); masters of language, such as Karl Marx, journalist and editor of the *Allgemeine Wochenzeitung der Juden in Deutschland*; and skilled observers of German bureaucracy and German mentality, such as Werner Nachmann and Heinz Galinski, both longtime chairs of the Central Council and chairs also of their own local communities, in Baden and Berlin, respectively.

It is through these figures and their counterparts in other Gemeinden, from Munich, Stuttgart, and Frankfurt to Cologne, Hannover, and Hamburg, that, by way of what we might describe as "bureaucratic patronage," West German politicians funneled financial resources into individual communities. Those that were politically more amenable and cooperative were likely to be rewarded financially within bureaucracies — funding for a new synagogue, for example — and also received other political and social recognition. This same pattern applied to levels of hierarchy within the Jewish community as well: individuals who were cooperative were likely to be rewarded financially and politically or were socially reorganized.

Yet, despite the important and indeed critical role played by a score of Jews of German origin, they remained exceptions, virtuosos in the interstices of the German and the Jewish worlds. This holds true not only for the political but also for the intellectual leadership. The majority of German Jews did not return to postwar Germany, and those who did and who were usually highly assimilated would often merge with

German society invisibly, without leaving a distinctive Jewish trace. Those, however, whose attachment to Jewish tradition had remained strong, and who returned nevertheless, often returned with particular non-Jewish agendas. Some worked for international, mostly Jewish, aid agencies, or worked as restitution lawyers; others assumed high public profile as academics — for example, Hans Joachim Schoeps, Theodor Adorno, Max Horkheimer — or in political life — for example, Jeannette Wolff, Josef Neuberger, and Herbert Weichmann, the latter a former lord mayor of Hamburg.

This was also the pattern in East Germany, the GDR: the small number of Jews or individuals of Jewish origin who survived or settled there after the war were absorbed by their German environment, assuming public positions in the universities and in political and cultural life. Among their numbers were the philosopher Ernst Bloch, the professor of literature Hans Mayer, and the writers Anna Seghers, Stefan Heym, and Arnold Zweig, the latter returning from Haifa. Those on the other hand who identified strongly as Jews gradually withdrew into private niches.[7] Others who were able to do so, such as Hans Mayer and Ernst Bloch, moved to West Germany. The DP community in West Germany, by contrast, because of their self-definition as sojourners, people who as a community sealed themselves off from the outside world, were the ones who could, precisely by rejecting their non-Jewish surroundings, elaborate, in this cocoon, new Jewish communal infrastructures.

Not all of what characterizes the DP community in Germany at large, then, is true for the Kalman family members, in both the older and the younger generation. In Germany, at the present time, only one of the German-born Kalmans is in any way involved with the organized community. That person is Lilian, who is active in WIZO, the Womens' International Zionist Organization.

Could we at least argue that the Kalmans are in any way involved in the much-proclaimed Jewish revival in Germany?[8] Dina in H. is a translator from Hebrew; Motti, also in H., is a sculptor and occasional photographer in whose work Jewish themes do play a role. There is probably not more to report about other family members. None of that compares to Jerry Guterman's Jewish communal involvements, so characteristic, to be sure, of North American Jewish life, or Esther's work on behalf of the Israeli olim (new immigrants) and her activity on behalf of the German Jewish heritage. The younger Kalmans living in

Germany are therefore quite typical for the majority of the average Jewish community membership in Germany today (but see "A Note on Methods and on the Text" at the end of this introduction).

Any study such as this multiple portrait points back to its author, thus I have to live with it. My first encounter with the Kalmans, around 1990, was through Dina, daughter of Ignaz, one of the surviving Kalman siblings. We met at a big party. Dina had moved to Israel and returned, and when I met her I had recently returned from Israel. I was fascinated by her story. Subsequently, we met a number of times and Dina began to tell me more about her family. At some later point—I was on my way to Munich—Dina suggested that I stop in F. to meet her father. From there on I met some other members of her family, and a possible research project slowly began to evolve.

It was a time of crisis in my own family, and Dina's story and the story of the Kalmans may have resonated with me particularly strongly, drawing me ever closer to dealing with and thinking about this family in relation to my own. It is therefore undeniable that my own situation has also guided some of this research. Throughout most of my adult life, I have lived within the framework of a moderately intensive Jewish context, in a large extended family of my in-laws, between New York and Toronto, and I found the similarities and differences between my own family and the Kalman family intriguing. Remaining a stranger, and at the same time attempting to understand the family, I made myself, in my own imagination to some extent, a Kalman family member.

I am the hidden other in this family. The Kalmans have become "my" family: they answered my questions, using my vocabulary and phraseology before they ventured into their own, and probably orienting their account to who I am to them. I am a peculiar "other," however. I have tried to be loyal to everyone whose story is told here, but by being loyal to everyone, developing sympathy for everyone's position, I am also, arguably, betraying all of them. This portrait, therefore, despite their participation/complicity, is my portrait, it is a form of fiction. As the teller of the story, I have authority over it, but not over the real world. I am excluded from their ceremonies and family events, and I have constructed a family that in reality, at least after 1945, has ceased to exist, partly on account of the Shoah. My effort is an imaginary tikkun: mending a family that in reality can no longer be mended.

This book is my view of the Kalman family, my constructed account; in editing the tape transcripts I added some significant fictitious elements and changes in order to conceal identities or in order not to stir up bad feelings between family members. Often I had to condense and edit lengthy sections of interviews. Nevertheless, it goes without saying that I have attempted to render my interlocutors' accounts with utmost care, including the translation of their words into English. I would nevertheless not be surprised if on occasion some Kalmans would not recognize their voices in what they said, even though I have the tape transcriptions to back me up.

My construction and the possible inability of some family members to recognize themselves in this portrait begins when I say that this is my view of "them," of "the Kalmans," because "the Kalmans" may well be fictional themselves. If we think of them as an ordinary family in sustained contact with each other, then they are certainly not a family today. Some of the cousins have not been in touch in years or even decades; often, their relationship to other, non-Kalman relatives is far more intense. This is particularly true of Jurek's family — Jurek, as we will see shortly, is another of the surviving four siblings — where ties to the Zysman side, the mother's side, seem far more important. I might be justifiably accused, then, of mending or even creating an imaginary microcosm that has long been shattered. I am also aware that my presence in the family has helped establish, or reestablish, some ties, such as that between Esther and Jerry. I have been a communicative link between individuals, bringing them news about each other which otherwise they would not have received. The book itself might also reignite memories, good and bad. With the passing of time, however, I would hope that this book will help the members of the Kalman family bring about a better mutual understanding of the basis of their individual and collective predicaments.

THE GEOGRAPHY OF TIME

This is decidedly not another Holocaust book, as it is the portrait of Jews born and raised after the war. I made no attempt to have my interview partners dwell on the Holocaust. I have tried to react against the easy and all too simplistic explanation that the lives and behaviors of all Jews, and particularly those of children of survivors, can only be "truly" understood and explained through the Shoah. This book is a comprehensive look at one family and not, therefore, yet another study of the psychosocial consequences of the Shoah on the survivors and their children and grandchildren. I have never felt that focusing on one aspect of someone's life, and dissociating it from the rest, is a sound approach. Jews are also not the people of the Shoah but the people of the Covenant, of the Bible, of the land of Israel, the Diaspora, and so forth. On the other hand, the genocidal past can be neither denied nor ignored, not only for "survivors" — whatever that problematic category may mean — because "surviving Auschwitz" is different from surviving in hiding, being given a loving — or not so loving — home with foster parents, or leaving Germany before the slaughter really began. The historical fact of the Shoah is therefore embedded in particular discourses, but in fact it has affected individuals in very different ways. Since I am dealing holistically with one family here, I am also not "looking out" for ways in which the Shoah has impacted one family, but I will certainly examine carefully those issues in which the Shoah has imposed itself on the lives of these people: the Shoah is indeed an undeniable presence in their lives, sometimes to a greater, and sometimes to a lesser, degree.

This book, then, does not want to be about the Shoah, and even though I have attempted to keep that history at bay, it has persistently broken into the story nevertheless. It might be compared to a boat that has run onto a rock and has suffered a leak, a leak which its mechanics are trying to fix but which can never be fully repaired; a boat always in danger of sinking with its passengers. The Kalman children have found different solutions to the fact that as Jews they were raised in the land of the murderers of their family. Whether they live in Germany today, in Israel, or the United States, the Shoah is the foundation of their calendar, the beginning of their time. In their majority, six of these ten Jewish men and women, now mostly in their forties, have, albeit tenuously, accepted Germany as their home without seeing themselves necessarily as "Germans." This enters those living in Germany into a debate with their sometimes reproachful cousins living in Israel and the United States who cannot understand why they are living in Germany. It also, to a greater or lesser degree, pits them against their parents who, after all, decided to raise the children in Germany. Where I might have given less attention to the Shoah, they have certainly given attention to the question of these Jewish lives in Germany, and the ever-present question, "How can a Jew live in Germany after all that has happened?"

Striking here, with the importance of "time," is the near absence of "place" for the Kalmans. "Geography," as I will show in the case of Ignaz and his daughter Dina, is translated into "time."[9] For several generations at least, the Kalmans lived in Slawkusz and its environs, but there has been a total severance with their origins. Only Motti, the younger son of the youngest surviving sibling, visited the town once, with his parents, and on his way to Auschwitz, where his mother had been. This was the real purpose of the trip, a pilgrimage to the past of sorts. The time they spent in Slawkusz was minimal. Ronnie had stopped in Cracow once, at the airport, which is not far from Slawkusz, but he "did not feel well at all" and he did not know exactly where his family had lived, nor did he know where his family's home had been; nor did he make any effort to find it. No one else has made any effort to visit Slawkusz, although the family is known to others as being from there; Slawkusz has become a virtual family name rather than the name of a place. This is especially the case for other survivors of the Jewish community of Slawkusz who, like so many other East European Jews, refer to their town of origin, even creating memorial books. Israel, strongest for Esther and Jerry, is a state of consciousness; the United States for Jerry, another such state, a promised land: a promised being-in-time. No one has found a true home in Germany or much attachment to place (and it is at least a question whether Haifa or Jerusalem and New Jersey have become "home"). The Kalmans today lack what Benjamin Orlove has referred to as "heimishkait," Yiddish for "homeyness," which invokes place. Their principal anchor is their own family.[10] The Kalmans, for the most part, inhabit worlds sometimes different from their immediate surroundings. Cornelia, for example, remarked at one point that her partner Motti Kalman sometimes uses "expressions and ways of saying things that are totally strange" to her, expressions she has never heard elsewhere.

The late Albert and his widow Eva's beautiful home in F. behind huge gates in a cul-de-sac represents time, not a place-as-home: the time of youth, vacation time for the Israeli grandchildren, meeting time for in-laws and parents, and of get-togethers for Jewish holidays. The other locations have been transformed into time as well: the camps, the towns of F. and N., where they settled after the war, Munich, or the city of H. in the north of Germany where several family members live today. Belsen is a book about time for Berthold, and Jerry, the amateur paleontologist, has stored precious frozen time, fossils, in his glass cabinet in the living room together with his sons' orthodontic plaster casts.

This being-in-time is particularly striking in the case of Dina in her marriage to Johannes. Dina has pulled Johannes into her family's calendar, has moved him out of German space, the space of K., and into Jewish time. In turn, however, Dina has found, through Johannes, some measure of space, because she has begun to "understand that I belong here as well." This does not deny that the principal coordinates are coordinates, or geographies of time, not coordinates of place; moreover, Dina's and Johannes's time is a different time from that of their German environment.

Albert Hirschman has coined the celebrated triadic concept of "exit, voice, and loyalty." With that, he describes strategies in relation to changes in organizations: leaving the setting; giving voice, in the form of protest or criticism, for example; and remaining silently loyal to it.[11] Disengagement, withdrawal, is a fourth possible strategy, and, lastly, deviancy inside the setting could not be adequately subsumed under the earlier rubric of "voice." All five of these patterns describe behaviors of the Kalmans in the second generation and, indeed, the behaviors of the second generation of postwar German Jewry at large. The story of the Kalmans who have remained in Germany shows, however, that in spite of the past, and no matter how conflicted they may feel about it, the new German Jewry is in Germany to stay — and is the most dynamic Jewish community in Europe today.

THE COUSINS

As noted earlier, of the eight children of Jacob and Esther Kalman, four survived the Shoah. Albert, the eldest son, married Eva Pincus, from Switzerland; they had five children. Gertrud, the second oldest, met Leon Guterman in the Landsberg DP camp in Bavaria; they married and soon left for the United States, with their baby son Jerry. Ignaz, the second oldest son, married Fela, a Swiss woman, and they had one daughter, Dina. Jurek, who married Rayna Zysman, an Auschwitz survivor, has three children. Two of their sisters, in their late teens when the Nazis marched into Poland, did not survive, nor did their two youngest brothers, who were under ten years of age when they were killed.

Except for Jerry, all the cousins grew up together in F., in sometimes closer, sometimes looser contact with each other, depending largely on whether their respective parents were getting along with each other at

Albert's family

ALBERT	==	EVA
(b. 1919 in Poland,		(b. 1930 in Switzerland,
d. in F., 1985)		lives in F.)

ESTHER   *daughter*
(b. 1953, gallery owner, lives in Jerusalem, married, two daughters)

BERTHOLD   *son*
(b. 1954, businessman, lives in Bavaria)

RONNIE   *son*
(b. 1955, physician, lives near Munich)

SALEK   *son*
(b. 1957, fitness trainer, lives in Jerusalem, married two children)

GABRIEL   *son*
(b. 1969, businessman, lives in Bavaria)

the particular moment in time. Considerable detailed discussion of all these figures follows in the individual stories; a brief sketch of the families here will suffice.

Of all four of the Kalman families, Albert's family is clearly the strongest and the most robust. All the individual accounts, taken together, reveal that Albert, as the eldest sibling who to some extent dominated the rest of the family, was the most powerful figure of the four. He was the principal force behind the firm, and in sheer numbers, with five children, Eva and Albert's family has the strongest presence. With his extraordinary devotion to his children, Albert was also particularly single-minded and pursued his goals as he saw fit. He was probably not the best listener, which might have been one of the reasons behind the difficulties among the three brothers, and the difficulties faced by the firm.

I suspect that his eldest two children, Esther and Berthold, were the ones who identified with their father most strongly, pursuing two different aspects of Albert's character. Esther's Jewish and especially Zionist commitments made her — in her own mind — complete the voyage her father had begun, that is, going on aliyah. The fact that she has also become an independent businesswoman reflects the other element in her father's character, the devotion to business. It is noteworthy here that Esther had left Germany by the time the firm began its downward slide, and Gabriel, the other sibling in business for himself, was too young to fully grasp that decline. Ronnie, the physician, Salek, the athlete and fitness expert, and Gabriel, the media person and business-man, all reflect another apparent inclination of their father, a devotion to sports and fitness.

The inclination toward business is most clearly evidenced in Ber-thold's life. He not only considered himself as following his father's footsteps but throughout his career might also have been attempting to correct his father's strategic business mistakes. Those mistakes include Albert's detachment from his German environment. Berthold, on the other hand, stresses how well he is integrated with Germans socially and within his world of work. His total immersion in his world of work might also, however, help him to forget, to escape from history.

Indeed, the career paths of all three younger brothers might be seen as further responses to their father's life: Ronnie's turn to medicine can be seen as a reaction to his father's long illness; Salek's total devotion to an athletic and fitness career — at least in his own self-presentation — ap-pears to be a reaction to the physical humiliation of the Shoah; and Ga-briel's path in business unmistakably incorporated some of his father's sense of "daffka" (defiance) in relation to his surroundings. Gabriel himself has detected that defiance in his father's character, especially in face of his experience with Nazism: "to be standing on the hill, and to be staying there where in the final analysis one had won the struggle."

Moreover, Gabriel might also reflect some of the ambivalence, en-tailing affirmation and rejection, his father had felt in relation to other Jews. Gabriel, as we shall see, with his Jewish jokes, presents us with an ironic Judaism; on one hand he lampoons Germans' mythologizing of Jews (Germans typically portraying Jews as religious orthodox with kippa and tallit), yet at the same time he invites Germans to participate in his Jewishness — and here, he departs from his father and the rest of his family with the possible exception of his mother. Gabriel breaks through the wall of political correctness toward Jews in Germany; he is bold and subversive and carries his Jewishness openly, "standing up for it." If all goes well between Germans and Jews in the next decades, then

Ignaz, Fela, and Dina

IGNAZ == FELA
(b. 1923 in Poland) | (b. 1929 in Switzerland,
 | lives in F.)

DINA *daughter*
(b. 1957, lives in H.) [1] == MARK ZIEGELLAUB

AVITAL *daughter*

[2] == JOHANNES RAUTENSTRAUCH
└── CLIFFORD *son*

Gabriel's interesting approach, informed by his optimism, might exemplify a possible future path for German-Jewish coexistence.

Where does Eva Kalman, the mother of the five, fit into this? From the vantage point of the outsider who has not had a chance to observe the family together face to face and in greater depth, it appears that, throughout, she has remained the strong anchor. Most of all, and often in a stubborn and defensive manner, she has kept the family together; indeed, she is the strongest integrative element for all four families. Her daughter, Esther, has developed this character trait further and has elaborated it, following in her mother's footsteps.

Ignaz, Fela, and Dina

Whereas Albert was the dominant figure in the firm, Ignaz was his perennial challenger. Like Albert after liberation, Ignaz also had first struck out on his own; later on, the two pooled their resources, bringing their younger brother Jurek into the new firm as well. Ignaz's major contribution seems to have been his innovative ideas, his intellect, and his willingness to take risks — an essential ingredient in any business venture and without which the firm would never have achieved its stunning success. It is also noteworthy that the firm went from crisis to decline only when Ignaz had left it, in 1972; of course, this is not a complete explanation of the decline. Nevertheless, it is ironic that neither Albert nor Ignaz, following Ignaz's leaving the firm, were successful on their own; Ignaz had to weather catastrophic crises before his financial recuperation.

Of all of the dramatis personae in this story, Ignaz's wife Fela remains a shadow, a tragic woman depicted as having profound personality problems. She is uniformly blamed for much of the conflict in the family and for a range of other problems, and she could never get along with anyone. I experienced her as a silent figure in the background, in the kitchen, preparing a huge amount of lettuce, while I attempted to interview her husband Ignaz in the living room, a room decorated with oriental carpets and a big television, with an equally big office chair in front of it. Ignaz and Fela live extremely withdrawn lives, without apparent friends or close ties to other relatives. Their nephew Berthold describes them as a couple who, without even being aware of it today, have constructed a "virtual world," an "imaginary ghetto world" as their only reality. Dina, their daughter, vibrant and outgoing, has grown up in this virtual world, cut off from other family and with only an immensely strong relationship with her father, a continuum of deep love and resentment, and an element of rivalry with her mother Fela as well.

It stands to reason that, given her intense relationship with her father, and without much family life, Dina would put great emphasis on attempting to have a family of her own. At twenty-seven, in a new country, Israel, Dina married Mark, gave birth to Avital one year later, and a few years after her divorce from Mark, married Johannes, with whom she had a second child when she was forty-one. Why did Dina go on aliyah? For her, as for other young Jews, Germany was not a desirable environment. Dina had spent time in the ZJD, which prepared her emotionally and intellectually for a life in Israel. Israel was indeed the promised land that she adjusted to with great enthusiasm. But in Dina's case, not unlike Esther's, personal reasons having to do with an oppressive family and social environment in Germany, and the sense of a "lost youth," as Esther's mother had diagnosed it, were significant factors as well.

Unquestionably, Mark, Dina's first husband, played an important role in her life. Dina came from a home without books and with a father "without a language," as she put it; Mark brought her fully into Israeli life and at the same time stimulated her cultural, especially literary, interests that would shape some of Dina's later career as a translator.

With her marriage to Johannes, Dina has moved to some extent from Jewish time into German space. Today she realizes that she "belongs here [in Germany] as well." Johannes, in turn, has severed ties with his own family, deeply rooted in Catholic Rhineland, and has been drawn into Dina's time, her calendar. It is possible that their relationship could only be made to work because Johannes had detached himself from his very large family, as was apparent at their wedding, to which only few of his closest relatives were invited. It would have been difficult for Dina to be confronted, especially at her wedding, with Johannes's older relatives, given their complicity with Nazism. She also found the asymmetry between his large family and her small one disturbing. Both Dina and Johannes, then, are detached from their respective families: Dina on account of the disturbed family relations with her parents and aunts and uncles, and Johannes more out of free will, as a reaction to the oppressive family climate back home and especially the seemingly overwhelming role of his mother.

What makes Johannes's case interesting in the story of the Kalmans and to us is that, while other Kalmans have taken Jewish partners—typically men with non-Jewish women—Johannes is the first non-Jew to marry into the Kalman family. This in turn has underlined his separation from his family, which had been merely tentative earlier, after he left home to begin his studies; it is also a window onto the severe gap and ethnic rupture between Jews and Germans, even among those born in the late 1950s.

Even at a considerable distance from the time of the war, Jews, as the biographies of all of the Kalmans demonstrate, are not merely "Germans like you and me," as many well-meaning Germans today, including Joschka Fischer, would have it. They like to see German Jews as Germans with just that minor difference of religious faith. In Germany, however, Jews are constituted as a different ethnic group with different memory, and Germans cannot simply ignore their altogether different history over at least the past seventy years. For Dina, Johannes's reaction to the film *Schindler's List* turns therefore into a decisive criterion of a possible future together. This parallels Motti's, Dina's cousin's, experience of starting a relationship with Cornelia, who is also not Jewish, just after he was profoundly shaken by the anti-immigrant pogroms of Mölln, in 1992: Cornelia bought tickets for a musical in order to alleviate the pain Motti felt. It was a clear statement as to which side she was on, a decisive criterion that established their relationship across the German-Jewish divide. There is a profound gap between both groups in Germany which, I contend, justifies, even today, the distinction "Jews and Germans."

Jurek and Rayna's Family

The psychoanalyst Revital Ludewig-Kedmi has written of a "divided delegation" in families affected by the Shoah, especially in coping with this ambivalence vis-à-vis Germany. In a case study of a particular family, Ludewig-Kedmi describes how one son "receives the superego delegation" not to live on a mass grave, thereby becoming an Orthodox Jew and emigrating to Israel, whereas the family's second son "receives the 'forbidden' or id-related part of the delegation, lives well integrated in German society and becomes the 'German' in the family."[12] This approach posits the family as an independent organism which, for adaptive purposes, for "coping mechanisms," delegates tasks to its members. While this notion of family as an organicist entity is highly questionable, the idea that children might react to existential contradictions and ambivalences at home is plausible nevertheless. I have argued for the case of Albert and Eva's family that their children's careers and outlooks on life can be seen as expressions of a sometimes open, sometimes hidden or subconscious debate with other family members.

This would hold for Jurek and Rayna's three children as well and is articulated as such by Motti. As far as Jonathan, or Jonny, is concerned, his intensive engagement with the ZJD during his adolescence helped to set him onto a path of aliyah. He rebelled and subsequently settled down, in Haifa, suspended in Israeli time. Lilian, on the other hand, follows, as Motti puts it, a traditional path close to that of her parents, whereas Motti, in contrast to his brother Jonny, appears to us as the actual rebel who remains unsettled and settled at the same time: "something in me is at home here." Where his brother has buried, forgotten, his past, Motti remembers. Where Jonny submits to the well-charted path of German postwar Zionism, Motti, insisting on an uncharted path of Diaspora, is attempting to map his way through the geography of time. In what could be seen as a direct response to his brother, he insists on the autonomy of Jewish diasporic life, and also on Jewish autonomy against his German environment. Not unlike Gabriel, Motti has attempted to chart an original path in Jewish-German relations. In

Jurek and Rayna's family

JUREK   ==   RAYNA ZYSMAN
(b. 1928 in Poland)   (b. 1935 in Poland,
                        lives in F.)

JONATHAN *son*
(b. 1960, lawyer, lives in Haifa, two children == EVA)

MOTTI *son*
(b. 1961, artist, lives in H. == CORNELIA)

LILIAN *daughter*
(b. 1964, businesswoman, works in F., three children == LEIBL)

Albert Hirschman's terminology of exit, voice, and loyalty, then, Jonathan took the path of "exit," Lilian that of "loyalty," whereas Motti is distinctly "voice," explicitly so in his conception of a Holocaust memorial with its celebration of the multiple voices of the Jewish people.

Jerry Guterman

What is there to say, then, about the "American cousin," Jerry Guterman, the brilliant, highly successful financial analyst? His decision as to where his family should live was made for him when his parents took him as a small child to the United States. Jerry took the celebrated American path of the child of poor, working-class immigrants, in his case immigrants with an experience of the worst oppression and persecution. He went on through top colleges and universities to an extremely successful career as a chief financial analyst, first for major financial institutions, and then on his own, as an independent assets manager. As one who does not have family to speak of, Jerry married into a very big clan of upper-class Jews from Cincinnati, of nineteenth-century German origin.

All the Kalman cousins, the history of their parents notwithstanding, have been astonishingly successful. Not a single one could be termed a failure, and yet, only Jerry's story fits the mold of the success

Jerry Guterman family

LEON GUTERMAN == GERTRUD KALMAN
(b. 1916(?), worker,   (b. 1917, housewife)
retired, lives in Brooklyn)

JERRY *son*
(b. 1947 in Landsberg, financial analyst, lives in New Jersey,
married, three sons)

story, embedded into an American discourse of optimism, without self-doubt and without ambivalence. There can therefore be no better country than the United States, as the truly Promised Land. This puts Jerry into a peculiar position regarding Israel, one shared by so many American Jews: Israel as the little brother of America, the land of the second-class relatives and/or of the idealistic Jewish patriots. It is therefore the duty of American Jews to take care of it.

Jerry's relationship to his German and Israeli cousins is of a peculiar sort. Like Dina, he is a single child, and moreover at great geographic and cultural distance from the other nine. As we shall see, however, as an American citizen he sees himself on morally higher ground than his German cousins. Dina, for one, resents this ("American") air of superiority; other relatives, Jonny and his father Jurek, seem to admire it. At this distance from the rest of the family, and not being dependent on it, Jerry may see things about the family that the others do not see; he has a greater ability to judge. In his account, for example, Ignaz, not Albert, is the more central figure in the Kalman firm, which no doubt derives from Jerry's mother's closer ties to Ignaz than to Albert. Ignaz, after all, was also the one who tried a new life in Brooklyn before he went back to Germany.

MORAL ECONOMIES, MENTALITIES, AND MEMORY

What conclusions, then, shall we draw from all these individual accounts? Clearly, there is an entire range of observations and conclusions that can be made about Jewish life in postwar Germany, its orientations between religion and Zionism, family dynamics in general, the role and transmission of family memories, diasporic Jewish life today under conditions of "globalization," and numerous others.

Moral Economies

To me, as to some of the Kalman children, the conflict between the three brothers is particularly puzzling. Why would siblings who helped and saved each others' lives during the persecution, even built a prosperous business together, get into such intractable conflicts, thereby destroying what they had so successfully created? As is often the case, there is no single and easy answer. It has been suggested to me that this family is exceptional because the families that emerged from the Nazi genocide typically have developed extremely close relations in the subsequent decades. Children of other survivors have also pointed out to me, however, that bitter conflicts have indeed developed in numerous families, breaking them into smaller, yet very close factions. The Kalman case is therefore by no means unusual in that it combines tight family networks with intense and bitter antagonisms.

The Yiddish term often used in Germany is "broiges," from the Hebrew *b'rogatz*, "angrily" or "not on speaking terms," and the latter precisely characterizes the conflict between the three feuding families. One explanation might be the "all one's eggs in one basket" argument in a homemade ghetto: that such very intense relations, strong ties, and the high expectations associated with such might quickly turn sour and even bitter when those expectations are not being met, which is the weakness of strong ties. A second explanation might point to the extreme family disruption that had occurred under Nazism, which saw the deaths of both parents, uncles, and aunts, and the concurrent loss of parental authority that might have been able to mediate conflicts between children. It is telling, after all, that the three feuding brothers, in order to reestablish cooperative relations and in the absence of parental authority and mediation, decided to arrange a type of family court, bringing in their fathers-in-law to mediate. Finally, a third explanation points to the radically different moral economies of the war period and the civilian life after 1945. Relations during the Shoah were dominated by the constant risk of violent death that united all who were persecuted: being discovered by the ss, being selected to die or to be sent to harder and more dangerous types of work in the camps. The willingness to risk lives for each other, to share food in order to help the other survive or to alleviate each other's burden, points to a type of camaraderie not present in normal "civilian" life; the absolute, unquestioned, self-sacrificing commitment to others during the war ceded thereafter to a greater interest in one's own advantage, to negotiation and perhaps calculation.

Difficulties arise where elements of wartime morality are brought into civilian society. Where one person still expects radical commitment (as during the Shoah), the other is already oriented to civilian life and refuses such commitment. When one person points to how he or she had saved the life of the other and could therefore expect rewards in return now, the other will regard this as a form of blackmail and will point to the different reality now, compared to the time of danger. The total love and unquestioned solidarity that had existed previously is often felt to be absent later, an obvious source of friction.

Mentalities

Despite all the deep divisions between the four siblings and their children, their many different experiences and spatial separations notwithstanding, it is the similarities in habitus, or mentalities, that are astonishing. The term *habitus* was adopted from Max Weber by Pierre Bourdieu, and Bourdieu defined it, rather cumbersomely, as "systems of durable, transposable dispositions, structured structures predisposed to function as structuring structures, that is, as principles which generate and organise practices and representations that can be objectively adapted to their outcomes." At a later point, Bourdieu speaks of habitus as "embodied history, internalised as a second nature and so forgotten as history" and as the "active presence of the whole past of which it is the product."[13] When we speak of a collectivity, the term *mentality* somehow seems more appropriate, and I am using both here, roughly interchangeably.

The most obvious mentalities are dispositions that travel from parent to child; we find, for example, that Albert's interest in sports re-emerges, very pronouncedly in part, in all five of his children; similarly, of all ten cousins, eight are, like their parents and grandparents, self-employed. Politically, the majority are strongly oriented toward Israel, and, while not necessarily revisionist Zionists like their father or uncle

Albert, none of them has a noticeable inclination toward the Zionist left. In terms of domestic politics, they are, as far as I could detect, centrist; the majority of the German cousins might vote slightly left of center, which can be attributed to the fact that the Social Democratic Party or the Greens are less likely to harbor anti-Jewish members and voters compared to the parties on the right.

Another intriguing continuity across the generations is that of the Kalmans' attitude toward organized Judaism. An often-told story is that of Albert refusing to work for the Judenrat, following the advice of his father, Jacob. As a member of the Jewish elite in town, he was expected to join. As a consequence, that very Jewish elite, which also largely formed the Judenrat, put him on the very first local list for a transport to the camps. This experience, so the generally accepted story goes, made Albert, throughout his life, harbor a deeply ambivalent attitude toward Jewish organizations and even more generally toward other Jews. In short, not only Albert but his father as well remained at some distance from the organized Jewish community in their town, and his children (and most of their cousins as well) have followed that path and are not involved with Jewish organizations. The only exception here is Lilian, who works with WIZO, and Jerry Guterman in New Jersey, who is active in his congregation. It is true, of course, that the majority of Jewish community members in Germany are not involved with the Jewish community; the point here is the astonishing consistency on this issue for the family at large, among the German-born, third generation.

Memory and Forgetting

It has been argued that memory can only survive in the long run if it is given shelter within institutions. Institutional memory, accordingly, is recorded and survives whereas personal memory is oral and disappears.[14] The case of the Kalman family demonstrates, however, that memories of key events are indeed transmitted from one generation to the next, albeit in a variety of transformations. The story of the family members' survival in the concentration camp is told and retold by the children, surely also because it gives individual meaning to the broader story of the Holocaust.

In some ways, however, these family memories are remarkably at odds with the generalized Holocaust discourse today, on occasion described as a "simulated Holocaust."[15] They are also at odds with such acclaimed accounts as those by Primo Levi, Elie Wiesel, Jean Amery, Jorge Semprun, and Imre Kertesz. The prevailing, baffling motif in the Kalmans' accounts is that of instances where lives were saved, even of the kind people in the SS and the Nazi police. Jurek, for instance, repeatedly tells the story of Herr Oppermann, the German policeman, friend of the family of sorts, who ordered young Jurek to run across the soccer field to a lineup that saved his life. Jurek also tells the story of hiding with his brothers near? under? a pile of corpses in the childrens' camp at Buchenwald, and about the death march from the East and his empathy with the German peasants who "understandably" kept the marchers, the *Muselmanen* with their horrendous appearance and deadly diseases, out of their barns and stables. Likewise, Ignaz's account of his survival during Nazism and thereafter, told by him to his daughter Dina and granddaughter Tali, reads like a success story — not a story of devastation and horror. After the war, Ignaz volunteered to testify on behalf of the kind SS-Unterscharführer, lovingly nicknamed "Uschi," in court. (Uschi is contrasted to the "strict" Oberscharführer; but even he, on the death marches, proved to be "exemplary" in contrast to the other camp commandants elsewhere.) From these accounts, one sometimes wonders whether there were any evildoers at all.

For all three brothers, the past was not laid to rest in 1945; remarkably, however, not even one of the three appears ever to have thought in terms of revenge. Instead, each remembers the goodness of those who belonged to the group of their tormentors. After the war, Jurek went to Vienna to visit the policeman, Herr Oppermann, who saved his life. Albert spontaneously offered his wristwatch to a former guard in gratitude, and Ignaz was willing to testify on behalf of "Uschi." Other than that, when he is asked, Ignaz attests that the most important events in his life have nothing to do with the time of the Shoah or his experiences before the war. For him, the key experience was the period of the black market that established his postwar business career.

Much of this does not fit the ordinary narratives of the Holocaust that we normally see in the media and memorial museums. Among themselves, with other survivors from particular concentration camps, the survivor-parents are overheard telling anecdotes from time to time, and there is hearty laughter about some of these reminiscences. How is that possible in light of the overwhelming horror of the camps? Why are the escapes, the life-saving moments being remembered here while the horrendous deaths and executions are often not being talked about? (A notable exception is Gertrud, who sobbingly talks about her sister's death.) These reminiscences themselves, paradoxically, are a form of forgetting, drowning out the nightmarish routine of the camps with its humiliations, while at the same time conveying the illusion of agency, being able to determine one's fate, to the victims.

To the children, understandably, such expressions of benevolence are unacceptable. Esther is particularly appalled by her father's stance: "Is that possible? Is that what you have to say about the Holocaust?" For Esther and the others born after the war, the historical events have been rewritten into the general, public discourse of the "Holocaust"; the story they tell about the Holocaust is not their family's story, and these survivors' dissonant memories about goodness among evil, will, in the long run, probably be unassimilable and forgotten. As far as the postwar Jewish generation is concerned, the family's Polish past is, or at least appears to be, forgotten as well, with the exception of a few genealogical particulars. Erased from memory with it are also the relatives who were murdered, their names for the most part unknown. Is that in any way unusual? Other traumatic experiences in entirely different circumstances are forgotten, and only this forgetfulness, as Nietzsche has reminded us, makes survival possible.[16]

A NOTE ON METHODS AND ON THE TEXT

The question that might be raised here is, how can the case of just one family, the Kalmans, stand for an entire community, how could this family, in sociological jargon, be "representative" for German postwar Jewry? I respond to this in two ways. We could, first, take the portrayal of this family as a case study. As a case, it stands for many cases; this family is embedded in structures, socially and culturally, and as such it both conforms to, and deviates from, the universe of cases—it is, in sociological parlance, isomorphic and heteromorphic at the same time. Especially insofar as this family or its members deviate from some presumed statistical mean, we will hear about it: from the family members themselves who contrast their behavior and situation with that of others in similar circumstances, and from the outside world which judges or reacts in other ways to such presumed deviancy. From there, we would gain a broader understanding of that universe — in this case, contemporary German Jewry.

My second response would move away from a claim of representativeness altogether. I would prefer to see the family as a guide, in this case, to the German and Jewish worlds, including the immediate environment of the Kalman family itself. Such guides take us into their world(s), sometimes into open spaces, and sometimes into dark corners, illuminating them with flashlights here and with strong beams there. They let us meet and get to know their friends, the spaces and times they inhabit, and they let us encounter their adversaries and whomever else they might be meeting along the way. This is, to be sure, an entirely fragmentary image of Jewish life in Germany today, an image of a community that, moreover, evolves, is in flux, and by the time this book is published, will have moved further along. What it does offer is, to borrow Clifford Geertz's phrase and use it slightly differently, a "thick description" of a microcosm within the German Jewish community today.[17] The "thick description" that is presented here, then, is quite distinct from Weber's "ideal type:" "the construction of certain elements of reality into a logically precise conception."[18] Of these "constructions," or "technical aids," Weber said that "they enable us to see if, in particular traits or in their total character, the phenomena approximate one of our constructions." The question, then, is the degree to which historical phenomena approximate the theoretically constructed type. The ideal type lays bare the essential, skeletal features, or it presents a technical reconstruction of it, the essence of a phenomenon, but it lacks the flesh, the color of hair and of eyes and skin, the particular shape of the body itself.

What I am attempting to present here is a biographical portrait of a family in its *multiple* voices. It relates to the ideal typical construction somewhat in the way that the kernel of wheat does to the royal pastry and the story that goes with it. In that story, a man from the mountains lived simply, sowing the wheat and eating the kernels raw. One day, he came to the city where he was offered bread, hitherto unknown to him, and he learned that it was made of wheat. Later, he was offered a cake, made with oil, and he learned that it was made of wheat as well. Lastly, he was brought royal pastry, made with honey and oil. Again he was told that this pastry was made of wheat, too. He concluded therefore that he was the master of all of it, because he ate the essence of all of these, which was wheat. The story concludes, "Because of that view, he knew nothing of the delights of the world, they were lost to him. So it is with one who grasps the principle but does not know all those delectable delights deriving, diverging from that principle."[19]

Nevertheless, both the ideal type and the case study, or biographical portrait, have more in common than meets the eye. While the ideal type presents only the important features of a historical phenomenon, without incidentals and ramifications, both are, in fact, constructions. Pierre Bourdieu, in particular, has spoken of the "biographical illusion" in this regard.[20] The individual who presents his/her life story to the biographer does precisely that: telling a story, not giving a detailed chronological account. The story is eloquent in some aspects, and silent in others, and both subjects and their biographers, unequal couples with divergent and even contradictory interests, attempt to construct coherences and meaning, "telos," in the subject's life — such as, "In his/her childhood already, s/he had demonstrated that . . . ," or, "As so often in her life, she had to confront once again . . . "

The biographical portrait, then, not unlike the ideal type, constructs coherences, erases or minimizes contradictions, and establishes consistencies. Both can be seen, furthermore, as heuristic tools. The ideal type, characterized by conceptual precision, helps to identify the incidentals, "ramifications" of a continuum of more or less extreme empirical cases, in relation to the essential, logically reconstituted features of the ideal type itself. The case study — here the biographical portrait — while presenting a unique empirical case precisely with all its ramifications and idiosyncrasies, will guide us to the universe of analogous cases, helping us to ask the right questions and, most of all, because of all its "typical" and "atypical" features, helping us to understand variabilities of structures and processes into which this case is embedded. It is one thing to operate with an ideal typical construction of the seventeenth-century Puritan, the great heuristic value of which I shall not dispute; quite another to analyze the behavior of the individual Puritan and observe how s/he operates within the structure and the contingencies of his or her existence. The ideal type, in contrast, renounces the "delights of bread, cake, and royal pastry," settling for the wheat kernel instead.

The case at hand, however, neither is a mere individual case study nor does it fit the oral history or "biographical research" approach. It is, instead, a *multiple biographical portrait* which takes account of the ways in which those portrayed are linked to each other — here by kinship — and the ways within which they continue certain relations, be they negative or positive in nature. These relations are grounded in their collective historical experiences and in the experiences of those outside the immediate family (spouses' families, friends, associates at work) to whom they are linked. I describe it as a multiple portrait because it is (a) like a group portrait in art, a set of individuals portrayed simultaneously in relation to others; (b) those portrayals are coproductions: they are my portraits based on their own self-presentations as communicated to me; (c) as they have attempted to portray themselves, they are also participating with me in the portrayal of the other members (cousins, parents, siblings, etc.); and (d) particularly important perhaps, by means of the multiple portrait, key family events and issues appear repeatedly, in different variants. This approach, on one hand, eliminates the absolutism inherent in a single voice and relativizes it; the different voices, on the other hand, illuminate different aspects of the same story, thereby putting it on far more solid footing.

I might put it differently: we could see this concrete case of ten cousins as ten attributes of the same family; ten individual vessels that are connected to the same source; one beginning with ten different endings. Our multiple portrait, then, presents a few out of a wider range of options available to family members and it unravels reactions to their common origin and their common history. This militates against any form of determinism: the argument that a given set of external conditions could only bring about a given set of results. Instead, this approach emphasizes the contingencies, and the ways in which these reproduce, react to, and transform the structure into which they are embedded. More specifically, this approach belies the notion that Jews living in Germany today — even those with nearly identical socioeconomic and cultural origins — would all have to arrive at the same appraisal of their situation, with congruent identities. What is so astonishing is how these children, from the same sociocultural background, have built such diverse lives in Israel, Germany, and the United States.

In order to improve the flow and cohesiveness of the text, I have usually omitted my questions. They appear therefore only occasionally where their inclusion is imperative, marked with a Q. Sometimes I folded my questions into the narrator's account. On numerous occasions, one family member's story is interspersed with comments by another family member, or with that of an "observer." Their comments, in important ways, corroborated, supplemented, or contradicted the family member's story. The observers, on the other hand, normally had intimate knowledge of some aspects of the Kalmans' family life; they have not been further identified, except for Frau Neuffer and Frau Widmayer, the two women working in the Kalmans' firm. Some early interviews date back to the early 1990s; some other brief ones were conducted as late as 2003 or 2004. I have indicated the year of the interview whenever it seemed important.

NOTES

1 Some of these names have been changed to preserve anonymity. Similarly, the names of some cities appear only with an initial.

2 Concerning these figures, see Y. Michal Bodemann, *Jews, Germans, Memory: Reconstructions of Jewish Life in Germany* (Ann Arbor: University of Michigan Press, 1996), 19ff.

3 For rich portrayals of that milieu, see Micha Brumlik, *Kein Weg als Deutscher und Jude* (München: Luchterhand, 1996), 33 ff., and Martin Löw-Beer, "From Nowhere to Israel and Back," in Bodemann, *Jews, Germans, Memory*, 101–30. See also reminiscences of time spent with activities of the ZJD in Cilly Kugelmann and Hanno Loewy, *So einfach war das: Jüdische Kindheit und Jugend in Deutschland seit 1945* (Berlin: Jüdisches Museum Berlin/Dumont, 2002).

4 Issues related to this are addressed in Bodemann, *Jews, Germans, Memory*, and Anson Rabinbach and Jack Zipes, eds., *Germans and Jews since the Holocaust: The Changing Situation in West Germany* (New York: Holmes and Meier, 1986).

5 The only detailed, but overly impressionistic and factually often problematic, account is by Fania Oz-Salzberger, *Israelis in Berlin* (Frankfurt/Main: Jüdischer Verlag im Suhrkamp Verlag, 2001).

6 See Franziska Becker, *Ankommen in Deutschland: Einwanderungspolitik als biographische Erfahrung im Migrationsprozeß russischer Juden* (Berlin: Dietrich Reimer Verlag, 2001); and Barbara Dietz, "German and Jewish Migration from the Former Soviet Union to Germany: Background, Trends and Implications," *Journal of Ethnic and Migration Studies* 26.4: 635–52; Ruth Ellen Gruber, *Virtually Jewish: Reinventing Jewish Culture in Europe* (Berkeley: University of California Press, 2002).

7 As her title indicates, Ulrike Offenberg describes this phenomenon in *"Seid vorsichtig gegen die Machthaber": Die jüdischen Gemeinden in der SBZ und der DDR, 1945–1990* (Berlin: Aufbau Verlag, 1998).

8　See especially Sander L. Gilman and Karen Remmler, eds., *Reemerging Jewish Culture in Germany: Life and Literature since 1989* (New York: New York University Press, 1994).

9　On time and space in relation to the Shoah and Zionist discourses, Haim Hazan's observations are of note here. See his *Simulated Dreams: Israeli Youth and Virtual Zionism* (New York: Berghahn Books, 2001). I had been under the impression that the concept of the "geography of time," discussed further in part 2, was my own original contribution. But I have found that same formulation in the highly stimulating earlier study by Ammiel Alcalay, *After Jews and Arabs: Remaking Levantine Culture* (Minneapolis: University of Minnesota Press, 1993).

10　Benjamin Orlove, "Surfacings: Thoughts on Memory and the Ethnographer's Self," in Jonathan and Daniel Boyarin, eds., *Jews and Other Differences* (Minneapolis: University of Minnesota Press, 1997), 1–29.

11　Albert O. Hirschman, *Exit, Voice, and Loyalty: Responses to Decline in Firms, Organisations, and States* (Cambridge, Mass.: Harvard University Press, 1970).

12　Revital Ludewig-Kedmi, "Geteilte Delegation in Holocaust-Familien: Umgang mit der Ambivalenz gegenüber Deutschland," *System Familie* 11 (1998): 171–78.

13　Pierre Bourdieu, *The Logic of Practice* (Cambridge: Polity Press, 1990), 53, 56.

14　See especially Aleida and Jan Assmann and Christof Hardmeier, eds., *Schrift und Gedächtnis — Beiträge zur Archäologie der literarischen Kommunikation* (Muchen: W. Fink, 1983) and Aleida Assmann and Ute Frevert, *Geschichtsvergessenheit, Geschichtsversessenheit: Vom Umgang mit deutschen Vergangenheiten nach* (Stuttgart: DVA, 1965).

15　Hazan, *Simulated Dreams*, 35 ff.

16　See Yehuda Elkana, "In Favour of Forgetting," in *Ha'aretz*, 2 March 1988, 13 (cited in Hazan, *Simulated Dreams*, 55), who argued that memory of the Shoah can yield no positive lessons.

17　See Clifford Geertz, "Thick Description: Toward an Interpretive Theory of Cultures," in *The Interpretation of Cultures* (New York: Basic Books, 1973), 3–30.

18　H. H. Gerth and C. Wright Mills, *From Max Weber: Essays in Sociology* (New York: Oxford University Press, 1946), 59.

19　Daniel C. Matt, *The Essential Kabbalah: The Heart of Jewish Mysticism* (Edison, N.J.: Castle Books, 1997), 134.

20　Pierre Bourdieu, "L'illusion biographique," *Raisons pratiques, Sur la théorie de l'action* (Paris: Éd. du Seuil, 1994).

Rita Volkov

GREAT AUNT IN TORONTO

I had known for some years that the Kalmans had a relative living in Toronto, but it took some time to determine the correct spelling of her name and to find her telephone number. Rita Volkov is the daughter of the four Kalman siblings' grandfather Berish, but from his second marriage. That relationship was therefore at a greater distance, and Rita views the Kalmans from that distance. Rita, almost eighty when I met her, lives in a modern high-rise apartment near upper Bathurst, a heavily Jewish area in Toronto. She welcomed me most warmly and, when the interview was nearing its end, showed me family photographs and offered me cookies and tea. I in turn could give her news from the various relatives whom she had not seen in many years.

They were very talented people

RITA: I was born in 1922, so I am about the same age as Albert, Gertrud, and Ignaz. My father was Berish, he was their grandfather; they were children of Berish's first wife, and when Berish's son Yakov had children, I came into the world. I was from the second wife. Their father Yakov had a tobacco store in Slawkusz, and the second was a grocery store; and that niece of mine, Gertrud, was looking after that particular store. I remember like yesterday. Then they had the leather goods store. Albert went away once to Zakopane, it is in the Carpatian mountains where people used to go away in winter, skiing. So Albert went away once and he saw women's purses, they used to be painted in different colors, it was a beige background and they were patched in designs and on this patched design they used to paint flowers or scenery, and he decided they could produce that in their store in Slawkusz as well. They were so talented, all the children were sitting in that room, I remember, and they were all painting and designing and putting it together, binding and sewing it, manufacturing it. They were very talented people.

Much later when I was already married, after the war, Albert told Eva that he was in love with me back then in Slawkusz, but I could not marry him. His mother, Esther, went to a rabbi behind his back to ask him if I could marry Albert. And the rabbi said, I am an aunt, an aunt is like a mother, and in our religion, no way could he marry. Later when I visited them, I said to Eva, "Eva, forget it. You are married, I am married, we are happily married, don't think about it."

My father had a tailor shop in Slawkusz. He used to make the uniforms when they went underground, he used to supply to the miners. He lived there for years and years, all his children were born there, in Slawkusz, there was coal mines, and they lived from those people. They opened a grocery store and people came in and they shop for two weeks; they used to come and buy everything for the village. They used to buy on the book, meaning they came the fifteenth of the month, they got paid, so they came into the store and they paid. Came the first of the month, they got paid and they came in and paid. This is the way it was working.

Don't buy from the Jews

When Hitler came to power, we had the store, and do you know that we had to close up the store? In 1936, 1937 the Poles were standing outside and calling, "Don't buy from the Jews." They did not buy their food from us anymore. Then a Pole opened a grocery store and they started to go and buy there instead. So slowly we lived from whatever we had; I was too young to be involved, but I can see how my parents could only live from what they had accumulated. We still had some customers, but it was not like years before. Sometimes when I don't sleep, I'm talking to myself and I am talking to my son, always remember you have to have something to fall back on. That means, you always have to have some money, a capital or whatever, because I remember, we couldn't work, we couldn't have business, my mother used to sell all her jewelry for us to eat.

Then the Germans came, 1939, and we were all running from the Germans. We were separated from our father, and a few days later, we came back, and I said to my parents, where are we going? How far can we run? We cannot run to Russia. We can, but what we're gonna do there? So we came back home, my mother with my younger brother, and we found my father isn't here. My father used to wear a beard, he was a religious man. He had to separate. There was a bridge, and the men had to pass that bridge, and when the Germans saw these people, they threw them into the river; people did not know how to swim. So a day went by and another day, and my father wasn't back. And we were worrying, did not know what to think. All of a sudden, we heard somebody coming into the vestibule of our house in the front, and we always knew the way my father used to walk, you get used to the sound of a person, and I said, "I think Daddy is here." Now a man comes in, your height, my father was your height, but that man was without a beard. All your life you see a man with a beard, you sleep with him, you eat with him, you talk to him. All of a sudden a man comes in without a beard. The only thing — my mother and I were standing up — he was wearing a type of shirt that my father wore when he left the house, and we recognized the shirt and we both start crying, my mother cried, I cried, because he came home without a beard. Well, I said to my mother, who cares, so he's no beard, so what's the difference?

Go, *and this will save you*

He was lucky. They could have killed him. There were people killed because of their beard. Since then I used to shave him, and we lived there until 1941. Then we had to get out, leave everything behind and go to Szenuszice which was turned into a ghetto. And I had to work in Bendzin because I did not want to go to concentration camp. And on Friday, I used to get so lonely. So I took off my *Jude* armband, put it into my pocket. They were afraid somebody would recognize me, I was Jewish. I was blond. I did not look Jewish. I looked like a Gentile girl, blond hair, long. I went into the train, went home, to my parents, to be with them, Friday night and Saturday. Sunday morning I had to go back. They would not let me onto the train, so I walked back, back to work.

One day there was an Aussiedlung [evacuation] in Shenushitz. I came home and my father, that Berish, was praying and I say, and I say, come on, let's go. And he says, no my child, everything will be okay. So he took a page of his siddur and he gave it to me. And then he says, go, and this will save you. He believed that God will save them. How do they save them? That was 1943. And wherever I go, I always have that page with me. It's crumbling because it is so old. I never saw him again.

I would kiss him to death

I was working in Bendzin, and we had to go out of the ghetto to work, so we were traveling with the militz, the Jewish militz [ghetto police]. I return home because there was no room in the place. We were her husband, her daughter, her daughter-in-law, her baby, and myself. Can you imagine, in one room? So I just came in when I had to go to sleep. One night I came in and I see nobody in. Aussiedlung. I said to myself, that's it. At four o'clock in the morning, the Germans ripped open the door, and I did not say anything, I just went out, I see hundreds of people sitting, and there are lines made with chalk, four different spots. And they tell you where to go. You had no choice. These people were sitting there all night already, women with children, other people, for different squares, and I say, why am I sent here with women with children, I am only twenty, I am such a young woman. They were throwing a baby in the air and shooting it. I see my friend's mother and father coming out from a bunker and they put them on a wall and shot them.

It was a hot day in July. And we watched. And on one of the lines made with chalk, there was a German walking back and forth watching that we shouldn't jump from one side to the other. There was a young girl in a nice black coat, and she said, that's it, my friends, we are going to Auschwitz. And I'm afraid to look at the German, because I am afraid of contact with his eyes, when all of a sudden, he hit me right by the collar, by my coat, and throws me over to the other side. Do you believe me? He's throwing me to live. And if I could see that guy, I would find him. I would probably, I don't know, I would kiss him to death. Here I am to go to the Auschwitz, and here he goes and hits me by the collar and throws me over to the side. And I went to a work camp. There was a German that saved my life. In that moment, he threw me over the line and he gave me life.

They got sick from overeating

So I went to the Arbeitslager and lived through working, day in and day out, and this is through 1945, May 8, this was my liberation day. I did not know what to do. I was more hungry after the war because I couldn't know where to go, no money, no nothing, and go to a German house to beg, how could you? We were liberated by the Russians. I was so afraid of them, because they were animals, they weren't human. So I said to the other girl I was with for these two years, let's get out of here. We went to another house and there were people in that house from concentration camp that I knew, and we survived a few days, and we left again, and on the street I see somebody that I knew from Bendzin, and this was Henry, who got to be my husband for forty-five years. With him, we went to a house, a whole house with men, and they went to German houses and they took whatever they could, they ate, they drank, they were living too much of a good life, because they got sick from overeating. You eat like a wild dog and you get sick because your system is not used to it. Henry offered me a can of pears, but I said, I am not hungry, just give me two of them. I was really dying of hunger!

After a few days, Henry fell in love with me. I like him, too, he was fine. He offered to also take my friend, the girl, to the house and we started to have something to eat, and there were men, they were coming and taking and bringing, so of course I married my husband, my Henry, and my friend married his brother.

I have ten fingers, we can make a living, we can go anywhere

From 1945 to 1948, we lived in Weiden, in northern Bavaria. In 1945 I found out that my niece and nephews, Albert and Gertrud and Ignaz and Jurek, were alive, so they came to my place from Landsberg. Jurek still was a young child, but Albert was the everything, he was the builder of whatever they achieved, he was a smart chap, and Ignaz always had an imagination. They were very rich people. They had the biggest kitchenware store in Munich and they had so many stores. Ignaz had an imagination, but they would not listen to him. They were always against him, the youngest and the oldest against Ignaz. But you know, I said to them, leave me out of it. My husband talked to them and said they should work together because once they won't work together, everything will fall apart. Albert had ideas of building on land somewhere in the city, everything in Germany. I said, get out of Germany. You made money, you enjoy life, get out of there. I said to my husband, I don't want my child to grow up in Germany. That earth is all full of Jewish blood.

We had twenty dollars in our pocket, I came to Canada, I have ten fingers, you have ten fingers, we can make a living, we can go anywhere.

1

Albert's

Family

Berthold

and His Father

1950	Albert builds house with hotel in F.
1952	Albert and Eva marry in F.
1954	Berthold born in F.
1967	family moves from the hotel to a new house
1960s	family arbitration panel set up
1970	Kalman firm at its peak: 81 stores
1975	Ignaz leaves Kalman firm
1975	Albert increasingly ill; first heart attack
1977–78	Berthold fully involved in Kalman firm
1978	Berthold completes his studies, diploma.
1978	Jurek leaves firm; Albert's family now sole owners
1983	Kalman firm in difficulties; Berthold arrested; house is searched
1984	Kalman firm in receivership
1985	Albert Kalman dies

No one would deny that in the Kalman family, Albert, the eldest of the four surviving siblings from Slawkusz, was the family's towering figure, "der Motor der Familie," the "family engine," as his son Berthold put it. Without him, there would never have been a Kalman Haushalts-geräte, and without him, the three brothers would never have come together in a single firm. Albert died in 1985, and all we can do to lend him voice is to try to reconstruct some aspects of his biography from how the rest of his family perceive him and his life's work, the Kalman firm. In the best position to do this next to his widow, Eva, is his eldest son, Berthold. Like virtually all the Kalman children, Berthold helped out in the firm as a youngster; however, he was the only one to work in the firm full time after completing his studies, and he was also the family member who attended to the firm until the bitter end. It is Berthold who provided the most detail about his father's life and family background. Where necessary, observations made by other family members will be added to Berthold's story. We met for the interview in an open air cafe in Munich's Schwabing district.

BERTHOLD: Let me try to pull this together somehow. My father was the eldest of eight children. He was a Zionist, and the way the Zionists were at the time, he was a follower of Jabotinski, he actually still knew him personally. About my grandparents, there are a couple of stories. The grandparents were Hasids, that was a very pious family, very pious. My father was member of Betar, and he knew all those things. My father was a bit of a revolutionary. In Betar, he was not that religious, but he had gone to a yeshiva, I believe he even wore peyes, it really was a strictly religious Jewish family. But as I said, my father was a bit of a revolutionary and he went to Zakopane in the Tatra mountains to go skiing. For a Jew at that time, before the war, that was exceptional, nobody was allowed to know that, he also ate treife there. He always told me, the best thing they had there was sauerkraut with smoked bacon. If someone had found out about that [laughs], I cannot imagine what a scandal this would have caused in his family. Also, his father sawed his skis in half twice. Because a Jew was not supposed to go to sports activities in Zakopane, to all these goyim and treife food and so on. That's how my father was at the time.

Eventually, my father's Zionist commitment brought about a conflict that had a decisive influence on his life. As I said, he was in Betar, and it got to the point, especially with all the preparations — he was madrich and so on — where he was selected, before the war, to go on aliyah, to Israel. And he kept telling his parents about that, he said, he was going to go to Israel. So the day arrived when he was to leave. And this is how Jewish life happens, Jewish fate: his mother started saying, if you leave us, you will kill us, and if you go, your mother will die. I am sure you know all those emotional assaults and blackmail. So he stayed home, and the result was that sometime thereafter, he ended up in a concentration camp.

EVA: He had an incredible love for his mother; he wanted to emigrate to Palestine, and thought of his mother so often and how he had to leave her. He was in Betar. And he went through everything, all the training, everything, and his mother — she must have been a very smart woman — she let him do it all. When it came to the point where he was supposed to leave for Palestine, in 1937 or 1938, she apparently said, and I can only quote what Albert told me, "If you do that, then I am going to throw myself out of the window." So he gave in and he did not leave. Later, when he ended up in the concentration camp, he said to himself, yes, yes, she did not allow me to go. And now I have landed here. For four and one-half years, my husband was in the concentration camp, he was one of the first they picked up. A concentration camp can change a person, a person's character.

BERTHOLD: My father was somehow involved in Jewish community affairs in Slawkusz, people wanted him to be elected to the so-called Judenrat in order for him to help compile the lists that would get other people picked up and sent onto the transports. At the same time, they promised that nothing would happen to him and his family. This my father did not do. He refused to compile the lists and so on, and so it happened that he was the first one in the area to be arrested and sent to the camp. My father said this was unusual because at the beginning they picked up only the very poorest and the social misfits, beggars and peddlers, a big group in Poland at the time.

But my father came from a well-to-do and respected family, they owned houses and a tobacco wholesale company, very respected and well-to-do people. Normally people from these groups were arrested and deported only much later. Despite all of that, he was one of the first to go, because of his refusal to enter the Judenrat. My father was therefore already in the concentration camp before 1940. What I don't know is when Jurek and my father's other siblings were picked up and when his parents got there, I don't know that, nor did he remember that.

EVA: We know little about my husband's time in the camps. Only in later years did he speak about how he was picked up. He did not want to talk about it. It was only when the children began to ask, around the time they were in school, he began to talk, very slowly and he did not like to talk about it. Only when he got together with some people, for example with the elder Schenfeld, the father, because with him he was in the camp. Then they started talking, "Do you remember when . . ." and so on. But with me personally and on his own initiative he did not like to talk. With Schenfeld they even laughed at times. "Do you remember what I did then? And then, remember, you had . . . , and I told you, No! and because you did that, I did not give you . . ." It was a communication into the laughable. Laughing, yes, but later, when the children began to ask, he started talking, but then it got to be serious. With tears, too. I really almost could not understand what a human being could suffer there, how a person could bear that.

BERTHOLD: There are very few stories that my father told from the camp. He told a couple of stories about where he had to work, in some clay pits, in winter without shoes and in water and so on, about all this forced labor, and he also spoke about beatings. Once in a while, he also talked about people helping him, guards, peasants, outsiders who slipped him a piece of bread or hid some bread for him somewhere, so he talked about these things, too. These things were important to him, I believe. That there were people who helped him. I believe my father was someone who could negotiate much by communicating. He also had some charisma and he was a skilled negotiator. That helped him a great deal at that time, saving himself by communicating. More than once he succeeded in saving himself and probably Ignaz as well.

As far as people helping him is concerned, he also told me a story once about the time after the war. Once he met an SS man in F., it was after the war. He urgently wanted to speak to him because, he said, this was an SS man who was okay I mean, I cannot imagine an SS man who was okay because they did not simply get into the SS by accident. But for him, this SS man was okay, he wanted to speak to him and perhaps help him.

I know that in 1941 Albert met his brother Ignaz in a labor camp. I know the story from how my father has told it, but Jurek might tell the story differently. I don't know what is right, because my father never told us the terrible things about that whole concentration camp business. He did not want to burden us with that. He only told us a couple of things where you can say, oh, well, sometimes you can also laugh about it. The terrible things he had buried before himself, he was pretty good at this process of repression. My father, as far as I know, worked in the carpentry shop in Buchenwald. Ignaz had been there already, and Jurek was there as well, I don't remember the sequence. It was an accident, at any rate, that all three of them met in Buchenwald. Earlier, my father and Ignaz were together in another camp, working at different ends of a rail line or road. It was a labor camp, and my father found out that his brother was working on the opposite end, so he tried to arrange it such that they could be together. Later, I believe, they ended up on a march to Buchenwald, and there they met Jurek.

At the time, Jurek was in the Buchenwald Kinderlager, and according to Jurek, he smuggled his two older brothers into the Kinderlager where they were hiding out underneath corpses, so they did not have to go on a death march. Buchenwald was being evacuated at the time, and one of my father's close friends, Schenfeld, whom you probably know, was sent on the march. My father, Jurek, and Ignaz were liberated by the Americans. The only reason they survived was because during the evacuation of the camp, they were hiding in this mountain of corpses, and so they were left there. Jurek also talks about how they were hiding out in some attic, but they were caught and then hid with the dead. And many stories before that one. Of the entire family, my father was the first one to end up in concentration camp.

THE BEGINNINGS OF KALMAN HAUSHALTSGERÄTE (HOUSEHOLD APPLIANCES)

They came crawling out of every hole and bought mattresses

BERTHOLD: So he survived after all, and after liberation, the three brothers and one sister ended up in the Landsberg DP camp. Not long thereafter, my father moved first to N. and then to F. I cannot even tell you why. Maybe he did not know that himself. N. was pretty badly hit by Allied bombing, so he ended up in nearby F. He wanted to go on to the U.S., right after the war, but that did not happen for some bureaucratic reasons. Evidently, he got entangled with something or other. It was the black market period, and he got caught, so he did not get a card, a visa. He wanted to emigrate. Ignaz, a few years later, went to the U.S., but he only stayed for a year and then came back. He had planned to emigrate. But then he would not have met my mother and so on and so forth, and the story would have gone very differently.

So let me describe to you how the Kalman firm developed. First, there were these three brothers. And this is probably a subjective account, because from one's own experience you will not get complete objectivity, even though today, after a distance of so many years, one can see things in part differently as well. There were these three brothers who started with different businesses. My father began in car sales, then he slowly slipped into the household appliances field; he bought used equipment in bulk from the Americans. At the time and from military supplies, you could make bids on wall to wall carpeting, fridges, cabinets, and God knows what. This is how the appliances business began. Ignaz he had with him, and they did everything together. At some point, when I don't know, they also took in Jurek, who until then was working a little in the textile area. Then they founded the Kalman firm, they bought a large piece of property, my father bought that also on behalf of his brothers, because he always included them. Maybe he did all this for reasons of, let's say, family welfare, because he was the eldest brother and because the parents were no longer there. He always brought his brothers into his business activities, he tied them in even where these were private affairs that had nothing to do with Kalman Appliances.

Somewhere, they bought a large piece of land near F. and he got his brothers into the deal even though they did not even want it. Yes, it was a favor to them. It was out of a sense of duty for the welfare of the family which he perhaps could not relinquish. He might not even have wanted his brothers there, but he felt this duty of caring for the family.

The firm — this was in the time of the economic miracle in Germany — grew in leaps and bounds, and very quickly, they had over seventy stores in Germany, from Garmisch to Kassel; it was a major firm then, with over seven or eight hundred employees, and after some time, they began to argue. In the 1950s, there were still real sales, you did not even sell, you distributed. The demand in Germany then was greater than the commodity supply. They said then, "Today we are selling mattresses," and people came crawling out of every hole and bought mattresses. The goods were not even unloaded often: a truck drove up, they pulled back the tarp, they said, "Today we have mattresses," and they sold them from the truck. And they were gone, finished. Out of that, the stores developed. In the early years they were not even real stores, more garages or storage facilities, not a store with a glass window. All this was built into a network of branches for retail. Those seventy stores opened and closed irregularly and so on, but later they were consolidated and ended up being perhaps forty stores, a real retail system with normal daily opening hours.

The business and family life were closely intertwined. My parents married in 1952, my father was thirty-three years old then. They lived in the hotel my father built in 1950; he was surely one of the very first people in F. who built a house after the war. I'd say this really indicates that they were settling down. First, they set up a hotel with my mother as the manager.

JUREK: The hotel must have been built around 1949–50. The house was bombed during the war, it was a ruin. It belonged to a Jewish family before. The previous owners in America were contacted, and it was bought somehow or other; I cannot tell you the details; they were Jewish owners who had lived in F. before the war and who subsequently emigrated to America.

BERTHOLD: My father was involved in entirely different business activities. It was a house that could be used as a hotel, and we moved into the house. Later it was turned into apartments pure and simple. So at first we lived in the hotel, but in the late 1950s, they gave it up because my mother did not want to manage that anymore. The house was turned into a complex of apartments and we lived on one entire floor. On the ground floor was a store of Kalman Appliances.

Until the mid-fifties, before they got married, my father's two brothers were part of our household. At the lunch table, it was us children with my parents and the two uncles. My mother stayed completely out of the Kalman business. There was talk about it at lunch, of course, and very early on we were all confronted with the business. We are, from the bottom, an entrepreneurial family, including all of my siblings, and we had this expression, "He must know that, because he sat at the Kalman's table," meaning the table at lunch. We always ate lunch at home, and for my father as well, this was such an important issue that at lunch time, he would have his family together. And so, business matters were raised then, which means that early on, we learned about all the issues; we knew about the arguments with my uncles early on. We also knew about future developments, what should and what should not be done, we knew all about that.

EVA: Lunch was one thing, but breakfast was another. My husband rose very early, at 4:30 or five. He made a cup of coffee for himself, Nescafe and left. Then at 8:30 he came back home again for breakfast, to have breakfast just with me. That was very important for him, having a relaxed breakfast with me. I'll show you the breakfast room, where we used to sit and where we had the time to talk, for half an hour.

ALBERT AND HIS JEWISH ENVIRONMENT

A deep distrust of Jewish institutions

BERTHOLD: My father was not only generous to us in the family; he was also a generous man in the firm and he had a social commitment especially for destitute people in the Jewish community. Occasionally, he initiated something, he was socially conscious and when he could help someone, he did help him, giving him money and helping him with a job, especially when the Gemeinde did not do that. So with that he did have a certain role. He felt responsible for Jewish people in F. This was a commitment, a Jewish commitment, but not within a political structure.

EVA: My husband's major social commitment had to do with Israel. We had an employee in the firm who used to be with the French Foreign Legion. A goy. My husband came to the office one day, he was very depressed, it was the war, the Six Day War, a catastrophe. But that man told my husband, I believe his name was Ebenhofer, "Herr Kalman, don't you worry, nothing is going to happen. I know both sides and how they fight, I was in the Foreign Legion," and so on. That is what he said, "I know how the Israelis fight. Don't you worry." Then all of a sudden, my husband is back home, "Imagine what Ebenhofer has said . . . ," so he was all happy. But he suffered a lot, he suffered because of Entebbe, he listened to the news, he suffered at the time of the Yom Kippur War, but he never wanted to emigrate to Israel. When he was ill he told me in an aside, "I don't want to be buried here. Not here." That is all he said, this sentence. I don't want to be buried here. He did not say, "I want to be buried in Israel," but I understood, Israel. Esther had been married in Israel by then and that was quite okay with him.

BERTHOLD: He also started the Jewish Sports Club, Makkabi F., but without much success, there was no foundation, no critical mass there for it. If you don't have ten guys, you cannot set up a soccer team of eleven people. So when there is no foundation, you can forget it. But at least it was an initiative and he tried. At the same time, he harbored a deep distrust of Jewish institutions, dating from his time in Slawkusz. He had this negative attitude because of the story with the Judenrat, because it was the Judenrat that had screwed him. Thanks to the Judenrat, he was one of the first to end up in the concentration camp. Or at least the Judenrat had a role in it. I don't know that precisely, but I accept it the way he told it to me.

EVA: He basically lost his faith in Judaism because he was betrayed by fellow Jews. He did not want to enter the Judenrat, because his father told him, "You are not going to do that. You will not rule over the life and death of people." He had discussed it with his father, and his father told him, you are not going to do that. The way Jews behaved, he spoke to me about it. He was disenchanted with Judaism, he did not want to have anything more to do with things Jewish and with the Jews. He could not relate to Christians. To the Jews he did not want to. Of course, the camps were an extreme situation and inmates behaved badly. But later, a couple of things happened with Jews after the war as well. He was disappointed with human beings. The things a human being is capable of doing. Later on, with our marriage and the passage of time, things balanced out a bit, but at that time, he already was disappointed with human beings. Jews and Christians. He was disappointed. He felt that people are like rats.

BERTHOLD: He was no great fan of institutions, he did not like politicking and intrigues, he had his experiences. It is true, he did once accept being president of the community. He could have turned it down. Had he taken it completely seriously, he would have had to stay neutral and not be in opposition, he would have had to stay out of things completely. My father was elected president of the Gemeinde because Mr. S., who was president before him and after him, had misused community funds for his personal use. My mother used to say, "Al Capone is nothing compared to him, he was worse even than Werner Nachmann." There were other community leaders like that elsewhere, of course, as well. Mr. S. had the classic mentality of the functionary and he had all the qualities that you need for that. My father did not have these skills. My father was stright, not a politician, and a politician is never straight. The result was that between my father and this S. and his relatives, there was always trouble because of inconsistencies, imprecisions, and wasteful spending, and so it came to the point where my father was elected president.

What happened was that S. embezzled funds, and while the synagogue was renovated he had his house renovated at the same time and stories like that, and they did mobilize the opposition a little, including my uncles. If you are the leader of the opposition, it might just happen that people approach you and say, okay why don't you do it better. So he had to accept getting elected. It did not make him happy, but that is another story. Later, he resigned, because this political level was not his cup of tea. He was not a tactician, making political deals the way that would have been necessary. This was different from being an entrepreneur where he could decide how things needed to be done. There he had to be a party functionary where you have to prepare everything in committee. For that reason, he was the permanent, the constant opposition in the community. He was respected, but the permanent opponent of Mr. S. So he was engaged and he was not engaged, always in opposition against the established structure of the community.

IN GERMAN SURROUNDINGS

My father basically did not have any friends

We then lived in the hotel building for many years until at some point we said, we want to get out of the city and live in a one family home, with a garden and so on. Because my father always wanted to have greenery. He wanted to have a garden. So we moved, in 1967. It is the house my mother is still living in today.

EVA: For him, the family was important, that is, our home on Berolzheimerweg here, that was his ghetto. A big fence, a big garden behind it. Here everything is intact, a wonderful world, everything wonderful, from inside. From the outside it looked different. Nothing, not even with the neighbors. No. Just Grüß Gott, hello, how are you, wonderful, nice weather, no nice weather, because it rained, awful, how is your health? That was too much already, he already walked away then. We had no social life. None at all. It was actually pretty bad for me. We went out very, very rarely, for carnival, for example. To the ordinary goyishe carnival. There were three couples, the Bergers, a Jewish couple, my sister-in-law, Jurek, my husband, and I. We went to the carnival dances, we went to the Madame-Ball, or we went to the ball of the film festival. If you live here and want to do something you have to go to these places. One has to do that, with the Christians, that is to howl with the wolves. A bit of howling is needed. I don't know how much and for how long, but you have to do some howling. It took a big effort to drag my husband to that, but he did it. Occasionally, we went out to eat. My husband did not like to go out to eat.

BERTHOLD: No sociability. My father wanted to keep us children away from all these things. In his own life, it influenced him to the extent that he did not allow any social contact with the Germans, over and above a certain limit. He drew boundaries for himself, and these boundaries were the fence around the firm and the fence around the house. This explains why my father did not have a political lobby. He did not want to have anything to do with politics, and he could never work his way into these circles, he just found it repulsive by nature. Realistically speaking, my father basically did not have any friends. He was a pure family person. There were two things in his life, the company and his family. He did not have a buddy where you could say, he would go fishing or something with him on a weekend. Such a thing did not exist. In his spare time, my father was there for his children, a very attentive father for his children.

EVA: He invested an incredible amount in his children. He loved the children, it really was an obsessive love, an apelove [Affenliebe], he did a lot with them. He went skiing with them, later. He taught them how to swim, how to play tennis, amazingly, taught them horseback riding, opened a horse stable, bought horses for the children, he did an insane amount, and he found time for all that despite his work. One day, he walks over to me and says, "Okay, I've just bought eleven horses. Two are in the garden." I said, "What?" I thought, he's joking or has gone mad. I sat at my desk, working on something, I mumble, "Yes, yes, don't worry." By accident I looked out of my window, and in fact, I saw two horses. So I said, "Albert, are you crazy? What am I supposed to do with the two horses?" So he says, "Now we have to look for a stable." I say, "But they can't be here," they had already started to gnaw on the trees, that was my husband. Within eight days, we had a stable in Hellenburg, on the grounds, and a stable with everything including a veterinarian. All the things he did for the kids, for the sons, it is incredible.

This obsessive love of his for the kids. For example, the boys in part slept with us in our beds. They were ten, twelve, or thirteen years old, and one of them always slept in our beds. Alternatively, my husband would lie on the couch, and my husband always used to say, "Berthold, come and lie down with me." Berthold answered, "No thanks, not I, you'll have to buy a teddy bear for that." So there was an amazing love and understanding and talk. They could call him in the firm. For me, he did not have any time. When I called, he'd say, "Listen, I haven't got the time right now." When a kid called, he'd say, "Come right over to my office, let's talk about that."

Let me tell you the Porsche story. My son Berthold wanted to learn how to fly. You know he flies, he is a pilot on the side. For my husband, this was a disaster, and he said, "Berthold, I'll get you whatever you want. I'll even buy you a Porsche—not a new one, a used one." So Berthold took the Porsche but still did not stop the flying lessons. Things like that. Later on, he actually welcomed it, "good thing you can fly," he said, because he could send him places, "could you fly there tomorrow, you'll have to take care of this or that," he started liking it after all.

BERTHOLD: For my father, there were only two sorts of time. The time in the business and the time in the family. He did not have friends for himself, he found it almost repugnant. You know, when we had guests at home, my father would see no problem in going to bed at nine o'clock and to saying, "Let them sit down there and celebrate, I am going to go to bed," he was not interested in all of that. The fact that my father did not play ball with the local elite was bad for the firm of course. It was a disadvantage, because in a small town such as F., and as a major entrepreneur, you have to associate with the entrepreneurial group and integrate politically and socially in order to be part of the economic developments of a city. Building your own lobby and networks. The political environment did play a role of course. For example, we tried to secure permission from the city to build a shopping center, a new building, and we put up a new building of 20,000 square meters there, for sales. We never got a permit. It would even have been of interest to the city, also in relation to its neighbor, the city of N. But there were political tendencies that worked against my father, and this project was blocked. On the part of the city and on the part of the bureaucracy. It was also a question of the competition. The smaller merchants had a lobby, they were represented in the political commissions. My father did not have a political lobby working for him.

Not only did he not initiate anything, he even resisted the entrees, the leads that were offered to him. It was not like he was never offered any entrees, numerous times he did get offers of entrees with various parties, he simply did not take them. He knew a variety of people in various high places who were also positively disposed and who probably would have supported him. But he never cultivated and furthered these acquaintanceships beyond what was absolutely necessary for the particular moment. Others cultivated such ties far more intensively. He also never tried to integrate with these circles of local entrepreneurs or small businessmen or whatever, because for him, they were Germans. So he never sought any access to the Germans. He had his business in F., and his family, and he just did not move outside these two spheres. Also, he never wanted to fraternize too closely with Germans at the personal level. For him, they were first and foremost "the Germans."

THE DECLINE OF THE FIRM

A business at times needs to be readapted in various ways

As I mentioned, Kalman Household Appliances grew from zero to a very respectable larger company in the 1970s, from an ad hoc operation linked to the U.S. military via the German economic miracle to a rather complex retailing and production organization and to one of the major firms in the region around F. The firm made a lot of money — during the good times. You have to realize that already in Poland, my father got involved in business ventures, he was active early on, he was producing there and selling and so on. But those were more merchant mentalities, not mentalities oriented to management; and the much larger and complex structure of the firm really necessitated that.

If you look at its basic structure, the company was excellently calibrated; with a lot of entrepreneurial courage and a great deal of initiative and especially a great deal of hard work, the brothers had built a large enterprise. What they did not realize is that a business at times needs to be readapted in various ways, that it needs restructurings and that you have to learn to let specialists take over particular jobs sometimes. This is something they could never do, they could never hand over control of this or that job to other people and every decision was made in the heads of these three. So they needed qualified personnel, but they never had them in sufficient quantity. I would even say that the three brothers were not necessarily the types to promote and foster their personnel; they did not necessarily give them enough responsibility the way a company of that size would definitely have required. The three of them were very strong personalities and got too deeply involved in the day-to-day operations, and because of that, there was a whole slew of management errors.

ALBERT AND HIS BROTHERS

Not always to the benefit of the firm because they also wanted to trick each other

The management problems and mistakes that were made, as well as the structural problems of the firm, in turn helped to increase the frictions between my father and the uncles. Certain decisions began to be made, not always to the benefit of the firm because they also wanted to trick each other. Many decisions were emotional and not rational. Every company can afford that for a period of time, and it is always more than just one thing that leads to a result. It is not just one story. The Kalman company earned a lot of money, my uncle took a lot of money out of the firm and financed his own private building projects with that. This was the first drain of the financial liquidity that any firm depends upon. Financial assets were gone.

At first they tried to set up a contractual framework to define who was responsible for what, but then these quarrels came to a point where the brothers attempted to remove each other from the business. Finally, Ignaz quit the firm, he got cash for his share, but at the same time, parallel to the firm, he had started these activities in real estate, and he badly miscalculated. The money that he got out of the firm was, from an accounting point of view, transparent, so you could not say that it was embezzlement. It was transparent and could be documented, but as a fully liable partner in the firm he in fact had control over the financial assets. To the disadvantage of the firm. At year's end, you could see how his capital account had developed, but when you lose these liquid assets, you diminish the flexibility of a company.

All this brought about a great deal of friction, and there are only so many hours in a day. If of those x number of working hours, 80 percent are spent on internal warfare, then sooner or later, a major company is going to suffer. Here in particular, at the level of hierarchy, they were the only chiefs, and below them only Indians. All that went to the detriment of the firm. Initially, the firm as an organization had developed explosively, then it stagnated, we began to have competition, but we had been the biggest such firm in Germany. We were the pioneers in the field of discount appliances. We were the first to have a wide net of branches. We were the first to set up big computerized equipment, but then we experienced a time of stagnation that evolved from these internal quarrels. Basically, the business was being ruined because of this internal warfare. At least it started to ruin it. What they really needed to do was to develop the business further. They also did not train other people to do the work they could not do themselves. The competition did not sleep, they developed and became bigger, they learned from our mistakes and they did a better job. So step by step, things got to be more difficult. Our organization did not grow along with the overall German development. And our liquid resources became thinner and thinner.

You may say that it is difficult for me to give an impartial account, being Albert's son. But you have to remember that in its last years, I was the only one to be fully involved with the firm. My father basically was the motor in the family. I would admit that Ignaz had certain intellectual abilities. He was able. Except that he had this big ego. And this got out of hand, and the abilities that he had began to go in the wrong direction.

Because of all the quarreling between the brothers, they set up an arbitration panel, a sort of family mediation tribunal; mostly, it consisted of the fathers-in-law of the three brothers. But believe me, it was not just the brothers' fault; while there was a problem with the basic structure of the firm, the wives played a role in this somewhere. Fela, for one, was not affected by the war and all that; like my mother, she had also grown up in Switzerland. I have never been in close touch with her because our parents did not get along from very early on. So we did not have much contact with our uncles and this in turn had rubbed off onto us children, which is why when we were young, we did not have much contact with the other children, our cousins. My business connection with my uncle Ignaz was such that, very early on, I had to mediate between the three brothers. I was not even twenty years old when I got to be a mediator in the arbitration discussions.

In the arbitration tribunal, the fathers-in-law were involved because they agreed that this should not go to the courts. This happened already in the 1960s, my grandfather was involved in this, and also the old Zysman, father-in-law of Jurek, and there was also a lawyer present there as well and involved. So early on, I had witnessed these confrontations, and you cannot get a great friendship out of that.

So Ignaz—this was around 1975—took millions of marks out of the firm in order to finance his personal projects and all sorts of things happened that brought about open friction. Of course! If there is no more cash in the firm. As a consequence—there is this system of complementary liability—Ignaz was paid out, and he was liquidated as a fully liable partner and shareholder.

EVA: My husband was very embittered. He was sad and embittered. He had the first heart attack in 1975, and prostate surgery in either 1973 or '72. He was so sad about how everything had turned out. He often said, "We survived a concentration camp, we were doomed to die, we threw ourselves to the corpses, we have rebuilt something, and it is all for nothing." My husband was very embittered. And I suffered with my husband.

BERTHOLD: At the point where there was no more liquidity for future investments, the company's wings were clipped and paralyzed. So there was a point where we said, the discrepancies between my uncle Jurek and my father had escalated so much emotionally as well, so my father should also get separated from my uncle Jurek.

AN OBSERVER: Jurek is a relatively calm and uncomplicated guy. But that was not enough in order to run a big company. He was not the manager type. They took him along as the little brother. They said, Jurek, here you've got your place, they gave him a couple of jobs, and Jurek worked along without much responsibility. You also have to know that Jurek, in contrast to Albert and Ignaz, was not a Komplementär in the company, not a partner with liability. In Germany, as a liable partner, you are liable with all of your assets. Jurek on the other hand, was a so-called Kommanditist, with limited liability, and he did not have the same rights. In the firm, he could never really assert himself as a leader, they always doubted him. They said, this may be our brother, but well . . .

In the company, they never really believed that he had these managerial abilities, and of course, Jurek suffered because of it, it is entirely normal. He did not have any great success stories that would have tipped the balance, nor did he have specialized expertise. At some point, Albert evidently had had enough of this constant holding back, from his point of view, it was like a brake on the company, and so for a whole bunch of emotional reasons he said to himself, I got rid of the one, and now I also have to get rid of the other brother. Whenever they would ask Jurek, shall we build a new factory or do this or that, then Jurek answered, better not. Because building a factory means more responsibility, more investment, more work. Jurek must be aware of this himself, no doubt.

BERTHOLD: My father always wanted to develop further, he wanted to expand, he was, simply, an entrepreneur and everything that got developed came from his head. They bought properties, they bought shopping centers, real estate, they built factory halls on it, right out of the ground, for kitchen equipment, it was never Jurek who did it, it was my father. Ignaz did not take Jurek seriously at all. In the conflict with Ignaz, therefore, Jurek was one of the weights that tipped the scale in favor of my father, because Jurek was more on my father's side than on Ignaz's side. Now Mr. Zysman, Jurek's father-in-law, who had some business experience but who was not part of our firm, also directed some of that from backstage, he could advise Jurek to some extent.

The business developed to the point where we said, we have to get out of this space, we had been in this space for years and years, warehouse, production, and so on. We had to get out of there because in that space, you could not build a modern system with warehousing, logistics, and dispatch. So we built a new complex, we wanted to move, but Jurek did not want to move. I have to add that when Ignaz left the firm, Jurek became Komplementär and therefore had more say. I got to be Kommanditist, and Jurek's wife Rayna as well. In other words, the weighting in decision making had changed. At that point, we said, as long as we don't agree in our philosophies, and have different points of view, we'll have to separate as well.

If you look at all this today, and from the outside, then you have to congratulate Jurek, because, of all of us, he managed to come out of all this with the largest fortune. He did it with less effort, and by staying more on the sidelines, staying out of much of the activity. This is the essence of the entire story or, if you like, the essence of that cabaret.

ON THE ROAD TO BANKRUPTCY

Unfortunately, I was not in a position to change course

The pending bankruptcy was a real blow, no question. Now we have to remember, while I was still young, it was not like I did not see that these problems were coming. I did have training in business management, but unfortunately, I was not in a position to change course. I simply have to admit that; things were too much at a dead end. I also did a lot of things in the firm that my father probably was not happy about.

Look, my father was very ill. In the years between, I believe, 1976 and 1983, my father had two or three heart attacks, he spent a lot of time in hospital; my father had cancer, so he had a high quota of absenteeism, and the company was in a situation where it needed to be directed. From 1978 onwards, Jurek was no longer there, so basically the people remaining were my father and I. Starting in 1978, there was only one Komplementär and one Kommanditist left; that was my father and I. As a stand-in for my father, I more or less took charge then and made decisions that my father did not like; for example, I shut down his factory.

My father built a factory, but this factory could no longer cover its costs. This had to do with developments in the market, with lacking investments, changes in the programs of what was being produced, reduced sales, and with a thousand other reasons. So against his will, and while he was in hospital, I decided to close the factory. I had to let go several hundred people, I had to set up social security benefit plans, and decide all these measures that were absolutely necessary. It was tough for me and tough for him, humanly speaking, this was a very hard thing to do. Because, there were people you had to dismiss, it was a hard thing for me to do because I made decisions which I knew precisely were against my father's wishes. My father was attached to that production, and to the very end he thought it was wrong to shut the factory down. But it had to be done, and it was done.

OBSERVER: Even these measures were not sufficient. It was not enough in order to reactivate the whole thing within a short time span and to reorganize it. In addition, Jurek at the time had the job to reorganize the electronic data processing, but for years on end, he only burned money there, then he quit the company and left the data processing area in total disarray, you cannot imagine. He bought machinery for a lot of money, machinery that did not operate even a single day. So it stood there for nothing. At that time, the machinery was more expensive than anything else: they had machinery there for 250,000 or 300,000 marks. Several of them.

BERTHOLD: My uncle Jurek was in charge of the data processing, but it did not function right, and he quit and was happy that he did not have to deal with it any longer. My father, then, dumped that pile on my desk and told me I should deal with it. So I started to get the data processing running, and it started working, but time ran out on us. As simple as that. So in a time when the economy was going bad for us already, my uncle was being paid off; in an economically difficult time, my father did everything to let my uncle go, and he compensated him extremely generously, with real estate and money and so on. My uncle built on that land later; today these are huge apartment complexes which he was basically given, in compensation.

My father's position was this: I am not making a value judgment; he argued, for the money it takes, I am buying my freedom, and my freedom is worth more than anything else to me. That was his decision. It was not based upon economic reasoning, but emotionally it was very important to him. This drain of cash in a period of restructuring was the first step into disaster, because when you restructure and when you rationalize, it takes money, and for a long time these savings measures don't bear fruit, and this return on investment shows its effect only later. We did not have that time any more. And since real estate was transferred to my uncle, the bank cut the line of credit, and called up debts, and that basically was the beginning of the end even though we tried to hang in from 1978 until 1983, with a lot of effort and private funds and whatever. But circumstances passed us by.

Concerning the bank, it was of course also my father's mistake. My father was a merchant of the old school. He said, "I have a bank that got me started, and I have remained faithful to that bank until the end. I never went to another bank to get another offer," and in the end, it was this bank that sent him into receivership. So in the final analysis, this age-old, if you like, Prussian merchant mentality also cost him a lot of money.

EVA: For my husband, his name was something sacred. The name Kalman was sacred. My husband is: one word, one word. His name was sacred, and his word was sacred. That is how he was raised. Saying something, promising something that he could not keep, this just did not exist. He always told me: never underestimate someone whom you meet. Even if it is the lowest worker. Or a maid. Never underestimate anybody. And keep your word. This is also how he raised the children.

BERTHOLD: There was not much left in the end. Had he still had anything, he would have reinvested that. My father was a flesh-and-blood businessman, his word was his word, worth more even than a signed contract, and this bankruptcy was for him — well, that is where he died. This was his life, his personality. For him, it was a huge shame, his personal failure, his failure as a businessman, as a human being, as one responsible for hundreds of employees, that is where he died. As for me, I was barely out of university and it was now my job to supervise the bankruptcy proceedings of the firm. It was a pretty tough time for me, there was much winding up to do in the company, then there were the problems with the prosecutor's office, we don't have to go into all the details right now, but it started with police searches in my house at five in the morning to arrests, simply the kind of things that you normally get in cases like that.

Luckily, my father was not arrested, because he was ill and they spared him. But I was arrested. So at six o'clock in the morning, and just the way it is supposed to go, we were led away with armed guard and in handcuffs. I have all that behind me already, I know the German mentality [*laughs*] from the other side as well. In 1983 I was twenty-nine years old.

EVA: It was a difficult time for the entire family. Outside the house, I behaved entirely normally, I went shopping as if nothing had happened, I don't know how I managed, somehow I did it. I was on the street every day. My husband did not show his face anymore at all. And I did not hear anything negative from anyone.

BERTHOLD: The question has come up as to whether there was anti-Semitism at play in this story. Subliminally, I know that it is there. I used to have a lot of dealings with various offices, also in relation to the firm, and again and again things emerged that one can imagine being said behind closed doors. Then you know that latently, it exists and resonates. This is not anti-Semitism that verbally or in some other way would ever have been directed against me.

I had been accused of a variety of things that later on were shown to be entirely untenable. In the end, all charges were dropped. And as happens with bankruptcies, there are of course also things that developed because employees had suddenly landed out on the street, and they tried to generate dirty laundry. They forwarded information to the prosecutors about money that had been secretly moved, about embezzlements, fraud, Israel, the Jews, whatever. The prosecutor had to take note of all of these things and had to react, because maybe there was something to it. So they moved with full determination. Some informed the company council [Betriebsrat], and the company council delegates went to the appropriate political levels of the employees, the labor unions, and the whole thing was played up. They tried to put everything in motion in order to finish the evil Albert Kalman, the man who defrauded all these people over all these years.

This could be done far more easily because they were dealing with a Jewish businessman who did not have a political lobby because he had never developed such a lobby. Here it could be done so much more easily because at the political level and with the political establishment, any other company would have been built up very differently. After us, some larger companies went bankrupt in F., but never with the kind of scandal it was with us. With the others, there was never a rally of employees with banners who called for their heads; it happened to us.

EVA: My husband made mistakes, but anti-Semitism did play a role here. Oh yes, for sure. It happened to them and it serves them right, the Jews. What had happened to the Kalman company, what happened to Albert Kalman, my husband said, that was pure anti-Semitism and envy. Our employees as well, people who had been working for us for twenty-five or thirty years, they behaved the same way. Very badly. But my husband made a mistake. He should have talked to them. But at the time, he was already very ill. He just could not do it anymore.

JUREK: The union lodged a complaint in court against Albert. The firm's council had accused him of having taken money from the firm, so they wanted to present this as a fraudulent bankruptcy. Nothing came of that, because it turned out to have all been false, and there was enough money left that everybody got his share and no one suffered damage. The bankruptcy was genuine, and more than enough money was left to satisfy the creditors.

RAYNA: The house searches, the reports in the press, all that took a terrible toll on my brother-in-law Albert.

JUREK: My brother put his entire life into this firm. One has to imagine, someone struggles for something, his whole life, and my brother struggled and fought for this firm. As for myself, I can't say that I fought for it the way he did. It hit him terribly that he was accused of embezzlement, because that is precisely what he did not do: he did not take out any money from the firm for his own benefit; quite to the contrary, he sold some of his own personal real estate in order to support the firm. He could not cope with all this psychologically and died shortly after the bankruptcy.

BERTHOLD: The press as well really did take heavy aim at the person of Albert Kalman and to some degree against me as well. This was not in the style of objective journalism and more like the yellow press. This hurt my father very much, because it was a question of his name which was so important to him. Emotionally, he dropped into the deepest depression. It accelerated his illness exponentially.

ARTICLES FROM THE F. DAILY NEWS

18 April 1984

FORMER COMPANY HEADS ARRESTED

In connection with the bankruptcy of the F.er appliances company Kalman, the investigating judge at the lower court of F. has ordered the arrest of the two former company heads Albert Kalman (65) and his son Berthold Kalman. Both of them were arrested Tuesday morning in their homes in F. The orders of arrest were based on the risk of an escape attempt, because the family is said to maintain connections abroad. The two former company heads are under suspicion of criminal acts in the context of the bankruptcy which has affected 160 employees.

11 May 1985

Legal proceedings in relation to the bankruptcy of the kitchen appliance firm called off

EX-COMPANY HEAD ALBERT KALMAN IS DEAD
Trial of his 29 year-old son because of alleged embezzlement

Albert Kalman (65), former head of Kalman Appliances which went bankrupt in October 1983, has died. It has been learned only now that the former owner of the firm had already died a few days before Easter. Albert Kalman was to appear in court shortly because of irregularities in relation to the processing of the liquidation of the appliances company. After the death of the senior head, the proceedings have been called off. As has been previously reported, Albert Kalman and his son Berthold Kalman were arrested in April of last year because of alleged criminal offenses in relation to the bankruptcy proceedings. Albert Kalman suffered a circulatory collapse and was taken to hospital. He was declared unfit to be held. 29-year-old Berthold Kalman, who is charged with embezzlement in relation to the bankruptcy, will appear before a jury on 21 May. According to the investigations of the prosecutor's office, one day before going into receivership, the former junior head of the appliances company had transferred 20,000 DM from company accounts to his personal account. In March 1984, Kalman had declared that these funds were in compensation for unpaid salary from his time as managing director of the firm.

8 November 1985

Events surrounding bankruptcy of the Kalman-firm revealed in court

CONSULTANT IN CHARGE OF RESTRUCTURING
SENTENCED FOR PERJURY

The occurrences surrounding the collapse of the appliances company Kalman in October 1983 were brought up again in trial by jury under the direction of judge Dieter Penkel. The accused was a 57 year-old industrial consultant from N. who was accused of favouring creditors and committing perjury. . . . The counsel for the defendant accused the prosecutor of an underhanded strategy against his client. According to the defense counsel, the prosecutor apparently needed to produce some success because in the earlier Kalman affair, this prosecutor's overblown case of business crime had collapsed entirely.

BERTHOLD: The morning I was arrested, my big problem was finding out whether they had also arrested my father, because I knew that if that happened, it would be a traumatic experience which he would not survive. And this entire affair had a negative effect on his health and I am convinced today that it accelerated his decline. What was interesting is this: later on I could look into the files, and in the files there were different expert reports. Reports in part written by auditors or people I think are auditors. At some point, I hit on a passage where they characterized the various people involved, and my father was portrayed as Ostjude, as somebody of typically eastern Jewish background. So some guy took the liberty of making a remark beyond the facts of the case, a remark that was really out of place. For me, this was a sign, and black on white in the files, where I would say, this is open anti-Semitism. In the newspapers as well, if someone is Catholic, they don't write, Albert Kalman, Catholic, but in the newspaper you find Albert Kalman, Jewish businessman or whatever, and they also construed this risk of flight because of our presumed ties to Israel. This idea that we were likely to escape to Israel was also one of the causes of these harsh prosecutorial measures. In the company as well, people spread rumors that we had been moving money to Israel, and that was published as well, and was brought to the attention of the appropriate officials to really have an effect.

So then I had the thankless job, after the application for bankruptcy in 1984, of overseeing the liquidation. There was so much to do, stuffing holes, fixing leaks everywhere. I had to speak to the banks, go to various institutions and offices, and there was no way for me to try to build some kind of network. I did not have the time or energy anymore to be developing political and social contacts in F. You need time to do that and a business that is in good shape and running well and that has a positive image, not one that is diseased and shipwrecked. It was one of the many weaknesses of the company, and time had run out for that. In the end, the firm was insolvent, and we closed it with all the things that go with that. And sooner or later, grass grows over it.

ALBERT'S DEATH

At that moment, for him, we were transferred into another time

When we were children, my father had never told us much about the past. Throughout his entire life, he massively repressed this entire matter and never let it come up. My own experience has told me that this past is much closer to us than we might believe. So this always swings inside me, along with other things, and it does not allow for a stronger bond to develop with the Germans. So when my father fell in and out of a coma, just before his death, and when somebody dies, at that point the past caught up with my father. He started speaking in Polish and only occasionally in German, but basically he was back in the concentration camp. This was on his death bed. Somehow he figured that I was near him and he told me, "We have to get out of here, because the ss is coming."

So at that point, after he died, there was the question of the burial and the funeral, and we had to deal with the Jewish community. Here now I also had a somewhat negative experience with the Jewish community, just like my father. When my father died, I of course did not want him to be buried in F. So we said, there is no alternative, we will have to bury our father in Israel. Basically, my father was a Zionist, and throughout his life, he never succeeded in doing what he originally had wanted to do, that is, going to Israel. So we decided that at least he had to be buried in Israel. So we started to get this organized, and, the way it is with the Jews, it is never easy, and certainly not easy in F., because there is no infrastructure for such cases. As you know, you have to have a Chevra Kadisha for these cases, and the people in F. made it clear they were not responsible for this sort of thing. So the guys in S. declared that they were responsible for this, even though they have nothing to do with the community in F. We wanted to take the body to Israel, and in order to do that, only the S.ers could do that, because they are the ones with the connections to the Israelis, to the Chevra Kadisha in Israel, and that is how it got organized. The result was that they asked me to come to S. and they said, okay, if I want my father to be brought to Israel, then we'll ask for a horrendous sum of money. You have to imagine, I was in mourning at the time, we were all traumatized a bit by his death, the bankruptcy, we were all emotionally shook up by all kinds of calamities.

Here now, we are trying to take our father to Israel, and there is a community there in S. with whom we don't even have anything to do. All we need is a couple of stamps and signatures, because otherwise, nothing would move at all. And they are asking us for a horrendous five-digit sum of money, because in their heads, my father was known to be a super-rich man. Never mind that there was a bankruptcy, he obviously must have enriched himself on it and must dispose of immense sums of money. So we can use that in order to take care of our financial needs. This was the opinion of the community in S. I had to fight emotional wars with them, you probably cannot imagine how; we told each other things that I need not repeat here. Except that now it was clear to me: how can a Jewish community in Germany of all places behave like that? The simple point was, to be of assistance to a family and to bury a deceased. How could they put up all these obstacles?

As the young person I was at the time, it was not clear to me — what else should the job of a Jewish community be? Is it their function to enrich themselves in cold blood? This was the point for me where the Jewish community as an institution had died. I immediately broke off all my activities in Jewish communities.

Working in

the Kalmans' Firm

What was it like working in the Kalmans' firm? After listening to Berthold's story, I asked his mother, Eva, to put me in touch with someone who had worked in the firm and knew it from the inside. She graciously agreed to give me the names and telephone numbers of two former executives, Frau Neuffer, the company accountant who arrived in 1956, and Frau Widmayer, chief financial officer who was hired in 1962. Here are their stories.

It is a huge story

FRAU NEUFFER: I came into the firm quite early, in 1956, when things were really starting to move. I had power of attorney, was Prokuristin, but soon, I moved into a management position, and from the start, there were the two brothers in the executive, that is, Albert and Ignaz. The youngest brother, Jurek, well, he was still very young and did not have much say. From the beginning, there were problems between Albert and Ignaz. Ignaz started competing for power and Albert did not like that. Still, Ignaz had good ideas, smart ideas, but with his ideas and decisions he was too impulsive, so it got to be difficult. So there were these problems between the older brothers; later on, Jurek married, and then he also wanted to be in first row, and so there was a lot of friction between the three, and that was our problem. Albert, the eldest, felt he had to be in a paternal role for the younger brothers, he felt he had to take care of them, which he basically did. But the younger ones did not feel as thankful for it as he would have deserved. So eventually the younger ones separated from him. The end of the story came with the controversy around the Stettenheim property in F., a controversy with the city administration of F. That really was the end of the firm.

Albert Kalman was a tolerant and even kind-hearted person. He was the brain and the heart of the firm; toward his people he was always fair, even in situations where you'd say, no, you cannot do that. It was surprising, in light of all that he had gone through. Take my mother, for example, when she called me at a very inconvenient time, I told her, "Mom, this is a bad time, I'll call you back." But Albert Kalman would say, "No, your mother has priority." The mother, the family, was extremely important to him, that is, not only his own family, in the firm as well. He also had a very subtle sense of humor. For example, at a trade fair, he sat down at a stand, there were large dressers and closets, and a young man asked him whether he needed any help. And he answered, with a smile, "Well, if you really want to help, I'd like this big dresser here, and we'd like to take it with us; if you could carry it and take it outside . . ." He really was a marvelous boss.

His past experiences, he barely ever mentioned them. Once, we drove to a trade fair, and when we were finished with our work, on an occasion like that, he might speak about the one or the other situation which obviously still moved him very much. He told us for example that when the Americans liberated him in the concentration camp, there was a little boy who, even though he was so small, he mimicked an ss man in tone and in gestures. He wanted to take revenge; this boy was liberated and now he wanted to get back at this ss man. Albert said, one cannot imagine how this little boy there had suffered, and finally he could give vent to his feelings. Or the story when Albert worked at a brickworks, and where he had to stand in water in the cold, and next to him was someone who was much bigger and taller than him, but because he came from a good home and did a lot of sport and had a well-trained body, he could keep up with the others. These things seemed to go through his head especially every April [the month of his liberation by the Americans] and he always showed his gratitude towards the Americans, the soldiers who were stationed here. For all his life, he was thankful for his liberation by the Americans.

Albert Kalman's two brothers were also quite nice, especially in the early years, but Jurek also had an easier life because Albert did all the hard work. Ignaz also was very nice; but after getting married, strangely enough, he turned 180 degrees. He became so jumpy and moody. Eventually, the brothers realized that it could not go on and they decided to separate. On his own, Albert Kalman would have managed, but he had to pay out his brothers, the banks gave him trouble, and then the issue of the piece of real estate, 15,000 square meters, perhaps, that the city had promised us in Stettenheim. There were powerful interests in the back doors of the city administration, and they simply had the area rezoned from commercial to residential use, and it could no longer be sold. Tellingly, a few years later, the rezoning was reversed again. Even very early on, Mr. Kalman wanted a big shopping center, but the brothers were against it. One said no, the other could not decide either way, then one wanted to know how they wanted to build the staircase, minor details, even though this was such an innovative idea. And Mr. Albert Kalman often gave in because he felt, as the eldest brother, he had to keep the peace and unity.

Albert's son Berthold then came into the firm, he was highly motivated, but of course he was inexperienced, and in his manner and mentality, he was not the father. His father told him you have to do things with your brain *and* with your heart. But he meant really well, and had he only been given enough time, he could have got control of the whole thing. It is a huge story.

It hurt me, because I was with
the Kalman firm for nearly twenty years

FRAU WIDMAYER: The basic idea behind the arbitration panel was to have a more neutral majority; bringing the fathers-in-law plus Frau Fela Kalman onto it was thought to bring about a less emotional decision-making process than just having the three brothers dealing with it. The idea was not bad, and the family was concerned not to have third parties, strangers, be the judges of their affairs. I was called onto the arbitration panel at times, but I did not have a vote. I was called upon when there was a technical business matter. The way these meetings went, it was a normal discussion, and they had to come to an agreement; but it was a three-partite constellation, and one always tipped the scales, and the one who always tipped the scales was Jurek's party.

And then, the children grew up and that, in part, was also a problem. A father who has four sons and who has to try to stop these sons from coming into the business if you wanted to keep the peace. But Albert definitely wanted to have Berthold in the business, and I could imagine that occasionally he thought of bringing Salek in there as well.

But it is not an easy situation once the next generation gets up onto the platform.

I would say, there was one personality in the firm, one who was the boss, and that was Albert. But at the time when Ignaz was still in the business, as Komplementär, not yet as Kommanditist, at that time, Ignaz was dominant. When I came into the business, in 1962, it was Ignaz who hired me. The business manager at the time was Ignaz. That the brothers fought among themselves, that's a different story. But at the time, Ignaz was fully involved in the business, and basically, things were still okay.

Did anyone tell you why Ignaz left the business? Of course, earlier, a woman like Fela Kalman, Ignaz's wife, had the feeling that her husband was the boss and that everybody had to follow his directives, and her husband let himself be influenced by that. But that is a different story. The real reason is because Ignaz pulled huge sums out of the business. That was the principal reason. That was the straw that broke the camel's back. The amounts of money that left the firm were in dimensions that could drive one into desperation. These were amounts that could not simply be ignored. That had to be stopped and it was the reason why Ignaz was pushed out. So it was not the previous fighting; things really only escalated with the horrendous amounts of money that were being pulled out.

Still, even that gigantic withdrawal was a blow that somehow or other could still have been absorbed. But when Jurek Kalman took out his share as well, that was, well, it was not easy. You cannot weaken the capital base of a firm by sixty percent. If you want to do that, then you have to do things differently, and for that, the company management was the wrong one. And the advisors were as well. I at the time said no. Don't pay out Jurek, but everyone else apparently was for it. Yes, it is true, Albert wanted Jurek to leave the business, but there were also a couple of people who warned Albert, who said, don't do it. This was also the reason why I quit.

When you are a senior executive, Prokurist, of a firm of that size, you cannot say, well it is wrong, but I'll follow the boss, and let's just go on with it. Albert Kalman's mistake was that he did not listen to a lot of people who knew the firm well and who could look at it objectively, his tax accountant for example, or the house lawyer, he just did not listen to them because there were a couple of, pardon me, nutcases, who told him, "Mr. Kalman, we'll manage that." Without knowing the figures, without being able to recognize the consequences. That was the demise, nothing else.

My quitting the firm, that is a very personal story. Some people who are still alive know that story. The bankers at the time tried to talk me into staying. Albert Kalman offered me a contract where I could determine my salary and everything. It was not a matter of salary. I was being well paid. My problem was that I could not afford losing a good reputation. I was known in banking circles, I was known for my expertise and evaluations, and I was known for making the right prognostications. So I told Albert Kalman that if he followed through with everything, then I had to clear out my desk. He did not believe me until the last minute. On the day I left, Albert Kalman did not come into the firm. We could not even properly say goodbye. His wife told me later that it had hurt him. It hurt me, too. After that, I started something totally different. I set up my own firm, and I was successful there as well. But it hurt me, because I was with the Kalman firm for nearly twenty years.

Albert Kalman was always very fair to me, very correct, very humane. Let me tell you an anecdote. A nice one. At a point, we opened a branch in Dachau. We had taken over a big appliances firm and went there to take a look at it. Kalman went, someone from purchases, someone from mergers, I was there and two or three other people. And now the following happens. We walk into the house, and someplace I notice a beautiful painting. So I told Albert in passing, you know what, buy this house, because the painting is beautiful. For me this was the end of the story. Two days later, Albert Kalman comes to my office, is setting up the painting in front of me and says, "That's for you." Do you understand?

Small things like that. Or, for example, we drove to the opening of a trade fair to Heidelberg, we drove off early, with two cars, and at six in the morning, I think, we were already in Heidelberg. So I said to Mr. Kalman, first thing is we have to go someplace for breakfast. So he says, "Let's go to the place in the train station. I'll have a bun and a coffee — does anyone want more?" You know, he did not mean badly, for him it was natural. Or this: we drove to a trade fair in Cologne, I am from Cologne, and I told him, "You know, as long as you're taking so many people to the fair in Cologne" — I don't know if you know trade fairs, but it is back-breaking work — "you should take everyone out for a nice meal." Mr. Kalman was a very thrifty man, with himself as well. He only drove secondhand cars, very thrifty. So he said to me, "Then name me a restaurant please." I said, "Fine, I'll organize that." After the fair, everybody went to an address I had given them, they could eat fabulously well there. After the trade fair, Mr. Kalman came to me and said to me, "I have to tell you one thing. You know something or other about good food, but not about the price of it [*laughs*]." I knew the restaurant, and I knew the prices there. He was also very polite and had a very pleasant personality. He would open the door for the cleaning woman. The other two brothers would not have done that kind of thing. These manners.

But I can also tell you a story about Ignaz Kalman. When Ignaz had pulled all that money out of the firm, and when he wanted to start a business in Schesselheim, he called me one day and asked me to come to his office. So I walked over there, Mr. Schmidt, our personnel manager was there as well, and Ignaz Kalman said to me, "Mrs. Widmayer, I want to talk to you, and Mr. Schmidt, please take notes. Do you want to come with me to Schesselheim?" I said, "Mr. Kalman, why should I do such a thing?" I live here, I am married here, my house is here. I cannot go with you to Schesselheim." Then he tells me, "The house is not an issue. Mr. Schmidt, please write: 'Mrs. Widmayer — I am hereby committing myself to build a house for Mrs. Widmayer in Schessel-heim, as long as she will go with me to Schesselheim." So I laughed. "I am sure you are joking." "No, I am dead serious." He wanted to lure me away, to hire me. Later, I saw Albert Kalman, and, still laughing, I told him, "Mr. Kalman, I am stupid. Your brother wants to give me a house as a present if I go with him to Schesselheim." So he said, "Mrs. Widmayer, he is crazy."

Q: *There is this story that Albert Kalman's bank, the bank that he was doing business with for years, abandoned him.*

There were two banks that canceled loans. And I don't want to sound arrogant, I need not tell you any stories. The director of one bank is still alive, and he could confirm that. Two days before I left the firm, this director said, "Mr. Kalman, we'll have to rethink a number of things in case Mrs. Widmayer leaves the firm." It is important for the banks to have a partner in the company from whom they knew that they would get the truth without embellishment, and reliable information. When you are in a firm for several decades, and know everything, and can weigh the risks, it is different from having someone new. And their contact person — me — was no longer there.

Stettenheim was a totally bad investment. It was a bad move by Albert Kalman. Mr. Kalman promised the city a lot of employment. It was illusory. They built this huge factory, for production, and to develop that production when you did not have the know-how and when you could buy cheaper than you could produce it yourself. You have to be realistic with a project like that. You cannot simply go and say, it is the city's fault. The city kept to certain agreements.

When I had the talk with Albert Kalman that I planned to quit, I told him the reasons why. I told him, "If you want to go ahead with all this, you'll be finished in four years." Later, when I had left the company, I watched it declining from a distance. Yes, it hurt me very, very much. I met him again when he was already very ill, just before he died. He told me at the time, "You were right." That was in the hospital, his wife was there and his son. I was hospitalized at the same time.

Berthold surely had the will, and the will to turn the wheel around, but in my view, he was too young. He will probably disagree. Then you have to imagine, in the firm, it was either father and son agreeing or father and uncle agreeing, and these were people who had suffered and who had accomplished something. No one would have said there, Berthold, this idea of yours is really brilliant. His father might have. Perhaps. But none of the uncles would have listened to him. For these things, you need a certain experience, a certain calmness, you also need to realize: hold on, I've got to take a step back. When you are that young and have the sense that, so far, the whole world has been courting you, then you think you are still the strong man. This is perfectly normal. You cannot criticize Berthold for that, these are things you do in your youth, experience comes later.

As far as the past is concerned, you could not tell what the three brothers had gone through, all three. My husband as well had a good relationship with the Kalmans. It was simple: I was in the firm, they respected my husband. Occasionally, we got together privately, including going to the theater and the like. But there was never any talk like "I was in Auschwitz." You knew about that. But it was not . . .

Q: *How did you know then that the brothers were in Auschwitz, in concentration camp?*

In the concentration camp, in Auschwitz. It was a known fact. It was known. But it was not talked about. Not even to me, although I came from Poland. It is clear that those years had shaped them personally, as human beings. But certain things did occur. Someone showed up at some point, I was introduced — it happened now and then, I also knew some of the acquaintances of the Kalman family — and then they said, "We were together in the concentration camp." Usually it was Albert who would say that. "We are friends, but already since the concentration camp." He could also have said, "We are friends, ever since we went to school together."

I grew up in Warsaw, and of course I speak Polish. Occasionally in jest, I would speak Polish with Albert Kalman. Especially when we were in relaxed company and wanted to make fun of somebody. I can tell you another story about that. For a while, Albert Kalman was active in the Jewish community here. He was, I forgot what they called that, a special expression. He was, at any rate, the boss of the Kultusgemeinde. There were a number of business issues to be dealt with. There was an issue with Herr S., the former boss. One day, Albert came to me and he said, "Frau Widmayer, you know, we have no clue about something — would you mind coming to the church this afternoon, that is, the synagogue, we have a meeting, and I would like you to be observing this and show them a bit how you do bookkeeping." No problem, I went there, there were a couple of gentlemen sitting there, and no one knew that I spoke Polish. Gentlemen, really typical, pardon me, they see a younger woman, they were all pretty advanced in age, and I was perhaps thirty-eight or forty at that time.

So everyone got together, papers were spread on the table, and they did not want that I understood everything, and they started speaking in Polish. I had to smile to myself and I thought, as soon as this is getting too confidential where they really do not want me to listen in, I will simply leave and tell them, gentlemen, I understand Polish. But they spoke about all kinds of things, banalities that they could just as easily have told in German or Yiddish — I also understand Yiddish. It would not have mattered. In that moment, Albert Kalman comes in and hears how they are speaking in Polish. He looks at me and grins and says, "You can just as well speak German because she understands Polish [*laughs*]." We both had to laugh, and they were embarrassed. "You also need not speak Yiddish, she understands everything."

Berthold

in His Life

1954	Berthold born in F.
1973	Abitur; enrolls in business management studies at the University of Munich
1977–78	fully involved in Kalman firm
1978	completes his studies
1984	works as management consultant
1987	management consultant for major German firm
2000	starts own consultancy firm

Berthold, as Albert and Eva's oldest son, and in contrast to his sister Esther and the other siblings, seems betwixt and between: with his father but critical of him; highly rational but with deep emotions; German but also Jewish on a visit to Israel; living with a non-Jewish, non-German woman but not marrying her; being engaged in German society but also being drawn to look up the register of names in Bergen-Belsen. I wish I could have talked to him more often.

GROWING UP IN F.

For me, the picture was clear

BERTHOLD: I was born in F. in 1954 as the firstborn son, just one year after my sister Esther. I was named after my [great-]grandfather, his name was Berish. Later, I went to elementary school in F. and then to Gymnasium which was just three doors down from the house in the center of F. where we were living at the time. It was the house that my father built as a hotel first. In 1973, I finished Gymnasium, did the

Abitur, and then studied business management at the University of Munich, with a special emphasis on marketing. In 1978, I graduated as a Diplom-Betriebswirt and then I returned up north to F. in order to work in my father's company.

Of course I had these dreams when I was still in Gymnasium, to get out of F., for example, and to go abroad. Especially as a young person, you are exposed to a whole range of impressions, also through your friends. This is clear. Then we had a relatively large friendship circle, especially in Munich, and a whole range of people had emigrated, not just to Israel, to other countries as well. People talk about these things. Why did they emigrate, and what sort of expectations do you have in life. In my case, things got firmed up in my younger years already; I have always been closely connected to the company. I did not just start working in the firm in 1978; even when I was a child, my father had always tried to involve me there. Even as a twelve- or thirteen-year-old, I went to industrial fairs and on purchasing trips. When we bought real estate, I was asked, as a twelve-year-old, what would you do? So very early on, for pedagogic reasons, I got integrated into the firm, whether it was important or not; just for the simple reason that I was supposed to go into the business.

It was not like that with any of my siblings. Of course, there was also an interest there on my part, I was really interested, and I really could imagine doing this for a job. So during university and even when I was still in Gymnasium, I have always been connected with the company. During my studies, I have also had projects, like an internship, that I did in the firm. So my path was delineated for me and I was a bit predisposed, and I thought: what would you do if you did not go into the company? What would you do if working there wasn't that interesting? And if your parents did not really expect you to work there somehow, and if I could really free myself completely, would I feel more comfortable going elsewhere instead? I really never thought that I absolutely wanted to go elsewhere. I was in Israel and in other countries and so on, but for me, the picture was clear, even from the point of view of what I was studying. It is for that reason that I studied that. Otherwise, I could have studied history just the same.

JEWISH ENVIRONMENT AND SCHOOL

*I had a strong affinity with the Jewish environment, but I was not
integrated into any of the organizations there*

In contrast to my brother Salek especially — Salek was a real organization fan — I was never that involved. I never joined the ZJD, for example, the Zionist Youth, but I did have a bunch of Jewish friends in
Munich. When I was sixteen, together with my friends, I went to Israel.
My father encouraged me to become active in sports and when I was in
Munich I was involved with the Makkabi sports club. I did a variety of
things there, but I never let myself get hitched up in front of that cart
and take on positions of responsibility that would have obligated me to
anything; that is not really something that I would have wanted. Even
as a child, I had many friends here in Munich, and on Saturdays, I took
the train down to Munich, a two-hour trip, and so we spent the weekend in Munich together. So I had a strong affinity with the Jewish
environment in Munich — which I did not have in F., but I was not
integrated into any of the organizations there.

Other than the Jewish environment, I certainly also had non-Jewish
friends. I definitely had a solid social life there as well, but I also stood
out to some extent. I definitely had good friends in school, one should
not underestimate that. My friends were all non-Jews, because you
have to realize, it was a school of about two thousand students, surely
the biggest school in F., and among these two thousand students, I was
the only Jewish student. I remember such things as when, at the beginning of the school year, the teachers asked: how many Catholics do
we have, and how many Protestants, and is there also anybody else?
[*laughs*]. These are things that I have experienced, because I had teachers that were from those older generations.

People ask whether I experienced any explicit anti-Semitism. No,
but what is explicit? We are a generation that is of course hypersensitive, those of us who are children of parents who survived. We also hear
things between the lines and the spoken sentences and perhaps also
things that we want to hear. If you want to call this hypersensitive, then
I would say, in the one or other case, yes. But this is a matter that
everyone would give different weight to. There was no persistently
negative attitude; I could only speak of a couple of places, of particular

individuals who at some point or other played it up in one or other incriminating manner. Let me put it this way: I certainly did not experience a genuine and persistent anti-Semitism in school. There was no anti-Semitism there that would have been directed at me verbally or in some other form. No one for example would have said "kike" [Saujude] to me or something like that; possibly in elementary school one time or another, we would all beat each other up, and the Kalman boys were known for getting into small brawls, we all got into fights. From that point of view, we were not the types who would go into hiding, we took care of things right on the spot. Because of that, we quickly had a good position in school, and from then on, there were no further problems relating to the others.

WORK AND SOCIAL LIFE

There is an entrepreneurial personality present here

I have my world of work and I had assumed a leading position in a major corporation. So while I am satisfied with what I have accomplished, there were dreams that were shattered, and speaking of the Kalman firm, my original ideas of what I would do with my life were not realized. There were also disagreements with my father, as far as the firm was concerned. We had a relationship that included confrontations; we had a business relationship and also a father-son relationship. And in that direction, there were many things that I could not understand, and where I had to say, boy, they have made mistakes there, why is it that I lost such a big company, a company that I got prepared for even as a child, where my entire life was oriented toward that company. All three, my two uncles and my father, if you like, have ruined my future in a way. And one can also be pretty annoyed about that. And I was annoyed, in fact.

As I mentioned, the entire firm was liquidated at some point, at the end of 1984, it was finished then. And there I was at the point where I had to figure out what I should do. I was thirty years old at the time and found an opportunity to become active as a consultant, and worked in a consulting firm until 1987. Our office was in southern Germany and I went to visit our clients from there, all over Germany. It was of course a precarious move, from being the CEO of a bankrupt company. On the other hand, my new employer did recognize that there is an entrepreneurial personality present here, with experience, multilayered, experiences in production, sales, marketing, warehousing, and negotiating with employees and dealing with benefits questions with the unions. I had gathered experience in the entire range which could be utilized. So I got into this job and I had another couple of years of an apprenticeship, where I learned a great deal, and also in every situation, you learn more. I have stayed in this consulting area until today. After this first consultancy job, I changed to a top German firm as a management consultant; later on I started to work for another very big German corporation as a vice president of one of their branches.

Recently [2002], I left this job and have now started my own consulting business. Working for German firms, incidentally, got me into interesting situations sometimes, especially when they sent me to Israel to represent them, a German firm. It is a neat feeling — there is a little story, for example. One of the biggest customers of this company is an Israeli firm. At some point, there was a small problem, which was delegated to the consultancy section, and the consultants said to me, hold on a moment, you are from Israel, isn't that your department. So I went there myself. Of course, they thought, it would be good to send Kalman over there, but there is no one in my work environment, I think, there is no perceptible anti-Semitism, but my environment knows about me being Jewish. And really, I was not sent there because I am Jewish, it just happened that way, it was a project that I would have taken charge of in any case. Let's say it was a coincidence. Now for the Israelis, it was quite interesting. They expected, of course, to meet a super German, from a big German corporation, and they thought, how are we going to deal with that German? So it was more their problem than mine, and for a while, I left them with that impression. It was a little game for me, I wanted to enjoy that for a while, of course [laughs].

So the Israelis called me in Germany, "We'd be glad to pick you up from the airport and show you around Jerusalem, so you'd have a nice weekend before we start to work, and you'd see a bit of the country." "I am not really interested in all that," I said, "I am coming to work." So they were shocked, of course: here is a German coming to Israel and is not even interested in seeing Jerusalem, and does not even pretend being interested. So I arrived in Israel, and they were a bit reserved, of course, until I let the cat out of the bag and told them, "Okay, I am going to go home now because I am going to my family." So they were all embarrassed, of course, and pale, and one of them said, "So you have family here?" So I told them, and there was a sense of relief on the part of the Israelis [laughs]. Well, it was very nice then and very productive. I just wanted to demonstrate with that story that I am very well integrated here.

GERMANS AND JEWS

I have achieved a certain integration here

The relationship between Germans and Jews really is a question of pragmatic realism. The Israelis who are cooperating intensively with Germany can see that from a more up-to-date perspective compared with the Jews living in France, England, or America. They look at things from a much more pragmatic point of view. The Israelis are also not as Holocaust-oriented; when you speak to someone who is not directly affected, it is different. Someone else, on the other hand, who does not take note of the new developments but who says, this is my image of Germany and who has closed the shutters at some point, then that is finished.

But there have been further developments, after all, I mean, excuse me, we can talk about the past, we can talk about the Germans, but when we talk about anti-Semitism today, then we have anti-Semitism in Germany one hundred percent, but we also have it in France, we have it in England and also in America. If I decide I want to go somewhere without anti-Semitism, then there is only Israel that is left, and even there I still have a couple of Ashkenazim and Sephardim who don't like each other either, and then there are the Arabs.

So my friendship circle, those are Germans. People who, except regarding me, have nothing to do with Judaism and who debate things with me, and who, from their vantage point, may quite well debate critically. They discuss Israel with me. Oftentimes, the two are tied together, Jews and Israel. So if in Israel something goes wrong, it is immediately also a matter concerning Jewry in Germany. The Germans come and talk to me because we are kind of the representatives of the Israelis here, we have a mission here, with the Germans. But I believe the Jews of France or wherever perhaps have that task as well. They may quite easily say to me at some point, "What is going on in Israel?"

There will be a discussion of the Palestinian problem and things are associated together that should not be associated together. How the Palestinans are being treated, how can Jews do such a thing, with the past they have, and so on. I mean, from different vantage points, one can debate many things, and such a discussion is not an anti-Semitic discussion. It is a discussion where I would say, here are people who for once are being given the opportunity to talk directly with a Jew about that kind of topic. They can speak without a bad conscience, where they need not say, I as a German am not allowed to even raise a topic like that. Nowadays, many are also emancipated enough that they might very well dare to discuss this topic, or they might also ask, how do I feel about living in Germany, why am I actually here — Germans ask that sort of thing. These are all topics that may very well be debated at some point quite bluntly, without embellishment.

Q: *There is a book of personal testimonies of young Jews, edited by Micha Brumlik, entitled* At Home without Home *[Zuhause, keine Heimat]; an earlier collection of testimonies by Jews in postwar Germany speaks of being "strangers in their own land." Where would you put yourself between the two statements?*

You know, of course I am somewhere one of those of the postwar generation with a rather restrictive attitude vis-à-vis the Germans. I also don't feel myself German. I have the same identity crisis as everyone who is part of that first generation. But, let's put it this way: I have probably accommodated myself, have come to terms with it. I stand by what I do, without getting into a personal crisis about it, I have achieved a certain integration here, both into the German, the non-Jewish, as well as into the Jewish environment. I have my work environment where I have assumed outstanding positions with major industrial corporations.

Being a "stranger in one's own land" — that I would not let stand without context. This is because certainly in my professional environment I don't feel like a stranger in this country; in my work world, which is so important to me, I feel accepted and established. In my personal, social environment, on the other hand, I am emotionally substantially more reserved from this Germany, because of the past; there I am more likely to feel like a stranger in my own land as opposed to my work environment. Of course, I have also established a social context that has a Jewish imprint but which nevertheless admits other social ties. Still, I have not come to the point of an unqualified German identity. And I don't want that to happen in any case. So I am not a German who is Jewish, but I am still a Jew in Germany.

So inside of me there is this feeling of reserve, a certain distrust in relation to things German, and I am therefore not someone who, let us say, thinks nationally. I can observe that in myself and I evaluate myself in such banal matters, such as when Germany plays soccer against Italy. There I am hoping that the Italians win. I can well imagine that in the next generation, the generation of my children, this will all be different. They are encountering entirely different generations, are subject to completely different influences, and also the transmission of the traumas from myself to my children will be entirely different from that of my father onto me, with that proximity to history.

A DREAM OF FAMILY

If children come out of it, then that's what is going to happen

Since about 1989, I have been living with Fiorenza, an Italian woman who works in marketing. We were introduced through mutual friends. She was only to stay in Germany temporarily, but because of me, she decided to stay, and this has developed really well. By now, she is well established, we have a common circle of friends, a common social sphere, we have Jewish friends, she has Jewish girlfriends, she has non-Jewish girlfriends just as I have non-Jewish friends, we have our little circles here and in a certain way we are settled here.

So for the past eleven years then [as of 2000], I have been living with a non-Jewish woman, not a German woman, with an Italian woman. In neo-German, you might call this a quasi-marital relation. At home, we speak Italo-German. I speak Italian with her, she speaks German with me. Out of solidarity. It is my contribution to the European Union [laughs]. She sees things much as I do. She also asks me, how can you actually live in Germany? It was really only through me, and gradually, that she became aware of this entire problem, German/Jewishness/ concentration camp/trauma and so on. It really was because of me that she came to deal with this matter, because how otherwise would the average Italian hit on that topic? Not spontaneously. The Italians, at any rate, have a primordial, somewhat ambivalent relationship to the

Germans, they've never been great friends. And her Italian friends as well have asked her, how as an Italian can you live in Germany? Even today, there is that image in Italy about Germany that does not correspond to Germany any longer; they still see the Germans in part as wartime Germans. So the Italian who has never left Italy has not changed his mind.

Living with a German woman would probably be far more difficult, because I am well aware that you don't just marry the woman, you marry the family. Personally and with my background, I would have much more difficulty with a German family. With a German father-in-law or grandfather who still fits into that period of history, I would have such a strong emotional problem that this probably would not work. It simply would not go, I could not jump that hurdle. Of course, I have never been in such a situation so far. The situation that I am actually in is as follows: my girlfriend's mother is ten years older than I, her father maybe is eleven years older. Her grandfather, who would figure here decisively, is someone who fits the antifascist resistance, from Piedmont, and they don't particularly like the Germans. In this regard, I have far fewer problems. Still, it was a maturing process because my father, my mother, even some of my siblings cannot really accept all of that.

So I am living with Fiorenza, and if children come out of it, then that's what is going to happen, and if according to Jewish law they are not Jewish, then they are not Jewish according to Jewish law. That does not mean that I would not bring them up as Jews. I have come to the point in my thinking where I am so far away from a Jewish institution that wants to tell me how to lead my life — I am so much liberated from this that today I can say, I am the one who is going to decide my own Jewishness. People who are telling me, I first have to pay before I can bury my father, these kind of people will not tell me what is Jewish and what is not. Because as far as I am concerned, Jewishness and a certain humaneness belong together. Where that basic premise does not exist, those people will not tell me what is Jewish and what is not.

Of course I would send my children to a Jewish school, even if they are not halachically Jewish. Fifty percent of the children in the Jewish school in B., for example, are not Jewish or are from mixed marriages. Just take a look. And in most cases, it is the women who are not Jewish. In fact, Fiorenza would even be willing to convert. At the same time she knows, because she is intelligent enough and because after eleven years of being together she is aware enough of the context, so she would say, even if I convert, I am still not Jewish, because I don't have the Jewish past. For us, it would simply be a legal procedure which we would put in motion in order to provide the children with an unambiguous identity. That is something we are debating. It is not an emotion-guided debate, but derives from purely practical considerations, from the point of view of "how can we organize that." So she knows perfectly well that she will not become Jewish, and will not be able to think really Jewishly. She knows, on the other hand, that I simply want to transmit to my children a Jewish orientation the way I know it, that I want to transmit to them a Jewish identity. Call it tradition if you like.

I am not a religious person. The only day that is of significance for me is Yom Kippur, it is just the way I have been brought up, it is basically the most important day for me. On that day, I go to shul, and I have never missed that, and nothing could stop me from fasting, although I would not fast just because it is prescribed.

People ask why couldn't I decide to have children much sooner, to start a family, and so on. This is a good question that I have often asked myself. I would answer that in my case, it is a process of accepting. The fact that I can marry a woman today who is a non-Jewish woman — that step is the result of a maturing process. I completely admit that. I of course had a different upbringing. So if I marry a non-Jewish woman, I will not start to think more or less Jewishly than before, and I will not relate to other Jews more or less positively on account of that. Period. No one, including your own family, can take responsibility for what you do; you have to do it yourself. This is a maturing process that you have to go through. Sometime in your life you have to learn that life has a beginning and an end, that time is limited, that you cannot just orient yourself by other people. You have to take life into your own hands and make your own decisions. Then you have to say, take it or leave it — either people around you accept it or they don't, and this concerns even the closest family circle. It is a maturing process that you have to get through yourself, and that I believe I have gone through. Today, we are at the point where we are saying, if we have a child, it will be a Jewish child, it will be raised Jewish, my wife will convert or she will not convert, we will bring up the child Jewishly and I will marry my wife in the sense of a legal procedure, case closed.

I believe my brother Ronnie has not come to this point as yet. In fact, Ronnie is hard to categorize. In his case the problem is perhaps

more extreme because he has not gone through the same kind of maturing process and because he does not have that kind of a relationship [in
2000]. If he were in such a relationship, he would react exactly the way
I do, because he as well has long since understood that our daily matters, our daily life is more important. This is more decisive as opposed
to somebody wanting to comply with a trivial framework that someone
puts in front of you, someone, however, who cannot assume responsibility for a particular life. You yourself have to take the initiative and
also take responsibility for your decisions. At times such a decision may
well go against one or the other person in the family; you cannot always
and in all your decisions please everyone. At times there will be areas of
friction, and you have to get through that. In my case, this has gone
further, and with Ronnie, it is going in a similar direction.

THE PRESENCE OF THE PAST

I had driven past that sign many times before

I have noticed that things of the past are moving me more today than
they did previously. Let me tell you a story about something that happened to me recently. I am on a business trip, only a few weeks ago,
going from Hannover to Hamburg. I am on the highway, and I am often
on that highway. As a consultant, I am on the road a lot. It was a late
afternoon, and I pass a sign, "Bergen-Belsen Concentration Camp Memorial." I had driven past that sign many times before. And all of
a sudden, at the very moment where I am driving past there, I see,
"Exit KZ Gedenkstätte Konzentrationslager Bergen-Belsen 2 km." And
somehow I got that feeling I have to drive out there. I don't know why, I
am not the emotional type, I am a pretty rational person, but somehow
I said to myself, okay, I am going to drive out there.

So I exited the highway and there was a sign, and I think I had to
drive another fifty kilometers, because the place is between Bergen and
Belsen somewhere in Lower Saxony in the woods. Something, I cannot
tell you what, drew me there. So I am right near that memorial — I don't
know if you know the Bergen-Belsen concentration camp — there is
nothing left there except a memorial and basically that huge area. So I
went into the memorial and I looked at all the exhibits and documents,
exhibits done by schools, these emotional things, and somehow it

moves you, of course, and then I hit on a book where the prisoners, as far as they are known, are registered. And as if led by a hand, I went towards that book and looked under "Kalman." And you will chuckle, I did find a Kalman. A Kalman. I found a sister of Gertrud of whom I did not know a thing. I knew nothing about that sister; I did not know that she was together with Gertrud in Bergen-Belsen.

Q: *Gittla died shortly after liberation.*

So she died in the camp. This was a kind of emotional story, when you stand in that place, in that camp, and you open a book where all of a sudden you find your own name, when you are not prepared for that at all; you stand in that camp all of a sudden and in that book it is listed, and where you stand right now there are ten thousand dead under ground. At that point I realized that this history is catching up with me ever more often, compared to earlier years. And this: how often did I drive past this camp, but only this time did it pull me away.

I am certainly traumatized somewhere as well. Yes. In the past few years, I have realized that the things of the past are stirring me more today than in my younger years. There are maturation processes, and you come to think what might have happened to you back when. I don't have to explain all this to you. Over the course of the years, you read more of the history, you take in whatever is available; when something is published, you read it, if there is a film, you watch it.

Dealing more with that history also led me to have a different understanding in relation to my father. As I mentioned, we did have a relationship that also brought certain confrontations. He could never answer my question as to why he is in Germany. I asked him that question and I believe every child of this war generation at some point asks his parents the question: "Why did you stay in Germany?" I don't know how many answers there are to this, but I have never received a clear answer. At some point I tried to answer this question for myself, and somewhere I have a certain idea what the answer might be. But from him, I could never hear that. Let us say, the sensitivity in relation to the events of the past has gotten greater in recent years, and I have begun to understand my father ever more.

Eva

SWISS MENTALITY,

POLISH COMPANY

1930	Eva Pincus born in Zurich
1950	completes training as dental technician
1951	sister Stella moves to F.
1952	mother dies at age forty-eight
1952	sister Esther moves to Argentina
1952	marries Albert Kalman in F.
1960	sister Stella moves to Argentina
1967	moves into new house on Berolzheimerweg
1985	husband Albert dies
2000	seventieth birthday celebration in Barcelona

My interview with Eva illustrates how the interviewee guides the interviewer and, later, the analyst and editor of the text, into particular courses of questioning. Berthold's world was ordered according to the spheres of work and sociability and his dual relation to his father as father and at the same time as the head of the firm. His mother's, Eva's, world, in turn, is organized around a variety of significant others in her environment: most of all her late husband, her children, her in-laws and other relatives, and non-Jewish acquaintances. Her work experiences are a thing of the past and marginal at best; her story is congruent with the way in which she has ordered her world. Any other approach would not do her justice.

It took me some time to find Berolzheimerweg and the Kalman family home, of the late Albert and of Eva, at the very end of this cul-de-sac. The house, in a large beautiful garden with many trees and shrubs,

set back from the street and behind a high steel fence, is guarded by two
huge, ferocious-looking dogs. Eva's housekeeper sent the dogs into a
big cage with steel bars and then opened the gate; the interview with
Eva, on a beautiful summer afternoon, was conducted on the terrace in
front of the house. Eva, a most gracious host, served cake and cookies
with tea.

EVA: Let's start at the beginning. I was born in 1930 in Zurich, Switzerland; around 1900, my paternal grandparents had arrived in Switzerland from Kielce in Poland; offhand, I don't remember where my maternal grandparents came from, but in all likelihood, they came from
Galizia as well. My mother was born in Switzerland, and my father
came to Zurich from Poland when he was a few months old. You have
to think of my family, the Pincuses, as a large, intact, very religious and
happy family. My grandparents spoke Yiddish, but my parents spoke
Zurich Swiss German with us children; and when we, the children,
were not supposed to understand, the grandparents spoke some words
in Polish. Still, my mother's mother tried very hard to speak Swiss
German to me and my two sisters; my sisters emigrated to live in
Argentina.

I went through a very protected childhood. It is probably because
my two elder siblings died; one died at birth, and the other fell from a
balcony. My mother really went through a lot. So when I was born, I
was well looked after and very spoiled. They practically put me into
chains so that nothing would happen to me. But I was a pretty wild kid.
Then my sisters were born. Now you will ask, how would anyone in her
right mind, a very protected Jewish girl from prosperous Zurich, move
to postwar Germany and to F. of all places? This is a story all of its own.
Let me start from the very beginning.

You have to know that my mother died very early, in 1952, at the
age of forty-eight. Now sometime before her death, in the fall of 1951,
my sister met my brother-in-law in Zurich. He had a wholesale business
in hosiery in N. and in F., he was working together with two partners,
and he was on business in Zurich. I don't remember exactly, but he was
invited to my grandparents' house for Friday night when the whole
family came together for Shabbat dinner. He was a guest there. And he
saw my sister, and something happened. My sister was very pretty, she
was a great beauty, and he fell in love with her, something clicked there.
Then they said, engagement at New Years' Eve, because my mother was

already very ill, she had cancer, and no one knew how long it would take. The family felt therefore that they should marry as quickly as possible so my mother could still experience it. The decision went back and forth and there was the question of the papers. But my mother was only there for the engagement; she did not experience the wedding after all. My sister got married in April of 1952. It was a very sad wedding.

Within a year, my family as I knew it dissolved. My mother died, then first one sister and later my other sister got married; one sister left for Argentina, and the other sister moved with her husband to F. Losing my mother was a very difficult experience for me. Only my father was still there. I have to tell you, life without my mother was unthinkable. I would never have separated from my mother. For me, to leave my mother was unthinkable, that my mother had to die, it was — a whole world collapsed. And then I lose my sister Esther who went to F., I had already lost my mother, and my youngest sister left for Argentina, all of that in 1952, and my father always away on business trips. I had to live with my maternal grandparents, which was very bad for me, and I was very sad, I suffered, I suffered.

I was trained as a dental technician, but never liked that job. I had also picked up secretarial skills and bookkeeping and went to work for a commercial firm. The director of the firm was a friend of the family. One day, my boss, this old man, he said to me, "Fräulein Pincus" — Pincus was my maiden name — "let me suggest something to you. We have a branch in London. How would you like to go to London for a couple of months, for a change of scenery?" Before I left for London, my father insisted that I visit my sister in F. I went there, reluctantly, and met my husband there, this is how it happened.

My sister picks me up from the train station, and I see the train station: destroyed, bombed, it was the first time that I saw a bombed city, it was all new for me, it was not like that in Zurich. I meet my sister there, it was on a Thursday, the 18th of December, I'll never forget that, these dates, an 18th of December, a Thursday. The next day, of course, it is Friday night, Kabbalat Shabbat, which we always celebrated; I am from a religious home. So my sister says to me, "Listen, every Friday, a friend of Tony's comes by, I cannot cancel that just because you are there." So I say, it is not a great idea, but what can we do, so go ahead. I had really wanted to discuss a couple of things with my sister alone before leaving for London. Well, and the guy who came to visit was Albert Kalman.

We were introduced, the following day was a Hanukkah dance, and that is how it went, and so I did not go to London after all. Instead of starting work there on the second of January, I got engaged on the fourth of January, my official engagement, and that is how I ended up in F. I lived with my sister, then I went back to Zurich to take care of the papers, the civil marriage was here in F., three, four weeks later, and the religious ceremony was in the synagogue in Zurich. Yes, it was a real wedding, a real chassene, with my grandparents. So I ended up in F., from Zurich to F., where I was really very unhappy.

EVA IN F.

This was the company, Polish company

I entered another world there. Completely different. Everything was bombed. Many things were not available, cosmetics for example. So I want to buy lipstick. I cannot get lipstick, it does not even exist. Just as an example. Anything. You go into a store and want to buy something. It simply did not exist. For me, this was terrible. Perfume. And I came from an intact world, you might say, Zurich, safe and sound — it was terrible for me here. In Zurich, they were worried about me, they were afraid that I would not stay, would return one day. Every time I phoned home, they thought I was calling in order to tell them that I was coming back; but soon thereafter I was pregnant.

My father also told me, "I am not at all happy that you are in Germany." Also, my aunts and uncles never visited me. I was the one who had to go to Zurich, because, "to Germany we won't go." They did go to Munich, though, to buy silver at Taucher's, or to go to Steinberg's for cutlery and silverware, they were always buying there. They came by plane, back the same day, they went shopping and left. The house that we built then, in F., made our life in F. pretty firm already. But we thought we'll see what happens when the house is all finished. Then one child after another was born. If we had at least gone to Munich, into a larger Jewish environment, many things would have turned out differently. But we were settled here. Sort of.

We did have company, of course, all the people from Poland who were there from the concentration camps. This was the company, Polish company. They were all Polish Jews. What can I tell you, I did not have a lot of contact. Because the women there were not . . . well, many were also older than I. I was twenty-two at the time, they were all between thirty and thirty-two or thirty-five years old; ten years made a big difference here. Among women. Also, they had no interests, not my interests, and I did not have theirs. There simply wasn't the right chemistry. Thank goodness I had my sister here, otherwise God only knows what might have happened.

It was a strange new environment for me, my husband's family and his friends. I had problems. I had a different mentality. I had a Swiss mentality: disciplined, precise, exact, the way it has always been in Switzerland, and perhaps it was good, perhaps it was not good. I found, at any rate, that I could not quite cope with it. Albert's sister, Gertrud, was jealous of me. Gertrud felt she had lost her brother, because she had her hand over the family, via remote control from New York. I could not cope with that, it might have had to do with me, too. I could not really slip into this mentality, the imprecision, it was all a bit gypsy-like. Today I assume that maybe it had to do with the concentration camp experience, but at the time I did not see it that way.

I was thrown into a chaotic domestic life. There was a coming and going, there was no time for lunch, there was no time for supper, nor was there a time for breakfast. Everyone came when he wanted, and left when he wanted, "do you have . . . , will you . . . , are you . . ." I did not like that. Then I had the two brothers at home with me, they ate here, lunch, dinner. I did not have an ordinary marriage in this sense, I had married three Kalmans. At that time.

It was a frenzied lifestyle, frenzied style of work. I was in charge of the hotel, I had the children, the family, my husband had the business. They worked that business, the brothers, day and night. All week long they were on the road, today in Freiburg, tomorrow elsewhere, the entire tour. It really turned into a rocket, a smashingly successful business. As far as I was concerned, I was soon pregnant, and my husband had the business, and so I settled down here, one child, and another child, and another child, I have five children, four one after the other, and my husband had already been building a hotel at the time; it was already under construction when we got married, and he really was the first Jew in Germany then who was building something; all the others were still sitting in low water at the time, had not been successful yet. That gave me a firm footing, and I worked in the hotel, day and night and had one child after the other. So I was quite occupied.

I really worked very hard, and that was okay with me. I had my family and was working hard, and my brothers-in-law were not quite living with us, but they were eating with us, and one day I said to my husband, enough, they've got to get married now. Here I was with my fourth child, it really was too much for me. They were always there in the evening, talking business and only business, and I had my work to do, I did night shifts in the hotel as well, it was too much, simply too much for me. One of them has to get married now. Better both of them. There was a Jewish agency, a marriage broker, matchmaker, whatever, I don't quite remember what it was. Ignaz met his wife there, and I said, it is fine with me that he is getting married. She was from Zurich as well, but I did not know her. But I have to tell you, when they got engaged, I said to my husband, "Listen, she is not right." He said, "What are you talking about. You are probably jealous." As far as Jurek is concerned, I knew his wife Rayna even before I got married, she was fifteen years old then. This was because my father did some business with Mr. Zysman, who was her father. It was felt even then that she would be the right wife for him, "made to order" as we say. She was in Auschwitz. She suffered a lot.

THE RISE OF THE FIRM

It developed into a roaring business

At the beginning, Jurek ran a textile wholesale business, he was on his own at first; later he joined his two brothers; they were more the ones with the initiative. Ignaz and my husband were in the auto business. Now I hope I am not telling you anything that is incorrect, but as far as I remember, they had from the Wehrmacht — no, it was from the Americans and the French occupation, there were tenders, and they bought cars, and my husband had a repair shop where the cars were being fixed up and then sold. This was Ignaz and my husband.

At the same time, the hotel was being built. Both operations were being run simultaneously. Ignaz certainly had initiative. He was a bright man. If he only had married someone else, someone who would have understood him. Because of their daughter, he could not leave her, and that had to bring about conflicts in the firm. If somebody is un-fulfilled in his private life, it will automatically lead to conflicts in business. That's the story. He could have undertaken a lot, Ignaz, he had many ideas, perhaps not like my husband's, but I thought of him as a smart man. A good-looking man, a bit nervous, a bit hectic, but he could have been guided.

I was right there from the beginning, with the hotel; I stood there when it was being built, with the brick layers: what are you doing there, and what is it that you are doing, and how about you . . . The hotel was a hotel garni, a bed and breakfast, for traveling salesmen. I had my regular guests. Every Monday, there was Herr Schmidt from Munich, every Wednesday Herr Huber from Düsseldorf, basically like that. During the summer, I also had groups, like bed and breakfast. I did everything in the hotel. I did the night shifts, I worked during the day, I did the administrative work. I was trained in commerce and accounting — basically I was raised the way in which in Switzerland the girls are raised, you have to know.everything. What you've got in your head, nobody can take from you. Money comes and goes. That's what my maternal grandmother used to tell me: what you have up there, no one can take from you. I rejected that at the time, but when I started working in the hotel, I thought to myself, my grandmother, she was right.

At the time, and this is how the business got started, my husband bought household appliances and furniture for the hotel, from the U.S. army. There was some kind of an outlet center, I don't remember what it was called, where you could buy household items. My husband had an address there, in Giessen, not far from Frankfurt, he bought furniture there and furnished the entire hotel with it. It worked like this: usually, when Americans returned back home and dissolved their household, or wanted to refurbish their house, their old furniture and appliances ended up in the outlet center where you could buy it. But not every mortal was entitled to go there, and I don't even know how my husband managed to get in touch with this place.

So my husband needed to furnish the hotel. They had very heavy solid mahogany closets and very big armchairs, solid walnut tables, a quality of workmanship you'll never get again, it cannot even be done. At that time, even the best was not good enough for the American soldiers. So my husband furnished the hotel with this furniture and carpets, refrigerators and kitchen stoves, all from the Americans. At that point, my husband said to Ignaz, hey, we could turn this into a business. Let's have the business in your name. This was because I had the hotel already, it was in Albert's name. That is how the appliance business started in the first place, they got the idea because of the hotel and the American appliances and the furniture. The appliances were being sold in the backyard of the hotel. We had big garages there, and storage, because of the cars from the used-car business. It was a big warehouse, and the sales were all done there. This was around 1954–55. Thereafter, as far as I can remember, advertising started in various cities, space was also needed for selling the appliances. Refrigerators and lamps, kitchen stoves and American furniture, whatever came from the outlet center. At that outlet, the wares were auctioned off; whoever made the highest bid got the whole lot. You did not know what was in it. My husband took care of that part. Everyone had their job. My husband was mostly in purchasing and sales and financial planning, he was the most capable one, my husband. But Ignaz was capable as well, he was clever, too, he was talented at organizing things.

From the mid-1950s onward, it was the time of the economic miracle in Germany, ads were placed in the local newspapers, let's say, the *Freiburger Tageblatt*, to announce that an appliance sale would be taking place on Monday from such and such a time, at such and such a place. They even had to call the police to control access, so many people were showing up. On such a day, normally two of the brothers would be there, or there was one of them in charge and there were already employees then who helped with the sale. All week long, my husband was on the road, and Ignaz and Jurek as well. Ignaz, however, stayed at home the most, because he was in charge of administration.

It soon developed into a roaring business, incredibly fast. It happened overnight. Later, new appliances were added, kitchen and electric appliances, step by step, an enormous development. Then, fixed branches were set up, with employees and so on, and so on. The business grew and grew, purchases were made in factories, they expanded further, it was the time of the sixties. Whether you liked it or not, you had to expand. Already in 1958, we had twenty-five big trucks, those big moving vans. Even in the fifties we had that. At its peak, we had about seventy branches, but this was simply too much. We consolidated to about forty. In Frankfurt alone, we gave up two stores. We wanted to concentrate things a bit. But slowly, also, things began to deteriorate somewhat.

FRATERNAL STRIFE

The wives played a role in that as well

The deterioration had to do with the internal conflicts. Instead of being concerned with the business, the brothers were busy fighting with each other. There is a virus in that entire Kalman story, and it started right at the beginning, even when I got married. The brothers simply did not get along. The wives played a role in that as well. Not me, however. But none of us got along with Fela, Ignaz's wife. This was transferred on to Ignaz, and from there, the frictions began. Among brothers. I suffered very much, I suffered. Because in my big family, I did not know fights. I had not known that, and I suffered. Rayna suffered as well, Jurek's wife.

It was not all Fela's fault alone. Ignaz was envious of his older brother and competitive with him; there are stories that go back all the way to their childhood. One day, Ignaz came by, this was early on, we had already opened a number of branches that were going well at that time, the firm was already well known all over Germany, but more in the south. Yes, he said, he'd like my husband to leave the firm, the firm is in Albert's name, but he, Ignaz, does not have any say in it. I said to my husband, okay, let him buy you out, I'll stand behind you, no more joint partnership, and we'll do something else instead. I was always in favor of doing that, us doing something on our own. I did not understand much of the friction, did not even follow it all, arguments like "This has cost a lot," and "Now you got married, it has cost us," "And now you bought this for yourself," and this is how it slowly began. I told my husband, you know, we can do a number of things on our own. There was also the hotel. But my husband wanted to be with his brothers. They were in the concentration camp together, and I understood that, but this was then. In the firm, everything looks different, and when they get married, when wives come into play it is always bad. Either the wives don't get involved and don't interfere in anything, or it will turn out badly. The husband has to have control over his wife and has to have the strength not to say a word about anything concerning the business. But that did not come to be.

In addition, Rayna had a father who also liked to get involved in the business a little, and Jurek saw in him not just a father-in-law but a real father, and so he consulted with him more and more. In this man, Mr. Zysman, Jurek found a father, and in his mother-in-law, a mother. And when Zysman gave him advice, he only advised him in his own favor, and not in favor of the business. It was like a cancer in the family: X did not talk to Y, this one not with that one, or went out of his way, there was something in there, it was a sickness.

THE ARBITRATION BOARD

They were not born, the Kalmans, for a joint company, together

As the conflict worsened, they decided to set up an arbitration board. Zismann and my father were the arbiters. Ignaz decided to add his wife, but that did not work. He sort of defended himself, but he did not stick to agreements. Then they wrote letters to each other, Ignaz to Albert, Albert to Jurek; they wrote letters to each other and spent so much time on this, rather than dealing with work. This is how the arbitration board functioned. The brothers and their representatives all sat around a large table, in a conference room. This was already in the 1960s. Once every month my father came from Zurich for these meetings. But what was so bad about this construction was that the fathers-in-law all defended their sons-in-law. My father was the diplomat type, and he always told my husband, "If you were only a bit more diplomatic, you would come a long way." But my husband simply was no diplomat. They were not born, the Kalmans, for a joint company, together — perhaps there was a certain lack of respect of one for the other. I believe that if you work together in a business, you also need a degree of respect and you need real leadership. You cannot have three bosses.

TOWARD THE BRINK

There was hate, and nothing worked well

This arbitration board, in short, did not make matters any easier. In 1976, finally, Ignaz was paid out and left the firm. There was a court case, and via a number of court proceedings the partnership was dissolved in this particular way. Even earlier, Ignaz had taken a lot of money out of the firm and had started to build. They let him do that;

they did not have to. Each one of them was entitled to take such and such an amount per year out of the firm. Ignaz was being bought out and needed a lot of money for that. He built big warehouses in northern Germany, and they did not do well, and we supported him every month: he needed to live, he did not have any money, then his wife became sick, what a story this was, his business was a catastrophe. There was hate, and nothing worked well, it was a catastrophe basically.

Once Ignaz was out of the firm, it continued with Jurek; it was good, and it was not good, Albert did not get along with Jurek. Jurek was always looked at as the little brother and he did not have the forcefulness to work his way up. He was more the slow type, thinking slowly, not as flexible. In business, you have to be very flexible, even doing things that don't seem necessary, you have to be venturesome; he was afraid to do new things. And they let him be like that, he was the youngest, and he was being pulled along. It was the same with Rayna; she did not think like a merchant either. A merchant has to take risks; without risk taking, nothing happens. A real merchant has to be able to lose sometimes. At Albert's request, then, Jurek left the firm: he wrote that to him in a letter in 1978. Jurek did not react well to this. It was a mistake on the part of my husband. It was not okay. It was also not good, because the banks did not go along with it. The banks get nervous when a partner leaves. At the time, I thought differently as well, but thinking about it today, I have to say, letting Jurek go was not good. But Jurek was very lucky. He ended up being the laughing third, laughing all the way to the bank.

My own personal problem was with the Kalman women, my sisters-in-law. When Jurek left the firm, I again tried to speak to Rayna, Jurek's wife. But I could never get close to her, she blocked me out. I could never, for example, go and say to my sister-in-law, you know what, my husband cheated on me yesterday, imagine, what shall I do, he is cheating on me. I could not have discussed that with her, nor would she have come to me to say, Eva, imagine, Jurek is cheating on me, imagine. No. The world was safe and sound and in order there.

THE KALMANS AND THE CITY OF F.

It was envy and anti-Semitism

From there on, things basically went pretty much downhill. Berthold will have told you, the strife between the three brothers was not the only problem. Another problem was the city, which was entirely unhelpful. It was envy and anti-Semitism. The city was supposed to help when my husband built something, in Stettenheim. My husband wanted to swap pieces of land, and it went back and forth and in the end, real estate was swapped, in another district. So my husband built office space there and warehouse space, but he was not allowed to set up retail space there; he was not allowed to do any more construction in Stettenheim. Afterwards, Siemens bought this land and expanded massively; to Siemens, the city was prepared to give a permit. They did not give us the permit.

Q: *Do you think it was anti-Semitism? Were there any remarks of that sort made?*

This is what my husband claims. Yes, it was envy and anti-Semitism. They did not have to mention the word "Jew." Speaking of Kalman was enough. Everybody knew who Kalman was; the name Kalman was enough. It was also my husband's problem, though. One would have had to howl with the wolves, basically. But my husband said, "Business is business and the private is private. I cannot sit down with them privately." But this really was a mistake. He should have gone into the Rotary Club perhaps or the Lions Club, I really do believe this today. He just did not want to do that, absolutely not. On several occasions, we were invited to the mayor's, but he did not go, or, for example, when the mayor turned fifty, we were invited to his birthday party, and Albert said to me, "Listen, I am going to stay there for ten minutes and then I'll leave." There were things where one would have had to push into a little bit. But he was not the sociable type. I believe he just could not get it together to be with the politicians. As far as the firm was concerned, he said often that it was pure anti-Semitism and envy. They tripped him, they succeeded.

FRAU WIDMAYER: You told me, Berthold said that there was anti-Semitism involved. That is not the case. No, it did not turn anti-Semitic.

The point was, somebody in the firm said that they brought their money to Switzerland. There was this search warrant for Berthold's house, that really should not have happened. The Kalman Company did not transfer money anywhere, but that was the reason for the search. That story was followed up, but it does not have anything to do with anti-Semitism. I know that these people are very sensitive on that issue, very sensitive, and sometimes they see a normal process as a personal attack.

Q: *So you did not, ever, have the experience with Albert Kalman and with the firm that there was anti-Semitism involved.*

FRAU WIDMAYER: No. Quite the contrary. They treated him very cautiously. Eva Kalman is very open with me, this has never been a topic. We are still getting together privately. It is also not true that Albert Kalman did not keep in touch with the influential people in F. He was one of the very well-known people there. One of the big taxpayers. One should not forget that. There was no one on city council, mayor and so on, who would not have known him. A particular party membership or a particular political orientation, all that did not play any role at all. It was Albert Kalman, a known and respected quantity who really had created something, and people did not deny that. They respected his accomplishments.

THE CHILDREN

This family will live in mixed marriages

EVA: As you can see, I live all alone now in this big house here, but three of my sons don't live far away, in Munich and in F., they are within reach, I see my grandchildren either here or in Israel and I am in touch with most of the rest of the family, more than any of the other family members probably. When there is a problem, chances are they will speak to me. When Ignaz has a problem, first thing he does is phone me. And complains. I am sick, I have this or that, could you ask Ronnie — Ronnie is the doctor — what should be done? I answer, no, there are no long-distance diagnoses. Ignaz has some story concerning his daughter Dina. He does not discuss it with his wife, he talks it over with me. So much for him.

Rayna recently called as well, she also is not feeling well, and her mother is sick and so on. So whenever there is something bad, they come to me. The fact that there is this contact nowadays is more my initiative. For example, in the last little while, I called Rayna three times. "I never hear from you," I said, "Oh, I am sorry, I have to run off to play bridge, I'll call you." She does not call back, of course. After a few days, I call again and she says, "Oh, you know, my mother is not feeling well, I have to go to the hospital immediately." Occasionally she calls back but does not have much to say. Nothing in particular. So we are in touch after all; also, I am of course a person who cannot stand fights. You know, to be walking past a family member without a greeting, that for me is the worst. I'd rather get lashed. But now I'd like to hear your honest opinion about the children, about all the children, mine included. You are a journalist, and I'd like to hear from you about that.

One of the issues you raised, an issue that concerns me a lot, is how my children and their cousins will marry and the families they will have. The question of mixed marriages. We are living in Germany, it happens, it happens, and I am not that opposed to it anymore the way I used to be. I am from a religious home, so it sounds strange, but I don't look at that anymore the way I used to. My husband, on the other hand, would not have accepted it. No. I am telling you, as long at I am alive, perhaps nothing will happen, but then, there will be one marriage after the other. This family will live in mixed marriages. The problem is simple: in Germany, the choices for a Jewish partner are very limited. My boys did not find Jewish girls. The girls that live in Munich, in Frankfurt, these spoiled girls, are just not right for them. My boys don't know that, throwing money around like that. They don't know that from me, and they certainly did not know this from my husband. They simply have not found the right Jewish girls.

I would not be opposed to them coming home with a non-Jewish girl. How could I turn my children away, even with a non-Jewish partner? You know the story with Dina and Ignaz. Dina wanted to come to F., a couple of weeks ago [i.e., in 1996]. I talked to her and I talked to Ignaz, I was the mediator between here and H., where she lives. She wanted to visit her parents together with her friend, she wanted to introduce him. But they said, "A goy does not come into my house." That's how it was, exactly.

All the girls that my boys went out with, including those of Ronnie, came to my house, for Pessach, for Rosh Hashanah, I have always accepted them in order not to lose the boys. And they took part, at a Seder, for example, and I explained it to them. Once I had a girlfriend of Gaby's there, and Fiorenza, Berthold's girlfriend, it was the first Seder, but it was also Good Friday, and they are both Catholic, we are starting the Seder, we are starting to eat, meat is being served, and what do I hear? "No, I cannot eat any meat today, it is Good Friday, we don't eat meat today." That was the first thing that I saw, that does not fit in, it does not work. For us, it was the first Seder, Berthold presided, and there is his girlfriend who says, no, I can't eat meat today, with chicken and duck on the table, and I cannot eat the meat soup either . . .

The question is what kind of a consensus will they find. Fiorenza, I believe, has no interest in running a Jewish home. I also don't think that she would come over to the Jewish faith. On the other hand, Berthold says, "I would have just as much of a Jewish home if I got married, not a kosher household, it is not possible in F. But there are the various traditions like Pessach, like Rosh Hashanah, the other traditions, that is where I come from, and that is how I will continue." Because, Berthold has a little bit of a religious side to him. That is the problem Berthold is having. It is a matter for both of them, they will have to come to an agreement; but so far, they have not come to me as yet.

EVA IN HER AGE

You have to be a bit selective about people

Ever since my children have moved away, except for Gaby, they are encouraging me to move to Munich for more congenial company. Berthold as well told me, "Why don't you move to Munich, you can socialize there." So I tell him, who? what? who? In my age, you have to be a bit selective about people. It is terribly difficult for me. There are people there, in part Israeli women, who have come out of the smallest, most miserable backgrounds, they barely even speak a proper Hebrew and who have become rich; men as well who got to be wealthy in the sixties during the time of the reconstruction. They are full of themselves today. I don't want that. I like to be with people where I can still learn something, where I can listen, where I can ask for advice — what would you do, would you do this, could you do that. Everything else is a waste of time.

Berthold has the same problem. He does not have any contact in the Jewish community; they only talk about money — this cost that much — and recently he told me — and I won't mention the name here — "Imagine, X told me, 'I only want to have friends who are on a par money wise, everything else is pointless.'" Berthold told me he could have vomited in his face, so he got up and left. They are not interested in you as a human being and in your character. All that counts is, how much money do you have, how much did your house cost, and this cost so much, and my vacation cost — only the prices count. As with the children, so it is with the parents. I am not interested in taking that, my time is too valuable for that.

Now that my children have left I am of course questioning my origins and my identity. No doubt, I am Swiss, I have to reorient myself toward my home country, I am neither German nor Swiss nor Israeli, I don't even know where I belong. Very disciplined I am, and the world must be in order, but I just cannot deal with these nouveau riche Jewish women. I am also bitter that the Kalman family was not very supportive when my husband passed away. So it turns out that my present friendship circle, they are all Christians. A Jewish woman, for example, she went over to Judaism, she converted. And her husband, he is Jewish; he even was a bit religious. He died nine years ago, and so we met. When my husband died, they were really helpful to me. They phoned, "Frau Kalman" — at that time we weren't on a first-name basis yet — "would you like to join us for a Sunday stroll, or would you like to come eat with us?" They really took very good care of me, and today, I am actually very good friends with her. It brings up childhood memories. I have to tell you something. When I was still in school, I had many Christian girlfriends. Because, in my class, there was only one Jewish girl, and she was very, very religious. I did not want to have anything to do with her, she was too much for me. Two Italians were my girlfriends. Sometimes they came to me on Shabbes, and on Pessach, they asked me, listen Eva, could you get us a pack of matzo, and on Christmas, perhaps, I would be up there with them, it was all easygoing; they knew about me and I knew about them. On the other hand, there was anti-Semitism there as well. I remember, when I was in school, it was during the war, a teacher said to me, his name was Herr Egeli, "You, Eva Pincus, you are only a guest here." I did not understand. Why am I a guest? At home, I told my father about it, "Listen, the teacher said I am only a guest here, what is that supposed to mean?" I was ten or eleven years old. My father went to school and complained. He said, "Please explain to me, explain to me please what does that mean, my daughter is only a guest?" The teacher could not explain that, of course, so he smacked him in his face. I had to change classes, and there was also a court case. I don't remember what became of it.

Before you go, I have to tell you one more thing, in spite of everything: anti-Semitism, envy. And something else I have to tell you. After my husband's death, neither the Kalman family, nor Schenfeld, nor the other Jews of F. helped me. Our friends, in quotation marks, Schenfeld, or the Karpls, they did not drop by or help, while my children and I had to get ready for the funeral; the goyim helped me. Or my husband's business partners, from Munich, no condolences, not even a phone call. Christian people invited me, my neighbors. People with whom I really did not have anything to do. So today, I basically have only Christian acquaintances with whom I go to theater. Also, nobody had helped Berthold or Ronnie find a job. The job Ronnie has, at the hospital, he got through a friend, a Christian, with whom he studied in medical school.

Ronnie

IN AND OUT OF HIS

FATHER'S SHADOW

1955	born in F.
1973	Abitur; subsequently travels through South and North America
1974?	begins medical school in Cologne
1976	continues his studies in Munich
1984	completes studies as specialist for dermatology in Munich and begins to work at a local hospital
2004	birth of son

I met Ronnie for the interview in his very personally and attractively furnished apartment. It reflects his wide travels and his various sporting activities and is located in a fine neighborhood in Munich's Schwabing district. He is an athletic, sportily dressed man. In 2001, we met briefly at a bistro on Hohenzollernstrasse. When I saw Esther in Jerusalem in December 2003, she mentioned to me that Ronnie's partner, a physician and not Jewish, was expecting a son — "the first non-Jewish Kalman in our family."

RONNIE: I was born in 1955, almost exactly one year after Berthold, two years after Esther and one year before Salek, so I was pretty much stuck in the middle. We grew up in almost total isolation. My parents did not like us having closer ties with anyone, and they did not like us bringing friends to the house or letting us sleep at friends' homes. I did all that, I did sleep occasionally at friends' homes or hung out with my friends or went places. But they were not happy about it. And my friends were not accepted at home. As far as I was concerned, my parents did not even encourage Jewish activities. I know, for some of my siblings, this was a way out of the house. My parents didn't encourage us to go on machanot [summer camps] or get to know other Jewish kids. They liked it best when we were at home. My parents' philosophy was "us against the rest of the world" — nobody should come in and nobody should get out.

To bring anyone back to the house was very, very difficult, and so I spent more time away from home. When I was in my twenties, I really had distanced myself pretty much from home. I only came home when I absolutely had to. I just did not feel comfortable. It was such a strange situation to be so cut off from the outside and that everything from the outside was somehow bad. Everything outside was bad, and one had to be considerate of our father, we could not discuss problems because he was sick. In fact, throughout my conscious life, he was always sick in some way. Problems could never be fully discussed or be dealt with and instead, one had to suppress them [wegstecken]. So in the period when I became more independent, after Abitur, it drove me away from home. I did not want to be at home. All that Jewish stuff I found somehow sickening. In school, I basically had German friends, and I got along with them really well. So I could not quite accept that I was not supposed to be friends with them, and out of defiance I did it even more. So I stayed away from everything Jewish. I really did not feel comfortable. After Abitur, I was hopping around the world a little bit, America, South America.

EVA: When Ronnie was still in school, I could not relate well to him. He was a bit of a revolutionary in the family. Very independent-minded. But since he was a good student in Gymnasium, I forgave him. After Abitur, he wanted to travel around the world, so I said, okay. Since I had two sisters in Argentina, he started there, and from Argentina all through South America, and so on, and in between, he returned because my husband had suffered a heart attack. In October 1975 he left, and a year later he returned for my daughter's wedding. As a hippie. With long blond hair. And when I picked him up at the train station I thought to myself, no, this can't be. I did not deserve that. I have a couple of sins, but this I did not deserve. Loud-mouthed, a terrible English, jargony, it was a disaster. Long blond hair. He always was a bit of an outsider. You could not tell him anything. He was a good student, so I forgave him a lot. But when he left, I told him, "Listen, Ronnie: in every consulate, wherever you are, there will be a letter from me, and if you need money" — He did not stay in hotels but had a pickup truck and slept in it overnight and with friends, not in a hotel. Under benches, in tents and so on, this is actually very dangerous. "And I only want to know where you are. You'll have letters in each consulate, call me collect from each consulate." And I also called every German consulate — in case my son such and such, if there is a problem, that they will be agreeable. So we actually were in touch pretty well.

AN OBSERVER: I believe the reason the parents supported this idea to travel was that they wanted him to get away from Corinna. They were very much in love, but she was not Jewish. I was friends with her for many years but now I am out of touch.

BERTHOLD: My father had a good pipeline to Ronnie, and if you have come to know Ronnie, you'll know he is always a bit of a revolutionary. Now, of course, since I was there, he was relieved of the obligation of the firstborn, kind of, to go into the firm. So he had a lot of freedom, as much as one could imagine, and he used it fully, and my father really saw himself in Ronnie. Ronnie was very much like him. Ronnie then went on a world tour, and what always very much hurt my father, he disappeared for an entire year. My father had had a heart attack, and Ronnie came back because he felt obligated, and then he went to the hospital, and my father said, "The way you are, I know you well, you'll be leaving again." So Ronnie said, "Can I be honest?" He says, yes, and Ronnie said, basically, I do want to leave again. So Father said, "Then get out." This shows that he understood that being free from emotional obligation towards parents was essential for Ronnie, because my father himself, towards his own parents, was exposed to that emotional obligation, being something of a revolutionary himself. And he understood Ronnie well, even though he always complained and would have preferred to have him around. But in the end, in the depth of his heart, he understood him.

RONNIE: When I came back, I began studying medicine, first in Cologne for two years, and then I moved to Munich to be closer to home and closer to my friends. In Cologne I did not feel comfortable, it was not my kind of city. I specialized in dermatology and completed that in 1984. At first, I worked in a hospital in N., I was not excited about it, but a friend helped me get that job, and then I transferred to the H. hospital in Munich. I work there in the intensive care department.

RONNIE AND WOMEN

But in my own personal matters, there seems to be
something really wrong

I don't know why, but somehow I am sick of all the traveling. I have led a very restless life until now, and I notice I am slowly getting tired of it. *Tired* is maybe the wrong word, but I have had enough of it. I would like to have a more stable life now. After all, I am over forty now. I am basically sick of my — I have had a very, very turbulent life, especially as far as my relationships with women are concerned, and I have had my relationships, a very restless life until now. So far, it does not look like I am going to have a family. I notice that I am running out of time, life is not going to get easier for me. To be getting this situation under control, this is kind of my difficulty in life; it is a hurdle that I don't seem to overcome.

EVA: Well, Ronnie may just demand too much of a woman. He's also had a couple of disappointments behind him. I don't know if he is the marrying type. He'd like to have children, perhaps, yes. He has a nice apartment, maybe you've seen it, very personally appointed, sports and motorcycle equipment. He loves this apartment and he is very orderly. He told me once, "When I have breakfast all by myself on a Sunday morning, I sometimes wonder whether this is not a bit odd."

RONNIE: In my case, I think this is simply a question of fate. In the meantime I started believing in fate. Now, I do have rather high demands vis-à-vis my partner, and I am a pretty emotional person — but the way things have been going in recent years, it looks as if everything is governed by fate. I cannot influence things, they go the way they go. And I have to accept that, as so many things in life. Now it is not as if I am totally unhappy. Many people are in much worse shape than I. For me, everything else in life is going well, I am healthy, am having fun, I've got my job, I have everything that is good for me. And I have my family whom I like, and while I am not extremely closely connected to them, it is still good that I know that they are there. But in my own personal matters, I can see that there seems to be something really wrong. I have really looked into everything and I have found that it is a course governed by fate, that I am just not supposed to have it. But I have, of course, high expectations of a partner and at the same time I always meet the wrong type of woman, a real vicious circle. And I meet the wrong type of women, because I have an affinity to flighty, spacy people. And I have different interests compared to theirs. I'd really like to get settled slowly, and those women who might have the same interests that I have, I am not really attracted to. I don't even meet them.

So this is my problem in life. Compared to other men, I surely have many women, but what I now really want is a stable situation, something with someone to get old together, and I am light years away from that. I want someone I can depend upon, the rest of my life, I mean half of it is over already, I am aware of that, and I can do the arithmetic. But someone with whom I could be for the rest of my life — that somehow does not come to be. I am beginning to accept the fact that I cannot have that. And to deal with it. One has to take life as it is. As I said, I am healthy, I have fun in life otherwise. I am not a sad character, but a stable relationship I cannot have, and I also don't want to make compromises. If I could not fall in love somehow, then I'd rather not get into it. Especially among us Jews, many people get into marriages of convenience and relations of convenience — I'd never do that. It must be passionate. If it is not, then I'd rather not have it.

BERTHOLD: In terms of planning one's life, Ronnie and I are hard to categorize. Ronnie even has a more serious case of that, because he has not yet undergone the maturing process, because he does not have such a close relationship. Were he in a close relationship, he would react the way I do, because he understands that one's daily life is more important than conforming to a trivial outline that somebody is providing for you — marrying a non-Jewish woman, for example. So you have to be able to take the initiative and take the responsibility and make the decisions. And these decisions may go against one or the other personality in the family.

RONNIE: Now I could not, for example — would you mind turning off the tape for a moment? Thanks. . . . [*Ronnie raises a point he does not wish to have recorded*] If they had not been Jewish women, for example, it would have been difficult, if not impossible. And you always have that in your subconscious somewhere and it does not admit total close-ness. That I have worked out with myself. You have the family in the back of your mind and you figure, this is just going to be trouble. It is in my subconscious and it does not admit real closeness.

Now, for my mother, it would be difficult, no matter what. Very difficult. My brother Berthold has been living with a non-Jewish woman, for over six years now [1996], for six years they have been living together, she is Italian, and right now I am trying to convince my mother that she should finally accept it. Because otherwise, a life, two lives are going to be ruined. That is not worth it. And it is really difficult for her to accept that. My mother is simply an incredibly dominant hen who is madly attached to her children. And she is madly jealous of any woman that comes into this family. I mean, Raya she accepts, Salek's wife, but Raya does not really count somehow in this regard. And lastly, perhaps it does not even matter if the woman is Jewish or not.

IN AND OUT OF THE FAMILY GHETTO

My current affinity for home developed much later

EVA: Today, I have a wonderful relationship to Ronnie, really fantastic, he also called tonight, we meet in Munich, he drops by, we talk, he tells me a lot of what happens to him personally, with women and so forth. A fantastic relationship. Super. We laugh, he says, just think, I was with this woman, dadadadadada, the things that happen, imagine, this woman, dadadada, and so on. Super.

Q: *Now Ronnie has had God knows how many women. Could it be that his problem is that he is very much tied to you?*

EVA: You are kind of making comparisons, and that is very bad. One should never draw comparisons with a mother.

RONNIE: Let me say that my current affinity for back home, that affinity developed much later, really only now that I have become an adult. I am a late developer, really only at age thirty did I slowly come to be an adult. Before that, I was a total child. During my time in medical school, I was not an adult, really. My attitude toward things was not responsible, and as far as my later life is concerned, all of that happened without me doing much about it, and I was not much concerned about it, I was busy more with superfluous matters at the time. So only for the last seven or eight years [since 1988–89] have I returned to the family. And as harsh as it sounds, my father's death was also good for the family. He was simply so sensitive, and we could not burden him with anything. It is unacceptable that if there are problems, you cannot burden someone with that. Problems can only be solved by burdening people with them. After his death, I was quite annoyed that we had put up with this for so long, including lying about his cancer and all that crap. He had leukemia, but we never talked about it, and he probably knew about it anyhow, but we still told him all this nonsense. I had to put a good face on it, and a number of things could not be articulated. In hindsight, this was simply wrong, I regret this very much. I would have liked to talk to my father about a lot of things, but it could not be done any more. At that time, I was still not mature enough to take things into my own hands. For example, not to be influenced by my mother's wishes. And perhaps it was not even my mother's wish, but I only imagined that it was her wish, and to contradict that, against better knowledge. Had it been today, I would have acted more independently, but at that time, I was still too young, too immature. It was too much for me then, I could not take a position then.

THE KALMAN FAMILY

All three of them caused an unprecedented wreck
of the gift of life that they received there

RONNIE: The environment I grew up in included my uncles and their families, and with them, my father fought all his life. As far as I know, we've always lived fighting, constant altercations between the brothers. They did not stick together. With Jurek we had more contact, Jurek was totally uncomplicated. But brotherly love and a feeling of togetherness — that did not exist. This applied to my mother's relatives as well. My father did not maintain contact with them either. He did not want us to have much contact with our maternal relatives. For my father, they were all idiots, and he did not accept anyone. As far as our contact with the cousins is concerned, it is true, we did have contact — what is his name again? — with Jonny and also with Motti, but as we grew up, it broke off. With Dina, there was no relationship at all. When we were

children, everyone bad-mouthed everyone else, but to be honest, this
also had to do with our parents. Our parents bad-mouthed the others in
front of us as well. For whatever reasons. These endless fights, they
were transmitted into the second generation, then; if you really think
about it, it is tragic.

So they all went through the camps together, and they built up
something after the war, and everything went to pieces. And because of
that, everything was wrecked. The whole business and everything. In
my opinion, all three of them caused, oh well, an unprecedented wreck
of the gift of life that they received there. To be honest, I find it awful.
And irresponsible. Despite everything that they did accomplish — but
they had lost the great idea [große Gedanke]. The great idea at issue in
my mind is, in all our misfortune, we were lucky, we survived the
Holocaust, now let us raise our families together and live and enjoy life.
I think they had to realize that they could not take this for granted. To
have a life like that. And even this life in business all three of them have
wrecked.

I find this horrifyingly awful. I find it tragic. It has a lot to do with
this being Jewish and not being Jewish and is also, I believe, a consequence of the Holocaust. I, for example, am aware that life is a limited
story and cannot be taken for granted. That we live here and today and
not at anytime, in the year 4000. They don't have that awareness. They
were only busy with crap. They were busy only with totally idiotic
pettiness, whether this one said this or that and whether one should
therefore be insulted, who is on speaking terms with whom and who
does not speak, who is friends with whom and who is not, and why one
cannot speak to this one or that one. It was total pettiness. It was awful.
So we had these intensely close and warm relations in the home and
awful relations outside. My father had a lot to do with this.

In the course of time, my mother was shaped by my father somehow. My father did not accept anyone. He did not accept my maternal
grandfather either. He thought that he himself was the best on earth,
and he did not need anyone. In this respect, as far as human relationships were concerned, he was very narrow-minded and intolerant.
From all that I have heard, he used to be an open-minded young man, in
view of the conditions he came from. He came from a supposedly very
religious shtetl family. In that respect, he apparently was very open-
minded and modern. But they did not carry this on, did not continue it.
He was Zionist-oriented, he was very sports-oriented. I am sure he

wanted to drive a sports car and all the kinds of things young men like to do. All of that must have been destroyed in the concentration camp. The way people described him is not how we got to know him.

We found out about this through small anecdotes here and there. He did tell us that he went skiing and that his parents did not like that, and other things like that. For me, looking back, all of this is incomprehensible: how they survived and how they actually lived. Also, after surviving the Holocaust, he did not have a relationship with my aunt Gertrud, it really did not exist, I don't know what else was going on there.

JEWISHNESS IN GERMANY

The Germans are so awful, and we are living here nevertheless

Both my parents came from religious homes, but in our home, religion did not play an important role. We did light candles, but not always, and it always sort of depended on the mood. Whether my father was in the mood or whether he was not. When something else was more important, then something else was more important. It was not conviction but rather family tradition. At home, everything Jewish was a matter of family tradition. They had nothing to do with religion, God, or what not, with spiritual things.

I myself don't have a particular interest in Jewish matters. I don't hang out with other Jews. I know a few people here and there, a few Jews I know, acquaintances from a cafe, but they are not people whom I would phone. I might meet them someplace, I might talk to them, small talk, but I have no Jewish friends. In Munich.

Q: *Let us say there is an interesting Jewish movie running, let's say Woody Allen, would that be something attractive for you?*

No. Well, I mean, Woody Allen and so on, this really addresses typically arch-Jewish problems.

Q: *Especially inasfar as women are concerned.*

Okay. I can identify with that. That is more interesting to me as it might be for someone else. But I don't find it to be something reasoned, I think.

Once I was even near Slawkusz. I was near Cracow once. It was totally by chance, I do air emergency rescues, kind of flying ambulances, and we were near there. We had to make a stopover, and I got out of the plane and stood around there for one or two hours in the Cracow airport, and it was weird, I felt really rotten. I don't know why, I did not feel well at all. Nothing reminded me. My family's home is still there, but I did not know where it was; all I knew is that I was nearby. And this is the air that I am breathing, and I did not feel good about it, I felt totally awful.

In F., for example, I don't go to synagogue, it is a real rotten feeling. Not for a million would I ever set foot in there again. Because of all the dishonest shit. This entire system of lies and of fraud that I grew up with. Where nothing fit neither in the front nor in the back. These lies, that we are all so different from the Germans, that the Germans are so awful, and that we are living here nevertheless. And please don't go anywhere. Best if we always stayed home and did not even go places. My parents did not even push us to go to boarding schools, even Jewish ones, to England maybe or to the U.S., they would never have allowed that. All they wanted was that we stay at home and have no contact with the Germans. This was such a sick business, and for the longest time I could not understand, how can my father hate the Germans so much and then stay here? And get his children to grow up here?

For us, all these Jewish things were only symbols somehow, that we are not like the others. All these ceremonies that we performed, in my view, were only kept up to teach us that we are different from the others. This had nothing to do at all with spirituality. I had nothing whatsoever to do with the Zionist Youth as well. I found all of that pretty revolting.

In contrast to me, Berthold always had Jewish friends. I didn't ever. And quite honestly, with that entire story, I turned into a real anti-Semite. I found all of that revolting. So in school, I basically had German friends, and got along with them very well and could not accept that I should not be friends with them. So out of spite, I did it even more. So this was also a reaction of defiance. I stayed away from everything Jewish. I did not feel comfortable. This whole Jewish thing is so sick and gets on my nerves so much, including now when I see it on TV, when they still discuss this victim question, which so many Jewish organizations are still keeping up, I hate that like the plague.

In no way can I follow that. It is my conviction that whoever is here, as a Jew, should either feel German to some extent or not be here. No one is forced to be here, and whoever hates the Germans — you can do that, it is entirely legitimate to hate the Germans, no question — should leave. But whoever stays here should see things differently. The Germans that I personally have dealings with I don't hate. People my age. As little as I hate any other peoples. I have simply been raised here. For whatever reason I did not make it, growing up elsewhere, going elsewhere, but it never bothered me much, because I never felt very Jewish.

Salek

1957	born in F.
1963	enters local elementary school
1973	active in ZJD
1976	goes to Israel, to continue high school
1978	returns to F., active in professional sports
1983	opens fitness studio
1988	brawl, legal trouble in F.
1989	returns to Israel, marries Raya

I first met Salek one afternoon in Cafe Nordau, a well-established cafe near Kikkar Medinah in Tel Aviv. The cafe and the street of the same name refer to Max Nordau, the German physician and Zionist leader who became known through his writings on physical degeneracy among Jews and as the proponent of the "new muscle Jew." The irony of meeting a Jewish bodybuilder in a cafe named Nordau occurred to me only later on when it was pointed out to me. Salek drove a car with a license plate of F., his hometown in Germany — the only time I have ever seen anyone in Israel driving with a German license plate. When Salek stepped out of the car to walk over to where I was sitting, people turned, whispering to one another, even giggling. Here was a Schwarzenegger look-alike, a huge muscular man who looked like no one else in this cafe.

YOUTH AND SCHOOL

From the beginning, and whether I liked it or not,
I was predestined to be an exception

SALEK: Well now, I was born in 1957 in F., and grew up there, first elementary school, then to the St. Hedwig Gymnasium. My career in school was such that basically I went through more schools than school years. I was a pretty bad student, a really bad, unstable student, also very influenced by sports, and they dragged me through Gymnasium as long as it was possible, because I was good at sports, but after a certain time, they could not keep me any longer, and I went to a private school instead.

This private school did not help much either. When I was eighteen, in 1976, and this was after my father's first heart attack and the beginnings of real trouble in the firm, I decided to go to Israel to continue my education there, via a pedagogically oriented system, to redo my high school degree there, which I did in part, but did not finish.

I remember my first day in school, in F., at age six or seven. The teacher takes attendance, reads all the names, and everyone says their first name and religion, and now you have to imagine the following: she calls my name, she says Kalman, I say here I am, first name is Salomon, and thirty kids turn around and ask, what? hah? and they stare. I mean, Salomon is not a German name. And I sink back into my chair. And for "religion" I have to say Mosaic, that is, neither Protestant nor Catholic like everybody else. There are thirty kids there and I sink ever more deeply into my chair. That you have to imagine, and I have to say, from the beginning, and whether I liked it or not, I was predestined to be an exception. And so I have given them a reason why I am the exception. I did not want it. But I was forced into it, basically. And that is how I saw it.

I had to face anti-Semitism all my life in Germany. Later, for example, a couple of things happened that hit close to home. It began in 1988. I was in trouble with the law, because someone in my fitness studio owed me money, and we had an altercation, and in the course of the discussion, and it got to be a bit agitated, he called me a dirty Jew (Saujude) which is nothing unusual because in Germany it happens often, and so, as usual, I knocked him down. This was not the first and also not the last time, and the matter went to court because he went to the police.

Q: *You could have gone to the police as well because of the anti-Semitic slur.*

SALEK: Sure, I could have done that, but I did not. For me, the matter was settled because I beat him up and threw him out. What else should I have done? And the court found me guilty of premeditated assault, and since this was not the first time — I was known to the police for previous assaults causing injury — I got two years on a conditional discharge, never mind the mitigating circumstances, and so I had a criminal record.

ESTHER: My brother Salek had several brawls because of anti-Semitic attacks. He was the one who said, *no more.* With him, there was no pity. Even today, people should not try to get into trouble with him, and earlier in his life, when there was anything, anti-Semitic or similar, he could have killed the person. There were two incidents in Germany where people ended up in hospital, with fractured chin, lost teeth, and so on. He probably also had, who knows, a criminal record because of it.

SALEK: There were still another couple of instances with Nazis in Germany, basically there were always anonymous calls or letters, abusing me, insulting me, or threatening me. But this was never particularly unusual, because I dealt with this entirely differently. If someone threatened me, I said, okay, make my day, because basically, for me this was always a great occasion, a couple of guys would show up and want to threaten me, and then I beat them up, and it made me feel incredibly good. Exactly. Make my day. They knew in town that if someone said something funny to me, I would not beat around the bush [nicht viel drumrum]. I am not the typical ghetto Jew.

The Jewish environment in Germany was not very satisfying either. In Germany I never had Jewish friends. True, I was in a Zionist Youth organization, but I never had any Jewish friends. I was even very active, I was madrich in the machanot, so I went through personal development there. They sponsored and supported me, but I was a militant type. Because discipline was important to me. I was raised in sports, was educated in sports and found that only through discipline can you accomplish something, and not with laxity. At the time, the ZJD was influenced by the antiauthoritarian movement, and I was always in the more right-leaning wing: more strict, more tight, authoritarian, and this was also my philosophy in guiding personnel in the ZJD. Now, the kids reacted in two ways to that, as you might expect. Some welcomed it, some rejected it totally. There was no middle ground. I was always more conflictual, I am not the smooth type. I have edges. I tackle problems, I am looking for conflict. And this was my problem in Germany, because I was looking for conflict, for account settling.

SPORT AND SHOAH

I was anything but a victim

I have always tried to understand, how was it possible that nobody resisted? With this strange discipline, they let themselves be shipped, be shot, they dug their graves, they got undressed and never defended themselves. Every Indian tribe, any Negro tribe has taken rocks and bats and defended itself, and only we, the Jews in Europe, with all our intelligence, all our dough, with our money, were not in a position to defend ourselves. This is why I developed my body the way you see me today. I am not exactly a weakling. I always had the pulse of new developments at my fingertips. And whenever there was anything directed against the Jews, I was super extremely sensitive.

I had nothing to do with the Jews in F. I despised the Jews. Because my premise was, it takes two to tango. You need a perpetrator and a victim. It was clear to me who the victim was to be. One has to be predestined to be a victim. I was anything but a victim. To this day I cannot imagine this: what is more difficult, what involves more suffering: this daily threat, this oppression, to see the torment and to experience it yourself — or, on the basis of this threat, because death is threatening me daily, every second, right?, to be taking things into your own hands, to say, I have to die no matter what, therefore I want to die like a human being. And there I would rip out one of the guards' throat with my teeth, and he bleeds to death and he shoots me dead. I am armed to this very day. Let me show you my gun, here it is. [*Pulls his gun out of his belt*] I am allowed to wear this gun, I have a special permit. This is my basic attitude. I am looking for conflict.

I am looking for person-to-person combat. This is why I chose handball as my sport, because it is a contact-intensive sport. It is a fight one on one. Only the winner survives. It is not track and field athletics. I started with that. In track and field, I run against someone else, but he runs. And I cannot block him, this is not really one-on-one combat. Handball is the absolute one-on-one combat, with hard body contact, only the stronger one survives. This is why I am the way I am, and basically this is why I am here in Israel. I did not want my kids to experience what I have experienced in school.

Q: *You are not the only one in your family, though, to be athletically oriented: Ronnie is, Gaby and Berthold are as well.*

Oh yes, but differently, totally differently. You just have to take a look and see how Gaby is involved in sports. He does not torture himself with it. I torture myself doing it. I am a fanatic. I am obsessed, I have an idea, I have a vision, this is what obsesses me. Now if you take Gaby or Ronnie or Berthold, my three brothers that are living in Germany, they are basically typical ignoramuses.

Q: *Why are they living there?*

For the basic reason, there is this psychological phenomenon of the consequences of error. If I admit something, then I have to admit that my entire development was in error. Can I afford that? They make a calculation. They say, I cannot admit my error, so I am not doing anything wrong here, everything is okay. That does not mean they are aware of it. They ignore their error, it is pure psychology. I have been facing this for a long time myself. My brothers are pursuing successful careers, but they are blind to what is going on around them, the anti-Semitism. Especially with Gabriel, and it has to do with the consequence of error. Because if he admitted this, if he felt this, then he would need to do something about it. But he does not do anything about it. So, consequently, he cannot admit that he feels something, he is sticking his head in the sand like an ostrich. One gets ignorant, one ignores that, just like it was with the German Jews before 1933 or until 1939 or until 1941. One simply ignores that.

Of course, mentality-wise, they would not really harmonize with Israel. Gaby and Berthold not at all, Ronnie more likely perhaps. Berthold is too straight and too German, but he is of course very successful, he is a top manager, I envy him; his job is a hell of a work. But they lack the kind of flexibility you need in Israel; their mentality does not harmonize with the Israeli one.

I should also point out to you that I am the only one of the Kalmans who has a son. An heir. Someone who (a) is a man and (b) carries on the name. It is obvious why my brothers cannot marry. They cannot find Jewish women in Germany, because the Jewish women who reside in Germany are basically a catastrophe. Both mentality-wise and in their looks. And to take a woman from Israel and bring her to Germany in most cases does not work, because you pull them out of their social acceptability, you plant them into a totally new and alien environment, and then you've got a job, and then work twelve, thirteen, fourteen hours per day, you barely see the woman, and whom does she see and meet?

SALEK'S FATHER

My father had absolute integrity

My father, my aunt, and uncles had the concentration camp syndrome. My father almost never talked about it. Only insofar as he said that there are no pictures, no books, and no films that could represent what happened. You see, when you look at that phenomenon and you ask yourself, six million Jews were killed, then no one can relate to that. What does it mean, six million? No one has seen a pile of six million corpses. Nobody has. You can also not imagine such a thing. But when you take a single life, for example, why it is that Rayna, my uncle Jurek's wife, why she is alive, then you'll understand what was perpetrated on human beings. Because Rayna was with her mother and her brother at the ramp of the concentration camp, and her mother had to decide which child does she take. So she decided to take her daughter, and her son was killed. Then you see and you are aware that this woman lives with the awareness that she lived because her brother was killed — when you see there the individual tragedy, then I have always asked myself, how was it possible that nobody resisted?

So I wanted to avoid my father's experience from the start. I suffered when I heard my father's stories, and how he was oppressed: his time in Poland, his time in the concentration camp, his time in Germany afterward. It had a great impact on my development. Later on, my father, being in Germany as a businessman, had two problems. The first one related to the problems that people make for Jews. My father had absolute integrity. Really beyond any suspicion of doing anything crooked or wrong. He had absolute integrity, he was absolutely correct, a cor-

rect businessman and very successful. But, like it or not, at a certain
level of success, in order to advance further, you need support at a
higher level, and that would also have to do with politics. And my
father never advanced to that level. My father could never overcome
that hurdle; he had no ties to the politicians, because he was simply
always the Jew. Before as after, he was the Jew for the Germans. And
they made sure that he did not become too strong. Our family was
isolated in F. We were an island to ourselves.

The second problem had to do with his brothers. There were times
when they did not speak to one another; in my view there were many
disagreeable things, but it is very hard for me to judge people, or to
evaluate their ideas of justice and injustice, to be judging people who
have survived the concentration camps. They have experienced an entirely different aspect in their lives, and I cannot even understand how
one can live after that. So in the firm, there were these conflicts sooner
or later, over who was in charge and responsible for what, who is the
big boss, and who has got how much to say. Since my father was the
eldest, he was the one, and everyone at first accepted that until the
women appeared and began exerting influence, because they did not
want to be the wives of the second boss or the third boss and wanted to
be the wife of the big boss. So there were these family quarrels that the
brothers had to go through, with arbitration and God knows what, this
was a really evil affair. It was a family arbitration court, they called the
fathers-in-law into that court, together with lawyers and legal sanction.
This was not a pleasant story for any of the parties.

All of this at some point led to a disaster, in my view; my father
simply miscalculated, and then, it was 1984. The firm went into receivership, basically it was politics because the banks canceled the
loans, in my view it was pure politics. But no matter what, my father
then died because of this bankruptcy, in 1985.

SALEK AND THE LAW

I had a wonderful brawl there. That was wonderful.

I had several situations with neo-Nazis in Germany, and this demonstrated that what happened to my father and to the ordinary ghetto
Jews would not happen to me. A lot of Jews in Germany today, and I

include my brother Gabriel, just don't react the way they should. You get to be ignorant, you ignore what happened under Nazism. They simply ignore it. Something like that could not happen to me, that's for sure. At the time, I had my fitness studio in the Tower Hotel in F., and next to the hotel was the congress center, and at some point the DVU, the Deutsche Volks-Union, had a party congress, and all the neo-Nazi big shots were there. There was an anti-Nazi demonstration there, and when I saw it, I joined them. They were leftists or anarchists or whatever, basically it was the same to me. I joined them, I was in total rebellion then, and the Nazis were also in the parking garage, and I waited, and I threw an egg onto the car, so they got out, and then I had a wonderful brawl there. That was wonderful. I had marvelous fun there.

After this event, I received a threatening letter, and my car was set on fire. This was 1989 in the spring. What happened was that this letter was stuck onto my car, my beautiful Chevrolet, this was on a Friday evening or a Saturday night, I don't quite remember. The letter said I should stay away from German girls, purity law or whatever, and soon F. will be judenfrei. I thought, well okay, anonymous threats, I was never particularly interested in that, but the following night, they blew up my car. In the parking garage. I assume it was with a molotov cocktail. They simply smashed the window, threw in the molotov cocktail, and whoops, at some point this thing blew up, via the gasoline tank.

So I had to make a decision. It was clear to me this was of a different caliber, and the German law, because I had been convicted, two years probation, and I thought, if this is German law, and that is how they see it, then I'll have to accept it. That is how German law is. So if I can no longer defend myself, then this cannot be a place for me to live. So in 1989 and on political grounds I decided to leave Germany.

MEETING RAYA

Here the ring was closed

The way I came to settle in Israel was different from that of my sister Esther. My route was a much more circuitous one. As I mentioned, I left Gymnasium in Germany and continued schooling in Israel. I was there from age eighteen to twenty. I played handball, as a professional, for three seasons and with a recognized team. But my father's health had already deteriorated, he had his first heart attack in 1975, and he wanted us to go into the family business. My brother Berthold started working there in 1977. In 1978 I returned to Germany because my father wanted me to, and he wanted me to start working in the factory. Household appliances. So I returned, but was working mostly on my athletic career. I played handball in the National League. In 1983 I withdrew from professional sports, intentionally, and opened a fitness studio, in F. I called it "Salek's Gym."

Nevertheless, I started playing handball again, as a substitute player, and then in 1988 I went to New York, and I worked in several fitness studios, with Sylvester Stallone among others. Basically, I started a career there as a personal coach. Then I came back from New York. And this is what happened. At my brother Ronnie's place, he gave a party and there I met Raya. She was an Israeli, she'd been living for eleven years in Munich, was married there, got divorced, she was already divorced for six years I think, and she got to know me there. At the party, she said to another Israeli, "Just look" — she said it in Hebrew, and I was standing right next to her — "just look, he looks just like Ronnie, it could be Ronnie." And I answered in Hebrew, "He does not just look like it and could be it, he really is his brother."

Now we are sitting here in Israel, and as you can see, I don't look like someone who would even speak Hebrew, certainly I don't look like an Israeli, not to mention somebody from the Middle East. I am not an Asiatic type; I am tall, have broad shoulders and blue eyes. Basically, I am the typical Aryan, and there we get these oppositions. My wife, it totally shocked her. That's how we got to know each other. And then we fell in love, and three months later, I asked her to marry me.

I looked at it practically, because at the time I was already almost thirty-three, and I saw somehow, after my period of Sturm und Drang that this is basically the woman who I could start a family with. But she turned me down, after three months, and I told her then, I will not propose to you again, and she accepted that. Six months later, finally, Raya made another overture and suggested that we get married, but by that time, I had already gotten used to the situation, it was not so hot anymore, I was comfortable the way things were, and at that point I did not want to become pinned down.

So Raya returned to Israel in May 1989. At that point, a number of things happened. It began such that in January 1989 a former player from my handball team also wanted to end his sports career. He wanted to finish it by getting into the phenomenon of the fitness studios. And he asked me whether he could join my studio. I said that was fine by me, so he came in as a partner, this was January or February, then my wife, my future wife, left for Israel in May. She basically left me because I did not want to get married. So I thought about everything: I saw that the right-wing scene got established, it became acceptable, they did not do anything about it. The DVU, the Nazis, they could hold their party meeting in the Congress Center, they were protected by the police and by a legal system that sentenced me instead. This is German law. So this cannot be my space. And then, there was this personal matter, this emotional matter with my wife, shutter closed, monkey dead, case closed.

And now you see, here the ring was closed, my future wife had gone to Israel, her actual home because she was born there and lived there and so on. I did not want to marry her, and she said, well then she does not have any reason for staying on, and then all those things are happening, and I recognize: (a) this cannot be my place here, (b) I have my wife — we were not married, but we lived like a married couple, I saw I missed her more than any other woman I have ever known. And I thought, this is once again such a situation that for two weeks I will have to get drunk every night, and things will pass. It happened often enough, in my life I really must have dated hundreds of women. Then I thought: just look, this is a signal of fate, you have to pay attention there.

So at the end of June, beginning of July, I decided to get over to Israel to figure out what kind of stable my wife was really coming from. Her parents, I found out, are from Rumania, basically Holocaust survivors, very cultured people. Simply Europeans. Her mother for a very long time had a hairdressing salon, a very successful one. This was in the south of Tel Aviv, and hers was the leading hairdressing salon in the entire area. Her father had a textile importing and exporting business, and now they are basically pensioners. So that is how that looks. Really cultured people.

She was pretty surprised about my visit and my checking everything out, and then we had a businesslike discussion together, and agreed, and then planned our future together. I agreed that we would live in Israel together, and I planned my future in Israel. And so I emigrated here to Israel then.

RONNIE: I did not know a thing about his marriage, that he would get married. He did not even invite me to the wedding. Maybe he was embarrassed. I don't even know whether it was a small or big wedding, I have no idea what it was like. I did not even get to see a photo from the wedding. I think Salek is uncomfortable about this. But he had to make a big show about it.

Q: *Salek, did the Israelis treat you like a Yecke [German Jew]?*

Less like a Yecke, Israeli society simply found my style very difficult to deal with, but this style is what made me successful, and that is my discipline, my sense of duty, and my view of life, which basically are very German. And this produces presentations and images that are appreciated very much here and that can be achieved only if you have this discipline and this work ethic and sense of duty. And with that, I have achieved a great deal of acceptance here, a far greater acceptance here than I ever had in Germany.

SALEK AND HIS FAMILY

We have also become aware, really, what family means

With my acceptance here and the success I have had, I have also gained my sister's acceptance. In earlier times, I never had much contact with her. But ever since I have been living here, since 1989, we have also become aware, really, what family means. It is also the Israeli environment. Here, you get to have an entirely different family relationship than in Europe. The mentality here is different. If you live here in Israel as a single person, you do not have the social acceptance that you have if you live in a family or with a certain connectedness. This is exactly the discrepancy between my sister and me on one hand, and my brothers on the other hand. You have to imagine that of the elder group of us siblings, the eldest and the youngest, my sister and me, are the ones who are married and have children. Not Gaby, not Ronnie, and not Berthold.

As far as the sense of family in Israel is concerned, I absolutely have to tell you the following story. At some point, after I had come here, I was working out at a fitness studio and I met and got to talk to this fellow. You have to realize, I was a giant body builder then, people really took notice of me. So we started having a conversation, I spoke Hebrew after all, and then he invited me to his home. Simply, "Why don't you drop by our house tonight, my wife would love to meet you," and so on. So I went there, Kikar Medinah number such and such. Now I realized I did not even have his last name, and I look at the bells with the last names on it and simply decided the ring the name Pincus, because this was somehow my family, my mother's maiden name. I get up to the third floor, yes, hello Ilan, hello Salek, yes, we talk, and I tell him how I got to Israel, and with Pincus, strange, this is also my mother's maiden name, and he says, "Really? Where is your mother from?" "My mother is from Switzerland." So he says, "Well, that's interesting, my family is from Switzerland as well." I said, "Perhaps we are even related," and he says, "Do you know, I have a relative here, a second cousin, as follows. She is from Germany, and has a gallery in Jerusalem in the Rehov Strauss." I said, "You know what, that is my sister." We had to really laugh, and our kin relations were all cleared up then.

Our family now meets on a regular basis, and in recent years, we've met fairly frequently. In the winter, we, my wife and I, were in Germany on a vacation. And in April, we were all together in Germany for Pessach, it was the first time that we were all together, after many, many years. So I met all my siblings, and then there was a big event in London because my sister organized her daughter's bat mizvah, so I saw all of my brothers there. So we really are in contact with each other now.

With my cousins, the other Kalmans, I have next to no contact. It is because of the trouble between my father and my uncles. What could connect one more than having survived the concentration camps together, having helped one another to survive? For thirty-eight years [1996] I have been in this system, this conflict, and I am party to it as well. I am predisposed, I have been subjected to a certain brainwashing myself, on the basis of the stories I was told, when I was a child. Naturally, you cannot be totally objective there. My aunt in Brooklyn — I am sorry, I just cannot remember her name right now, it is on the tip of my tongue, she is not involved in the conflict, but we don't have much contact with her either. She has also been wrecked by the concentration camps. Just think, I cannot even remember the name of my aunt. She has a son by the name of Jerry. He once came to F. He is a real American.

With Dina in H. and with Jonny, who is a lawyer in Haifa, I have zero connection, but I do have Jonny's phone number, and if he ever called me and needed something, it would never even occur to me to say no. Never! But it would not occur to me to just call him. Dina's mother's the one who has the most responsibility for the family feud. Now Jurek and Rayna, on the other hand, I see quite frequently, despite all the family trouble. Rayna was the power in that family. She is not only the wife. First, she is very educated and second, very smart. You can't underestimate that. And they come to visit me. Whenever they are in Israel, they visit me, and they are very friendly. From that side, there is no problem. They also came to my father's funeral. Ignaz was there as well, but Fela stayed away.

AN OBSERVER: Salek did not have much luck, neither in school nor with his fitness studios. But he always was a good body builder. Now [2001] he has a sporting goods store in Jerusalem. He saw the success of his siblings, so much so that they had difficulty talking to him. He suffers because of that. He wants to show them how successful he is. So he is looking for stability in his family, and he sees the children that he has put into the world as his sign of success.

Salek, among all the Kalman siblings, is the most colorful one, he has got real character, and of all the siblings, he is liked the most and in some ways even particularly admired. I don't know what his problem is. He might well be more able, have more abilities than any of the others. He has great intellectual and personal abilities, but they went totally in the wrong direction. These are personal problems, they have nothing to do with his capabilities. He has got the capabilities of a genius. And he is an incredibly nice guy, a real charmer, really witty.

Esther

THE ZIONIST PIONEER

IN OUR FAMILY

1953   born in F.
1969   first visit to Israel
1973   Abitur/ moves to Israel
1976   marries Aurel
1982   birth of first daughter

I interviewed Esther in her art gallery on a busy stretch of Rehov Strauss in Jerusalem; some parts of the walls are covered with exquisite lithographs and paintings and others are lined with floor-to-ceiling bookshelves, packed with rare and fine antique books, mostly related to eighteenth- and nineteenth-century Palestine, to Zionism, especially German Zionism, and to German-Jewish art and culture; well over a hundred paintings and lithographs sit in racks in the middle of the gallery, with additional precious, more or less worn books and folios piled on tables and in various corners. This gallery, founded by Esther's father-in-law, who had emigrated from Rumania long before World War II, exudes comfort. Its history is known to just about anyone in Israel who collects Israeli art, lithographs, and rare books. Esther invited me to sit across from her desk in the rear of the gallery, with my back to the street; she sat opposite me, looking out onto the street. Her desk was pleasantly cluttered with books, note pads, business cards, two telephones. Some customers, her daughters, or perhaps her husband, called a number of times, temporarily interrupting our interview. Esther is a resolute, attractive businesswoman with reddish hair; she was dressed somewhat conservatively in shades of orange, beige, and

light brown, accented by gold necklaces and bracelets. Her manner
conveys the sense that she has no time to waste.

I saw Esther last in her gallery in Jerusalem in late December 2003.
She had hoped to come to a lecture I gave at Ben-Gurion University.
She asked me what I thought of Sharon, whom she supports strongly.
She also told me proudly that her eldest daughter had just become an
officer in the Israeli army, and she showed me a photo of her daughter
next to her horse: an attractive, athletic-looking young woman with
long blond hair, smiling into the camera. Esther's father had bought
horses for his children as well.

ESTHER: All right, I am the eldest born of the eldest brother, that is, I
am the first of that generation, of the second generation. I was named
after my grandmother, and Esther is of course the quintessential Jewish
queen. There is also my cousin Jerry in the U.S., who is older than me,
but unlike us, he did not grow up in Germany, and he is a Kalman on his
mother's side, not of one of the brothers who stayed in Germany. I went
to elementary school and Gymnasium in F. and graduated there with
the Abitur, in 1973. I had firm goals and interests in school early on,
history and art history, but sociology and politics interested me as well.
Social-psychological and sociopolitical matters, political science, and
especially the history of the Jews. This fascinated me very early on, at
the age of fourteen or fifteen already.

I was totally, like in the worst Middle Ages, totally in the ghetto

Just imagine the kind of childhood and adolescence I had, in a southern
German town after the war. Especially for me as a girl. It was one thing
for the boys, but I am the only daughter of five siblings. And I was the
eldest. I was not allowed to date non-Jews, and basically I could not
have any non-Jewish friends. I was totally, like in the worst Middle
Ages, totally in the ghetto. There was also virtually no Jewish life there,
in F. or in N. We were very few children, perhaps ten children of various
ages. We were kind of organized, first in the Jewish kindergarten, all
thrown together. But it really was a very, very strong Jewish identity,
and we simply were not allowed to go out with non-Jews, during adolescence. So at best I was sometimes in N. or sometimes in Munich, but
we were very, very restricted.

Long before my first visit to Israel I had decided that I wanted to live in Israel. The *idea* of a Jewish state was important to me, especially with the Six Day War. I remember that well, I was fourteen at the time of the war, in '67. I was in school, we were incredibly emotional then, and very proud of course. There was a very old teacher, she was close to retirement, she got up and congratulated me to my proud countrymen. She was actually the first — I mean countrymen is really — well, somewhere we belong to Israel, true — she congratulated me.

But I did not just have positive experiences like with this teacher. I had many negative experiences in school, and it always drove me mad, this slander, this nonexistent Holocaust. I was very strong in history, and pretty pushy. At the age of twelve or thirteen, perhaps, I read *Exodus* by Leon Uris. It impressed me tremendously. I got to be very interested in the Holocaust and there was no book that I would not have read, at twelve, thirteen, or fourteen. It wrecked me completely. You have to imagine that at that time, it was the late sixties in school, they discussed the Hitler period without talking about the Holocaust. It did not exist. This always made me very angry, very upset, and I always raised it in class. I was very involved there. I also had several anti-Semitic experiences. Children called me dirty Jew [Judensau] or things like that, there I really defended myself. Once, it was in third grade, there was a boy in my class, he called me a dirty Jew, and I hit him with my fist in the eye, so he had a black eye for a couple of days. I never just swallowed that, I always reacted.

Well, there were not really very many, perhaps just two experiences, but my antennae were incredibly sensitized. When somebody — and this I still do today — if someone said something wrong in any shape or form, we probably also noticed that in an exaggerated manner. Not everyone, but I did. It is because I was the eldest, and I was very influenced by my father. Well, I can tell you stories, stories that happened much more recently. For example, I once had a German au pair girl, only ten years ago here in Israel. She noticed the mezuza at the entrance of our apartment and thought that there was Christian blood in there. She had learned that in her Catholic village. With the Jews, she had learned, you have to watch out, there is Christian blood in these things. Sometimes there are these things that are being transmitted from one generation to the other, it is scary how deeply ingrained this is in people.

Even today, I still have very many discussions. My husband and I are often in Germany for trade fairs, and we have many colleagues there. We have known them for ten, fifteen years. Whether you like it or not, we always get into discussions about the Holocaust, about Holocaust denial or about Israel. There is always so much in what they say, and latently at least a certain anti-Semitism although people don't even realize that. It is in their genes, it is simply present, there is nothing you can do about it. The only exception was that elderly teacher of mine, the great exception, an extraordinary teacher. She produced that ovation around the Six Day War, but it really was the only experience of that type.

First thing in the morning, in school, there was a prayer. I did not pray with them. We had our own course in Jewish religion parallel to the Christian one. There was not really a problem there, and I could not say that there was anything about school — the only thing that bothered me was that they did not address the Holocaust issue, they did not deal with it at all. It made me incredibly furious. As far as the teachers go, I never felt any anti-Semitism. I could not say that there was anything. I was a very good student, I was highly respected in my school, and I was very active in a number of things including the student newspaper. I cannot really complain about that.

All I can say is that I did not feel comfortable with the Germans. There simply was a barrier there. You create that barrier probably yourself as well, it is also a matter of one's upbringing. I was never in German company. In my class, I had a Jewish girlfriend, for example; she grew up together with me, but she always had German girlfriends, and she always felt much more comfortable in the German environment than I. I never let that happen to me, I did not feel comfortable there, and my father would not have permitted it anyhow. When I was seventeen years old, for example, I had a dance partner, as was customary in school, but I could not go out with him. My father really blocked the door there: "over my dead body."

You might think that because I left Germany right after high school, I really did not spend that much of my life in Germany. But it was not really just a short amount of time. Most of all, it was pretty awful, I'd say, being in a golden cage. I don't like to think back to that time. I can only say that I had an unhappy youth, very much burdened by all these stories. And just those years, between fourteen and eighteen, which ought to be carefree and lighthearted years, were totally burdened. I don't like to think back to that. I hate that town, really, it is a trauma for me. A couple of times per year I have to be there, and when I drive into that gray town, I am getting — I hate that place.

When I look at that so-called Jewish society in Germany today, it only confirms how right I was to leave Germany. In part I still have friends, or former friends, in Germany, in part they are spread all over the world; they've emigrated to America, to Paris, all over the world, but the ones that have remained in Germany, in Frankfurt or elsewhere, what a life! They go from a Keren Hayesod meeting to a WIZO meeting and so forth, just because they want to preserve a Jewish social life at all cost. I really pity these people. Just because they want to preserve a Jewish life they have no choice but to socialize with second-rate people, with people they really would not otherwise want to be around. It is pitiful somehow, especially pronounced in Berlin. I look at that with a skeptical eye, the hysterical way in which they are forcibly trying to consolidate a flourishing Jewish life there. It is a big lie. They need a justification for living in Germany. Because of that, it must be packaged well. It is almost hysterical how they are absolutely trying to rebuild a Jewish Berlin the way it was before the war.

Can you imagine the kind of people you have to live with as a Jew in Germany, or that our parents had to live with, Kapos for example, people who were traitors on their own people. We had that situation in F. But the new Jewish generation is being shielded from the problems of living there. I am thinking of friends of mine who have children the age of my children. As far as I can judge, these children are being brought up with as little conflict as possible. That is my impression. Especially, speaking as little as possible about the Holocaust. "Please don't talk about that," even where the grandparents suffered through it. Because they don't want to create a conflict with the Germans. They are being sent to German schools, they are members of German soccer clubs, they are German soccer fans. These are only minor points, but there you can see where they stand emotionally. I know this from a girlfriend of mine, for example. In our generation, it was unheard of to be for the German soccer club. One generation later, it really does happen.

AN OBSERVER: Esther's been talking about Jews being German soccer fans? Her brother Salek in Jerusalem is the greatest German soccer fan in Israel, more even than this professor there, Moshe Zimmermann. Salek even has a German flag, in Israel, which he raises in his own garden when there is a soccer game with a German club. This is crazy.

ESTHER: My brothers in Bavaria continue to live this crazy life as Jews in Germany. Ronnie, the one who is a physician, he has turned into a bit of a hermit, he is getting on in age, and he is social only with Germans and has nothing going with Jewish history or with Israel. The other one, who is one year younger than I, Berthold, he has almost only Jewish friends. However, he has a non-Jewish girlfriend. But he does not marry her. That is again one of these stories. I believe they have inhibitions somehow, you can see that with Berthold and Ronnie, who are really pretty isolated. Here are two men in their mid-forties, they still don't have a family, and I don't think they even dare to face that and to think about that.

The major reason why Ronnie and Berthold are in this situation has to do with that so-called Jewish society in Germany. It is a rotten society, and it is not only rotten, it is sick. You must not forget that. These are people who in part made a lot of money very quickly, they are not necessarily always the most refined individuals. If you have a choice, they are not really the people you want to socialize with. But sometimes you have to, for lack of an alternative, you do the best you can. It is very difficult, and the girls are all terribly screwed up and spoiled by their parents. So these girls, as partners, are out of question and it is not easy. In Germany you are limited to a narrow circle, and if you don't like anyone within that circle, then you are out of luck. And you always have to ask first, "Are you Jewish?" "Aren't you Jewish?" — this is crazy.

I have not been in Germany for a while, but I always get the Jewish publications from there and I know who is active there, and all the things they are trying to do: this festival and that festival and so on. I am not quite sure if that is good or bad. To be doing something like a festival in Berlin, that is a very ambivalent business. On the one hand you could say, we are doing it in spite of everything, let us show the Germans that we are here again. On the other hand, you are doing them a favor somewhere, because you are telling them, okay, we are starting again where we once left off.

I know the background to the idea of setting up this Jewish culture in Berlin and elsewhere. I know the attitude, and I know it is a big lie. They just need a justification for staying in Germany. So they are putting a nice wrapping around that idea and are building a blossoming Jewish cultural life for ourselves in Germany. It is a band-aid because people really don't like being in Germany. Nobody can tell me that they do. They are in Germany mostly for financial reasons or they cannot leave for other reasons. Often, their children are leaving nevertheless. I have just met someone from Munich again, he is very assimilated even and he told me, "It is again very bad in Germany, and I am glad that my children live in London."

In Germany today, something entirely different has to be considered as well: the immigration of the Russians, even non-Jewish Russians. Especially in the smaller congregations, they in part have taken over already. Take F. or another small community in Bavaria, and you find ninety percent are Russian immigrants and only ten percent are old residents. So my mother, and I quote, when she goes to synagogue, she thinks she is in "deepest Russia." Russian is spoken everywhere, and the Jews who have built these congregations in postwar Germany, they now feel like strangers in their own communities. Now just think how the Germans should view the Jews. Take the Jews who came after the war and who are not now recognizable as Jews. Then take the second generation. They were born in Germany, they speak perfect German, they went to German schools, not to Jewish schools, not to religious schools, and someone like myself or my brothers is indistinguishable from Germans.

Here now you have these immigrants from Russia, they are basically the Ostjuden of the 1920s. It is the exact comparison. When the Ostjuden came in the 1920s, the German Jews said, we don't want to have anything to do with them. They really did turn up here in pretty weird outfits, speaking only Yiddish, and perhaps they smelled of garlic and whatever, and the German Jews then thought, anti-Semitism is not because of us but because of them. Now we have a similar situation in Germany. We have the settled Jews, let us call them the German Jews, they are my generation, around fifty or above, you cannot recognize that they are Jewish. They are partly integrated into German society, and where they have money and success, they really flourish in German society. Everyone invites their bank manager to parties, and so on. And now we get these immigrants who don't speak German, they are pretty poor, and we have a similar situation to the twenties, because it breeds anti-Semitism, because they get all kinds of financial support.

When you really think about it, all of us are always against the right-wing radicals and against Jörg Haider and so on. But we should not forget, there is a problem in Europe today: it is immigration. In France, for example, you have a lot of anti-Semitism today, because there are now more than five million Moslems in France. This is the anti-Semitism from the other side. In Germany and Western Europe — and no one really wants to speak about that — you have the danger from the Moslems. Wherever they go, they change the urban landscape. They wear different clothes, they are veiled, they build their mosques, usually very big, then they call out *Allahu akhbar* — so this is destroying the city core and it is putting barriers up in the population.

Quite honestly, I can understand xenophobia. I believe it is something human. I can really empathize and understand, even personally. If some gypsies were to move into my neighborhood, or next door, Ethiopians or something, in my house or in my neighborhood. I can understand turning away strangers. I can understand xenophobia. But it is a very long and far road from xenophobia to the Holocaust. I need not love them, but that does not mean that I want to kill them, to murder them.

ESTHER AND HER FATHER

My father lived a life of contradictions

The basic element, where everything began, was my father's Zionist commitment back in Poland. We are talking about a man who grew up in Poland, who was a member of Betar, totally Zionist oriented, and who wanted to emigrate to Palestine. As a young man in Poland, and under Jabotinski, my father heard Menachem Begin speak, and that influenced him greatly. He even made hachshara, in preparation for his emigration.

My family, back in Slawkusz, was a very wealthy and respected family. They had a license for cigarette sales, a tobacco license. They had a beautiful house, my uncle Jurek, by the way, visited the house some time ago, when he was in Poland. He told me it is a house with several baths, and all sorts of extras, it is still standing there in the marketplace in Slawkusz. Very respectable people, and especially my grandmother after whom I am named, she was a businesswoman and an important figure in the Jewish community there. My father, then, grew up in a merchant family, and he was a merchant. He was not interested in going to university. Still, he wanted to leave this settled lifestyle, this well-to-do environment, and so he did this hachshara, he wanted to do something with his hands, maybe it was saddler or leather craftsman, I don't know, and so he prepared for his aliyah to Israel. But his mother was totally opposed to it, she did not permit it, and she said, "You as the eldest son, if you leave, then I'll kill myself." Later, my father used to tell us again and again, "If my mother had only let me go, then I would not have been sent to the concentration camp." This was always the overarching story.

The other story with my father was a certain conflictual situation. As far as the Jews are concerned, he experienced a very, very deep disappointment. When the Germans came into this town, into Slaw-kusz, my father's father, my grandfather, was the first to be asked to become a member of the Judenrat, because the respectable families were the ones who formed that council. My grandfather resisted that with all his strength. He said he would not cooperate with the Germans. That is how he saw it at the time. Normally, on the first transport that was sent to the camps, they always — that is simply the way it normally was — they used to put the people from the poorer and the ordinary families. It went from the bottom up, not from the top down. But on this first transport my father somehow was right on it. It was in revenge for the fact that my grandfather did not participate in the Judenrat. This resulted in a deep bitterness that my father carried with him through his entire life — that he had been betrayed by Jews. An incredible bitterness toward Jews. In the camps as well, he experienced a fair bit concerning Jews. It was not all rosy-red.

JUREK: The matter with the transport — you probably did not quite understand that. This had to do with being drafted to the labor camp, a so-called RAB camp, because they were building the Reichsautobahn. They were asked to appear for a medical, and those who were able-bodied, they packed a suitcase and left. It is true, however, that my brother Albert refused to cooperate with the Judenrat. His boss from Betar at the time was also a member of the Judenrat, a lawyer. I can still remember that, but don't remember his name; he recruited people from among his friends to set up a Jewish police force. So he asked my brother, and my brother said, "I am not going to do that." Since he did not, and on the basis of his age, he automatically fit into the category of people who went to the labor camp. People had to go somewhere. So in his age group, they either went to the police, but because Albert was not in the police, he did not have a task, and so they sent him to the labor camp.

Q: *Esther says that because of the Judenrat story, her father was very embittered and therefore did not want to have anything to do with Jews after 1945 because he said he and his family were betrayed by other Jews.*

Esther must have misunderstood that. When I get a chance, I will speak with her about it. At her age, she should not keep living with such a misperception. It is an error. In hindsight, it was even fortunate that her father got in there. Camp life, in contrast to what happened later. It was where my two sisters and I went voluntarily. You really have to let this melt in your mouth: volunteering for a concentration camp. It saved us. Labor camp instead of death camp; not "death camp," but death.

ESTHER: My siblings and I tried to find out about my father's actual experiences in the concentration camps many times, without much luck. I was very interested in the Holocaust. I think it was mostly on account of my father and what I call the "Black Hole," because he did not speak about it, and this black hole drove my imagination. I hear that often from people, where the parent did not talk. We did not even know the names of my father's siblings that perished. That topic was taboo, it was always being fended off. Whenever someone touched on it, even lightly, my father started crying right away, and my mother asked for a halt, and I got incredibly curious. It was always that game; a small stimulus, then a tiny bit was returned, and then it was fended off right away. It was a game where you could never really learn anything. My father actually talked more about life before the Holocaust, still with his family. That was very, very painful, too.

My father was so burdened with that Holocaust story, and had such strong arguments against relations with the Germans. This was very difficult for our family to handle, because it was not talked about. When I was little, I read all the books about it. When I was fifteen or sixteen, there was no film, no book that I had not read about it. You have to imagine, there was this vacuum for us, a black hole, and this maddening pain; for me to identify with that pain, that was very strong. It is still strong and it does not get any better.

The other major problem for us was, why, after all that had happened, did my father stay in Germany and not leave like most of the other survivors? Personally, I think it was out of a certain inertia. My father was in a Displaced Persons' Camp, in Landsberg. I believe he wanted to emigrate to America, but somehow he screwed it up. In more recent years, I got to be more tolerant and I said to myself that we should not be judging anyone who has gone through such stressful situations. Who knows what led my father to stay in Germany. Because he made a lot of money fairly quickly, by the early fifties he had already made a fortune for himself. He started with the American forces and used equipment he bought from them, then it was used cars, then it was used household equipment, and the whole thing really developed amazingly fast commercially. Already in 1950 he built a three- or four-story building right downtown in F., the first major new building to be built there, and so within the first five years he was already so well established that he did not want to throw this overboard and start anew elsewhere.

My father, then, could not get a visa for the U.S., but he also did not want to go to Israel. He thought Israel was a socialist country — we are talking about the fifties — he did not want that either, and he felt very conflicted there, his bitterness toward other Jews came into play. He probably thought, he would simply go on with his life in Germany. Most importantly, he could make a living, and the children for him were supreme.

My father lived a life of contradictions. Overall, he was anti-German, but I believe he had also had many positive experiences with Germans, including during the Holocaust. Here somebody helped him, there someone once saved him. A woman who gave him something to eat across a fence, two or three key experiences where Germans saved his life or where they had helped him, and several things that were not talked about. After the war, one or two years after 1945, for example, and this was also a key experience, he saw a German in a department store who had helped him with something, maybe he saved him, and my father ran after him. The German recognized him and ran away, he fled because he probably thought my father wanted to get him. But actually, my father wanted to give him a gift. He had already pulled off his wristwatch, but the other one was gone. My father probably had had positive experiences that he did not fully articulate, but they did exist, you could sense that.

Ironically, my father remembered the "good Germans" while at the same time, he remembered the Jews who betrayed and cheated him. This disappointment about Jews played an important role, and he always talked about it: he was put on the first transport. It was totally unusual to put someone from a leading family onto the first transport.

He had been betrayed and it was very painful, being betrayed by one's own people. We knew some people, in N. and in Munich as well, Frau S. for example, I don't know whether you know, she was a Kapo. So she was a Kapo, and with these sorts of people you had to be — well, not really together, but they were there, you had to live with them. This was the story, you could not simply erase it. Jews who were traitors to their own people. You had to live with them, but there was that story in Munich, I don't remember exactly, at one point people who were Kapos were attacked, but it did not concern Frau S. I believe. She actually had a terrible fate. One daughter has MS, and people said that God sent it. So she was punished differently. That is how people interpreted that.

SETTLING DOWN IN F.

There is no greater hatred than the one between brothers

As far as the family business is concerned, my father was the draft horse. First, because he was the eldest brother. Then, from the business side, he was very talented, he had the right instincts, very hardworking, a very strong personality. He was a real eldest brother, the way you picture a dominant personality. He pulled all three families along.

What is strange is how the siblings were so close to one another during the Holocaust, there was so much solidarity, and then all the conflict thereafter. It is not uncommon in survivor families, though. I have seen it frequently. It is a more general phenomenon, not only in our case. It is very, very sad, but I have seen this with other families here in Israel: some people who went through the Holocaust often do not have the strongest family ties in normal times. There are two explanations for that. First, these are often not very strong ties in the first place: in difficult times, you stick together, and once things improve, the different characters emerge. And then, I believe, there is no greater hatred than the one between brothers. This hatred between brothers, and what we call in Yiddish *broiges,* carrying grudges and not speaking to one another, these things are very strong. I see this with all sorts of families; you can love just as much as you can hate.

AN OBSERVER: I know, Esther seems to feel that her uncle Ignaz and Ignaz's wife Fela were the ones primarily responsible for the rift in the family. It probably did contribute in fact to Albert's health problems and his two heart attacks. Put bluntly, some in Albert's family feel that Albert would have fared better without his brothers around his neck; but Albert was a very authoritarian type in relation to his brothers. Esther herself admits that Jurek has always been a rather good-natured fellow, which made that relationship a bit easier. Albert had always felt that since he did survive, he also had a special responsibility for these three families. He felt that he was the head of the entire family, and had he not had his brothers on his back, he could have gone still much further in his projects. Instead, he always also took care of his brothers, but they were not always happy with what he did, and therefore the frictions developed.

ESTHER: In addition to the disagreeable family atmosphere, for my mother, coming from Zurich to provincial F. must have been a terrible adjustment to make. She said she experienced a disciplinary transfer. But my mother somehow adjusted herself to my father's circumstances. He was the one who set the tone, and my mother was perhaps the opposite pole. In other families in F. and environs, when both parents were from Poland, people spoke Polish and Yiddish. But although my mother could speak Yiddish, we did not speak it that much. So we were more assimilated than families where they spoke only Polish and Yiddish at home. Also, my mother was not psychologically affected by the Holocaust, which gave our family a certain balance, which is why we children got through the whole thing without getting too screwed up. She did not carry that burden.

Matters were made even worse for my mother because not only did my father isolate himself from the Germans, he also stayed away from the Jews. Socially, he was totally isolated. He did not want to have anything to do with anybody. So basically, we did not have any social life. Concerning my mother, he did not, how shall I say it, it's not that he did not allow her to socialize, but he did not make it possible for her, because he would not have gone along with it.

For my father the children were the absolute, the apple of his eye. The children were more important than his own life, and to build an existence for them and to experience a beautiful life, that really was his raison d'être. That was for him the most important thing, the children. And I have that, by the way, that story with the children, that must be a Holocaust thing, because at some point I was with my uncle Jurek on a plane, on the way to the birth of some grandchild, and we spoke about this, and he said: "For us—you don't understand—our children are Wunderkinder, miracles. If anyone would have told us back in the camps, you will get out of here and will have kids, and perhaps grand-children, we would never have believed that. The fact that we could experience this once more, to have one's own kids, and that these kids would have kids again, and perhaps even these kids in Israel—this was a total wishful dreamy illusion."

JUREK: After liberation, some people got married without any eco-nomic security, any financial base. I don't know why. At the time when my brother Albert had married, we were already reasonably estab-lished. The urge to have a family and to have children was probably different with different people. You know, people were not even sure they could ever have children. There was a long discussion among the survivors, whether one could procreate. This could not at all be taken for granted.

ESTHER: And therefore this business with the children. So the children are much more important than the wife. The children are, this is a totally obsessive—a totally crazy obsessive love [Affenliebe], this love for the children. And with my father, it was totally madly strong, it was an all-inclusive, total love for the children. He would have done any-thing for his children, in fact he did.

ESTHER'S ZIONISM

I told my father, I am doing what you really should have done

As I mentioned, we, whose parents were survivors—and I am speaking especially of those families that came from Poland—we were forced to live a schizoid existence in Germany. Here we had this conflictual situa-tion: you live in Germany, but you are really not supposed to have anything to do with the Germans. Here is my father who lives in Ger-many, but he hates the Germans; in soccer, he was always hoping that they would lose—a minor point but it demonstrates precisely where you belong. It is a totally paradoxical, schizoid situation to raise kids in. It is a miracle in my opinion that with all that, we managed everything somehow psychologically, because normally, one would really freak out completely. So when I was between fifteen and twenty, I had these problems with my identity. I decided it cannot go on like that, one has to make a decision somewhere. You either stay in Germany, and then you cannot go on living this ghetto existence under any circumstances; I was against assimilation, but this would have been the extreme other route, or one must emigrate. And when you emigrate, you don't emigrate to just any other country where you have the same situation all over again, in some variation; rather, you go straight to Israel. That was my logical conclusion.

This is how I got to Israel. I had been visiting Israel earlier, but after Abitur I wanted to go and live there, this was my plan already at age fourteen or fifteen; even before I had ever visited Israel I knew that I wanted to emigrate there; I was the Zionist pioneer in our family. There were a number of reasons for that; first of all, because we basically had a Zionist upbringing at home, because of my father; and secondly, we were organized in the Zionist Youth, the ZJD. The ZJD was a beam of light in our dismal ghetto existence in F. It gave us confidence and a positive identity, in contrast to everything else in our life in Germany. At least in my case. I believe this was a very good framework and helped us resolve these identity problems. I was influenced also by this heroic spirit there and by the shlichim that came from Israel, they were very well trained, they really could inspire us. I was emotionally very charged because of it, it really had a great impact on us when I was there.

The ZJD, as you know, also organized camps, especially summer camps, the machanot. But I never went there. I was not the machane type. If on the other hand I think of my daughter, she only hangs out with the scouts, she wouldn't mind living there forever. Not me. I was the pampered daughter type. I was about sixteen when I came to Israel for the first time and on my own. I was sent to relatives, to an aunt, and I lived with her and her daughter who was in her early twenties. At that time, they had the contractors in the house. That was a key experience, because I asked my aunt whether these people were Jews as well. And she said, yes, here they are all Jews. So there were these craftsmen, wall-paper hangers, house painters who were Jewish, everyone was Jewish. The idea that everyone here, everyone running around on the street was Jewish, that was a phenomenal idea. I sat in the living room and there were these handymen, and they sang and painted. It was incredible.

That visit impressed me deeply. From there on I knew that I would emigrate to Israel after Abitur. Although this was just a vacation, it impressed me most deeply. Somewhere it was the fulfilment of my wishes, because as a young person, I had all these big identity problems: Where do I belong? Who am I, where and what? In Germany, we grew up and were brought up in a totally schizoid and paradoxical situation, everyone else will have told you about that.

It begins with the provincial character of this town. My mother came here from Zurich because of my father, imagine. I hate this place. I was and still am very bitter about having been raised in Germany. What has happened to my family is a very, very, very great hurt, it is unforgivable. I always told my father, "I don't understand how you could stay on in Germany. How can, how could you stay in Germany of all places?" And I also told my father, "I am doing what you really should have done." I simply had to do it.

So I left for Israel, and you can say, this was the fulfillment. This was simply the step to take. I am still a Zionist today, and I have made it possible for the other members of my family, Salek, for example, to come here. He saved his soul with that, psychologically. The others, in my view, are lost. Except they don't see that yet, but they are lost. Gaby especially worries me a lot. How are things supposed to go on with him? Deep down, I am carrying on a debate with the rest of my family.

So I picked up from where my father left off before the Holocaust. Imagine a father who grew up in Poland, a member of Betar and totally Zionistically oriented, who wanted to leave for Palestine and so on. On one hand, my father had an enormously passionate love for this land, for Palestine, for Israel. When he saw an Israeli soldier on the street, he could have cried, he was emotionally so charged up about it. On the other hand, he did not want his children to emigrate to Israel, because he was afraid there would be war somehow and then something bad would happen. So when I wanted to emigrate at age twenty, it turned into a very serious conflict. On one hand, he had to admit that his mother did not let him emigrate, which is why he ended up in the concentration camp. On the other hand, he said, "If you emigrate, you'll automatically marry an Israeli, you'll get pregnant, and there will be war." That is exactly what happened later on. When I was pregnant with my first daughter, my husband was in the war in Lebanon. My father absolutely wanted to spare me the experience of being married to an Israeli who at some point would have to go to war.

This was our dilemma: we had a Zionist father who however did not tell us to go to Israel but who wanted his children to be around him instead. He had them, moreover, grow up in Germany, which was the greatest punishment of all times, and we, and especially I, always blamed him for that. I believe it was unfair to us children to let us grow up in a ghetto, because we grew up totally in the ghetto.

ESTHER IN ISRAEL

I settled down here in Israel really very well, I'd say

When I came to Israel, I had to face the problems of all immigrants. First, I did a preparatory course at the university, then I started to study. The first year was very, very difficult because I did not know the language and I did not have any friends. I was pretty much alone, I also did not get to know people, also because of the mentality — I mean, we were brought up quite differently. But after the first year and then at university it got to be better.

I was studying art history, and there I did have real advantages in my courses because of my background, also because I knew German and I could read books that the others could not read. Especially in my field, it was a great advantage that I had a European background, and it paid off later on, professionally, as well. Then I got to know my husband, Aurel, and then we married and the rest is . . . I married in 1976, I was twenty-three then. I settled down here in Israel really very well, I'd say, at least after the first extremely difficult year. I should also say that I had a great amount of idealism and I was very much involved and very happy in Israel. It is true of course that you always have some problems with the mentality here; things are different here. I have always managed to use my European background to my advantage: that I am very precise, that I am punctual, that I am reliable — those characteristics that are not Levantine, and they always helped me in my work and in my career.

At the same time, I have to admit that I don't have that Yiddishkait in me here, because I have something else. I got involved here working as a volunteer in all sorts of things. I did a lot for the new immigrants, I ran a big project for thousands of families, I really was responsible for this, a project of adoptions, where Israeli families would chaperon a Russian family, kind of adopting them socially. I ran a huge project for over two years, and I am very much involved that way, but Jewishness and Friday evening, that is not absolutely necessary.

Basically, I turned myself into a combination of two positive elements: the Israeli element on one hand: spontaneity, to push things through, to press for and to reach goals, that you have to be pushy — those are the Israeli things that I have adopted. On the other hand, I have preserved my positive European qualities. But in Germany, I would be considered very pushy. My mother keeps telling me, how can you, what are you doing, and so forth. I just don't have the patience any longer to be standing in line and to yak with everyone until something starts to move. That sort of patience I have not had in a long time, and in Germany, that is all slow motion. Here in Israel, we are much quicker, much more active, much more spontaneous, and we improvise much better. That is what Israelis are good at, improvising. It might well not be a hundred percent perfect then, but it will work somehow, whereas in Germany, if it cannot be done perfectly, then it cannot be done at all. This combination of the good Israeli side and European preciseness, that dependability and what we understand in part as German preciseness, this combination has helped me a great deal in life. On the other hand, I was still young enough to adjust to the Israeli mentality, and I have accepted that. At the same time, I never denied with what I came here. Many others who immigrated did just that, they said, now I am going to be different and I am going to start completely fresh. I don't find that quite right, because you cannot make over an American into an Israeli. Somewhere you have to preserve your own culture, because it gives you certain advantages, something that the others do not have. Aurel, my husband, also comes from a strong European tradition; his father came from a German-speaking family in Rumania, and there are cultural similarities there to my own.

My children, by the way, have also been brought up like that. They are not your typical Israeli kids, although they are sabras. For example, they have German table manners. My children know that they are not like the others — at least not like most, we should not generalize, but they have been brought up differently. They grew up bilingually, Hebrew and German, and they also speak English. They are trilingual. Their German they got through their grandma: they spent a lot of time in Germany, and my mother speaks only German. Also, when my kids were small, I forced myself to speak German to them, even though I did not like it, but my mother put a lot of pressure on me there. So they grew up bilingually, and they spent a lot of time with my mother when I was away traveling or when she came to Israel.

On the other hand, my children resemble other Israeli kids in that they are much less burdened by the past. They know, of course, grandpa was in the Holocaust, I have told them that and have taken them here and there. Of course I have not burdened them the way I have been burdened. But I do want to burden them at least some. Somewhere they have to know about that. Then again, they have their grandma in Germany. So I have to take care that they don't hate Germany to the point where they would not want to go there anymore. My little daughter, for example, she has something against goyishness. She says, and this in turn is racist, anti-goyish, they have pointed noses, and she is bothered by them wearing crosses. My big daughter is much more relaxed about it, she is more the bohemian type.

Someone once asked me whether my daughters should not spend some time studying at a German university. I would not want that, for a number of reasons. First of all, I would be afraid that they would somehow marry a German then or something like that, and that would be the biggest catastrophe of all time. This would be totally unacceptable for me. I have not come to Israel so that my children marry a German, it would be a total paradox and my life would have gone wrong. My big daughter was on a vacation recently and met a French boy there, he is not Jewish, and she was not bothered by it at all. For me, this is something of a problem. But with a German it would be worse.

But we were talking about the use of the German language in Israel. Here you can see a considerable change in the past few years. As little as ten years ago, the idea that anyone here in Israel would actually learn German would have been totally taboo. For example, twenty, twenty-five years ago, I would have been ashamed to speak German in public. I simply did not do it then. I am always being asked whether I converted. With me, everybody believes that I converted. They ask, "So when did you convert?" "Did you convert?" No one ever believed that I am Jewish. Other than Berthold we are all blond and have light eyes. In the playground, for example, I never spoke German with my older daughter. Never in my life would I have done that. I would have been ashamed, and perhaps people would have thought that I was a . . . Never, never in my entire life did I ever say, "I am a German." I have never said that; instead, I am Jewish. Not a Jewish German. Never, never, never. Not even in Germany. "Where are you from?" — "I am from G- I grew up in Germany." But I have never said, "I am German." I would never say that. You'd have to kill me first.

As far as German history is concerned, I believe there is now a certain interest. In the past couple of years they had lectures, there are the events at the Goethe Institute, and here at the university there is a fair bit as well. Now they also teach German in some high schools, with German as an elective second foreign language, and there is a growing interest in learning German. I know all that in part from people who I know around here, people who work at the Goethe Institute or at the German embassy. It really is not taboo anymore. Incidentally, I do have to deal with German diplomats here in the gallery. We also have many visitors from Germany, both goyim and Jews, and then we have the fairs in Germany, we've got a lot to do with Germany.

If I look back, I can see that I have become far less Jewish since I have been living in Israel. That is one thing. My national consciousness, on the other hand, is much stronger now. My main point of being Jewish has always been that I belong to the Jewish people, more a kind of national pride. I am not a religious person — what shall I do? I simply cannot be religious, and we were probably brought up in such ways that today we are not religious. I do not necessarily have to exercise my religion in order to be Jewish, do you understand what I mean? You cannot explain that to other people. You are either Catholic and go to church, or you are not and do not go there. On the other hand, you can quite well be Jewish and not fast on Yom Kippur. I am very, very Jewish, but I don't have to fast on Yom Kippur, especially since I have come here to Israel. I don't need to; I can, but I don't need to. Had I stayed in Germany, this would have been a different matter. Somehow, it bothers me that I don't give my kids enough Jewishness, simply because I don't have that anymore. I just don't. I cannot pull this out of me, because I just don't have that anymore within me. Yiddishkait and Friday evening are not absolutely necessary any more. Whatever I had, I cannot transmit to my children.

ESTHER AND HER VOCATION

We have come to the conclusion that if we don't return this art and these books to Germany, then this cultural legacy will be lost

We are not only dealing with art in our business, but also with books, and we are a piece of a culture chain in some way. Here I have to tell you something very intimate, because it is revealing about various conflicts. In the early years, when we went to German book fairs, we took a lot of books with us to Germany, books that originally belonged to German-Jewish immigrants; I am not speaking of the Holocaust survivors, because they did not have anything left, but the people who left Germany in the thirties. These Yeckes who emigrated in the twenties and thirties still brought their libraries with them. We are selling these books back to Germany. I had a lot of problems with that. Books that these people brought with them, as refugees, in flight, they are now going back to Germany, that can't be right, no? I talked to my husband about this issue many times and for a very long time, and we have come to the conclusion that if we don't return this art and these books to Germany, then this cultural legacy will be lost. Here in Israel no one reads this, no one wants it, no one knows it. In this generation, no one reads any German and they are not at all interested. Why should they be interested in the writers-in-exile? In Germany, these book and antiquarian fairs are very much visited by institutions, museums, libraries, and private buyers, because there is this vacuum. You can get these books only from immigrants' collections, because in Germany they had been burned. In Germany we are dealing in part with very young people, between twenty and thirty years of age.

MOTTI: I visited Esther in her gallery. Part of her professional work consists in dealing with the European cultural legacy. In Israel, this job is basically getting superfluous because the number of people who owned and used artwork, books, and prints in, say, German, Dutch, English, French, and so on, is getting ever smaller. Now this is simply a part of the European cultural legacy that became available in Israel. Esther and her husband, let us say, acquire this and then reimport it to Germany in order to sell it there. That is a pretty lucrative business. I don't really want to judge this from a moral perspective, but I just think that this is entirely a business question, even though Esther presents it differently. I just don't know whether it would not be better if these books would be staying in exile, in Israel, and in a garbage dump rather than being imported back to Germany instead.

ESTHER: I was talking about the German antiquarian fairs, that is a curious story all of its own. It is an entire establishment, an elitist club, and in order to get admitted to a fair and to exhibit, you need incredible connections. You have to be a member of the association, you need people who recommend you and who back your application. We had to wait for fifteen years in order to exhibit there in the first place. Imagine this: I am going there, basically as an Israeli, but I speak perfect German and I have this entire German background. So the people are totally confused and embarrassed, and when they get to our booth, there are always discussions with the customers. Most people say, it is nice that you are here. There are many conversations with older Germans who had Jewish friends, and believe it, they have tears in their eyes when they speak with us. They say it is nice that you are here, and how come you speak such good German, and all these questions.

Many customers ask me whether these books might not have belonged to Holocaust survivors or Holocaust victims, in that case they don't want them. These encounters in Germany are extremely charged and overburdened. But they are really also very interesting. On one hand, it is simply also a get-together with our German colleagues whom we have known very, very well for twenty years now and for whom it was usually the first meeting with a Jew. So I was the first Jewish woman whom they have ever gotten to know; somewhere, I am sure, they are predisposed to anti-Semitism. It is like I am always on a mission there. It is never just a normal trip, I am always there with a message, and I — maybe it is only me — I always feel in charge, with a mission.

In Germany, they always see themselves as being in a conflict: on the one hand they know, they have to behave toward Jews and Israelis, simply because this is politically correct, and on the other hand, especially the TV in Germany is in part totally biased as far as the Palestinian problem is concerned. You can see that with this new intifada. Here you get these anti-Semitic statements that are not seen as such, but that are coming right from their guts. I'll give you a brand new example, it is incredible. It is from Germans who have lived here for a long time. He was with the X chemical corporation. Same age as us, their daughter the same age as my oldest, we took a pregnancy course together. Later, they went to Japan and elsewhere. Recently, at the height of the trouble here, they came back on a trip to Israel, they had been planning this and did not want to cancel it now. One night, they came to visit and we started talking about politics. Now when I have people here from abroad, I do take care to represent Israel a little and to explain things to them differently from what they see on German television.

At one point the woman said she believes that Israeli politics are being strongly influenced by the wealthy American Jews who give money to particular politicians and who strongly influence Israeli politics that way. I told her, you know this is totally wrong, and she said, how do you know that and so on. So I answered, "You know, your remark sounds outright anti-Semitic, it is like the Elders of Zion, it has got that flair." And she responded, "With you, the moment someone says something against Israel, you call them anti-Semites." So here you see old anti-Semitic sentiments hidden in new packaging. Many of our friends have found that. It is elsewhere as well, in France, for example. But they are much more open about their anti-Semitism, much more relaxed about it. In Germany it comes in a new package, with a pink bow around it. I am finished with that couple now, they don't know that yet, but the friendship is finished.

So much for the new anti-Semitism. But in our gallery as well, I am meeting many Germans with affinities for things Jewish. I remember, in your book, you have written on that, you called it the "Judaising milieu." They are mostly younger people, interested in twentieth-century German-Jewish culture and especially also German literature in exile. I would say that the literature of the 1920s was seventy percent Jewish; German Jews produced that literature and the consumers were Jews as well, it is a known fact. After the Second World War, there had developed this vacuum, and especially young people, even up to fifty years of age or so, are extremely interested in replenishing that. There is an amazing eagerness there to learn about it. One can see that. I really have to say that.

So we are dealing here with very young people, between twenty and thirty. For example, a customer from the M. family, this assimilated banking family, they are of course, for several generations now, they have been Christian, but in the nineteenth century, they were Jews. He is very interested in the Jewish writers-in-exile. They are aristocrats, their name today is von M. I am not sure what his relationship to Judaism really is, but perhaps he is looking for something. He does not express it, but he is interested in pacifism and exile. He is totally occupied with that, a young man twenty-five years of age, very intellectually oriented. There are several of this type. I always find this very fascinating, and I want to encourage that. This is exactly why we consider ourselves as guardians of this culture. I don't want to calm my conscience with that, because I did have these pangs of conscience. I had a problem with that. Can you see this problem?

Take this Jewish immigrant, for example, who is now around ninety or more years old and who, at the last minute, lugged these books out of Berlin. When you ask him, "Would you like this book to go back to Germany?" then maybe he would say yes, and maybe he would say no. It is the fate of a book, but that fate is linked to a person. It is a fact that we are sometimes asked, is this book of a Holocaust survivor, or from someone who perhaps perished? Then they don't want anything to do with it, they don't want to touch blood. It is all not so simple. Books somewhere are people as well, and you cannot separate the one from the other. But this was our decision. We are saying, we have to do this; only this way can this cultural legacy be preserved, if it gets back to Germany.

Gabriel

POSTMODERN JEW

1969   born in F.
1987   begins work in advertising agency and work in radio
1988   breaks off Gymnasium six months before Abitur
1998   sells share in radio station, works exclusively in advertising
1999   sets up new radio station

As I have pointed out, the ten Kalman cousins can be seen as embodiments of particular messages. Esther might agree with me: "Every one of us has a different message." Coming from the same root, the cousins nevertheless represent vessels of diverse content. Without that common root, that of the Kalman family of Slawkusz, these cousins cannot be adequately deciphered, and all family members — but also the author who is attempting to portray them — are being turned into its messengers. We can see the cousins as being in a partly silent, partly open debate with each other where one message challenges the other. Esther and Gabriel are in such a debate with one another, often with quite different positions. Despite all differences, this debate at least is carried out in friendly, and even loving, terms. Esther calls Gabriel, in a motherly manner, "our prodigy" (unser Wunderkind). Part of the particular character of their relationship has to do with the fact that, in terms of age, they are so far apart. Gabriel was just four years old when his sister left for Israel, in 1973. Their worlds are very different, both the worlds of their respective childhoods and those in which they live today. This is the case with the other siblings as well. Even Salek, the second youngest, is still twelve years older than Gabriel.

I met Gabriel for the first time in the summer of 1995 in a garden restaurant in F. He had driven up in a fire-engine-red Ferrari — difficult to overlook in a provincial town such as F. I last spoke to him at length in February 2001.

GABRIEL: My mother says I was born on April 28, 1969. I guess I have to believe it. It also says so in my passport. I am a Taurus. Now we had, and still have, a very tight and loving family life. For my father, the family was everything; my father loved his children really almost too much. My father simply tried to give his children what he did not have, because of the war and the concentration camp. This is how he wanted to make up for it. And I, as the youngest member — me and my older siblings are twelve to sixteen years apart — I was the baby and was very, very spoiled. So my father's love for his children was extreme. My father never raised his hand against us.

BEING AN ENTREPRENEUR OUT OF FUN

It was such fun and so enjoyable and then became an
ever more serious business

Later, I went through the classical school career, from elementary school to Gymnasium. To be honest, I did not take school that seriously, there were far more interesting things to do. Half a year before Abitur, I dropped out, because of my professional career that had developed alongside school. I simply had to decide what to do and whether I wanted to seize the job opportunity that I had, or whether I wanted to further pursue the classical career via school. It was simply that at age eighteen, parallel to school, I worked in an advertising agency, specializing in the radio broadcasting sector, conceptualizing text and doing creative text for classical style radio advertising. This went quite okay parallel to school, nice earnings on the side, and it was fun.

Somehow, this was a creative environment, it was such fun and so enjoyable and then became an ever more serious business. So this resulted in the situation with the "Radio for N.-F.," we got a broadcasting license, and from being a fun hobby it got to be pretty serious business and future-oriented. At some moment or other, this came to a point where one had to say, okay you cannot do this any longer concurrently with the school. I missed school more and more often, because of meetings at work, and I really just could not concentrate any more on studying. Also, I never was the good student type, and I just could not manage to go on two tracks at once.

Quite honestly, one can say that the whole thing developed from a combination of inclination and luck. There was a friend of mine there, who had been working there already and who knew that I had always had a good ear for advertising, and that I found advertising very entertaining. He asked me at one point whether I would not be interested in writing a couple of texts because I always had witty ideas. This was in the "mini-style" at the time, and I had done a couple of nice commentaries in my class in school. I was known as the clown of the class, and they were looking for someone exactly like that as a junior copywriter. Well, and then I presented my texts at one point, and I wrote the first few items, and they were of course a disaster, and gradually, we came closer to what they needed. This is how I slid into this advertising text and radio broadcasting field. This was all by chance, nothing was planned, I did not look for a particular job, they simply came to me. Total accident.

Not going on to university was a problem, of course, which I had to face, because three of my siblings, Esther, Berthold, and Ronnie, went to university. But for us today, for my generation, it is like this, going to university does not guarantee you job security and a good income. My brother Ronnie was always a good example here — he was studying medicine at the time, and I believe he'd been studying for ten years; for a while he was in South Africa [*sic*], for a while in New York, in America, and that was a never-ending story. Even then I thought to myself: studying for ten years, if I don't take this opportunity now, rather than taking the classical route via school, if I wanted to earn two thousand marks per month just like any waitress, and if I calculate that over ten years, it makes 24,000 marks per year and 240,000 marks in these ten years, that is a quarter million. I would have to give that up, just in order to hope to be something sometime that I might not even manage being then, or which I cannot be, because the problem we have today, and which had already begun then, is that people in a variety of professions cannot find jobs. On the other hand, because of the route I took, I could not travel as much and I could not live in other places like my siblings have done.

With that decision, grabbing this opportunity and moving into business life relatively early, I did not have these great times my brothers had, spending a year here or there abroad, and this nails you down, of course, a situation like mine. Of course, if this agency grows further, one could move it to Munich perhaps or into another large city, but because of the radio station, I am very much tied down here. I am tied down also because I am responsible for programming, and I am also the moderator of my own show, every day between 6 and 8 o'clock, a show that I am producing myself. This show is called "Bread and Circuses" [Brot und Spiele], and it is an entertainment show. You can see, I am an old Latin expert, and we are trying a bit of the original bread and circuses for the masses here. Now that Anglicisms run rampant in radio, it is something special to use a German name for a change.

It means the radio show is going purely toward comedy, entertainment, is an evening show, is not geared toward news or information, is purely comedy, two-hour broadcasts from Monday through Friday which I am hosting myself. Otherwise I am staying out of the radio business and now [2001] I really only do the advertising agency. And I am a shareholder. Around 6:30, my agency existence ends and I switch gears and start playing the clown.

So I don't travel as much as my brothers, but quite honestly, I don't miss that traveling very much. I have great fun in my job, it developed very nicely. In the meantime, four of us are running a twenty-four-hour radio station in N., which according to the latest polls is the number one in listeners. And N. as a city is also larger than one might think. Apart from the radio, I have the advertising agency which I am running on my own, and this is of such a size that things will never get boring.

Our entire broadcasting area is a forty-kilometer radius around N.-F., our potential listenership is 750,000, and the advertising and economic region of N. has become very interesting, for large firms as well, we have very large firms here in N. and F. Now, we are independent people in this area, that is, we are not publishers like our competition. Our competitor is a mere subsidiary of the N.er Allgemeine Corporation, one of the newspapers here. For that reason, we had to be profitable from the start, because we have to make a living from it. Our project, then, is not a tax write-off project, but truly private entrepreneurship, and everyone has to earn his money with it. This is why we are so delighted that in this struggle of David against Goliath, David has finally won out, after seven years [1995]. This is also in relation to the listening figures as against the big corporate station of the newspaper publishers. Our company had to make a profit, right from the start.

As far as business is concerned, today [2001]: I have sold the radio station I told you about, over two years ago, and did quite well, thank God. Of course, I built this station over a period of ten years, and it is a baby that I had grown emotionally close to. I am still doing the radio show. When you've done a radio show once, you want to go on with it. It is the salt in the soup, a radio show, a comedy show, and I am not just announcing the titles of the songs and the temperature outside, it is just nice. I reserved this show for myself when I sold the station. We produce this radio show and basically sell it as a product to the station which once belonged to me. But the firm that I still have, that is a normal advertising agency.

Well, and now [2001] we've just founded another radio station. It is a music station. It is called *Smart Radio* and is digital; this is like moving from records to CDs, it is one of the very first digital stations and we're practically playing only *easy listening sound,* drum and base, soul, jazz, twenty-four hours a day. We take in the money entirely via advertising; no words, no hosts, only news and music. When I spoke to you first [1995] I still thought of taking this to Munich. But the new station as well is still in N., and I am more than ever an N.-F.er, because I really like living here in this place.

Q: *I understand there was an article about you in* Forbes *magazine, as a new star among young entrepreneurs, and your Gymnasium made you an honorary graduate even though you quit school before Abitur?*

Yes, every once in a while they write something. Whether there was something in *Forbes,* that I don't know, it is quite possible, but I myself have not seen it. And honorary student? I don't really know, that is, I heard that once I had been invited to a special exhibit, because all honorary students were invited and other somehow special people. I found that a real pisser, which is why I did not go there. Because, at the time when I needed these guys, they threw me out of school. Now they find it pretty good that I am kind of a well-known figure. This is why I did not go there in the first place.

AN *ARS VIVENDI*

*In my head, I am really after owning a country house
in Scotland one of these years*

Even if I have a lot of work and even though it is hard to reach me, I certainly surely don't live a puritanical life. I am a private person and relatively withdrawn, or in a very narrow circle of friends, and I am glad that I have a counterbalance to my job. At my job, all day long, there is a lot of shouting and lots, lots, of action, and in my private life I have a need to rest. I am pretty sports-oriented, do a lot of sports, I have also started playing golf, like my brother Berthold, by the way. I like to eat and to cook, I enjoy smoking cigars, and I'd like to get to know more about malt whiskey, and about Monte Christo cigars, and Italian food.

Still, I don't want to be a workaholic like my father. I'd really like to get more out of life. For me, an ideal future would be that at some point in the not all too distant future I would stop working. I am the type of person whose life at some point will be — I mean, I do have some kind of an *ars vivendi*. I am not somebody like my father who until the end of his life worked for his family, including Saturdays and Sundays. We benefit from that today, but he basically ruined himself doing that.

True, some of it looks like this was transferred onto me from my father, but I react to it in opposition. I am very busy right now, have a lot of work. My head really is after owning a country home in Scotland with three horses and a four-wheel drive and a boat where I can do some fishing. You will ask, why Scotland of all places? It is because in two weeks' time [1995] I will drive to Scotland, and because Scotland is a place that is getting ever bigger in my head, and because I appreciate Scotland, or England, very much, because of the nature, because of the people, and because of the entire life style.

Q: *In 1995, when we first spoke, it was two weeks before your vacation in Scotland. You said then, your dream was to have horses and a home in Scotland. How was it?*

Magnificent. Scotland is fantastic. I have a real old English car, and basically I started driving there from here, up the east coast, and returning back across the Highlands downward. It was one of the most exciting vacations. And my dream about horses has not changed.

FAMILY

It is a familial love all right, but not like we have to phone each other on a daily basis

I am quite close to my family, although my job does not leave me much time. And my mother is here in town, we are the few leftovers, and therefore I am particularly close to her. My mother keeps trying very hard to hold the family together, and all of us basically have a pretty close relationship with our mother. Among ourselves, that is a little — it is like with all siblings. Let us say, we don't idolize each other. It certainly is a familial love all right, but not like we have to phone each other on a daily basis, or else we can't survive. But you'd be surprised, sometimes I have more contact with my sister or with my brother Salek in Israel than with my brother Ronnie in Munich. It really does not have much to do with being geographically close. Sometimes those who are closer by are further away than someone in Israel.

My mother also makes sure that the holidays are kept. Less from tradition or on religious grounds, and more so that the family has a reason to get together once again, and we all try to observe that. At those times, my Israeli family comes pretty regularly and my brothers from Munich, and at least these five times a year we see each other. Most of the time.

When I was still little, candles were lit on Shabbat. Always. But in the later years, when my father was not well any longer, it was less so. And when my brothers began to be away from home, studying in Munich and so on, then it was only me, and everything was rolled back somehow. We did have Seders, although we run the fastest Seders in the world. But we did have them, and it was more than just sitting together and eating.

It is of course difficult for the entire family to meet on all occasions, with our job obligations and all. But important family celebrations always. Not too long ago [1995], I saw my sister Esther, we celebrated a bat mitzvah. It was her younger daughter. It was a bat mitzvah celebration in June this year in England, in London. Well it was not really a bat mitzvah celebration proper, but rather we met there on occasion of that bat mitzvah. The family, for the first time in ten years, was once again complete; the time before, tragically, on the occasion of my father's death when we all met in Israel. This time, ten years later in London, with our Israeli branch and my brothers from Munich, all together. We met in London because it was kind of midway; we had the idea for once not to meet either in Israel or in Germany, but in London, and Aurel, my brother-in-law, was busy with his paintings in London at the time, so we combined all of that together. Now, in December 2000 we had a millennium celebration in Jerusalem, and for my mother's birthday, we all went to Paris. Esther organized all that.

ESTHER: I organized all that. This was an amazing party. Since last year, since the millennium, I have initiated something new. It is a kind of family reunion, and what is new about it is that it is intensive, a three-day workshop. They liked that so much that I've said, okay, more of that. Before the party in Paris, there was the question of the millennium; what should one do for the millennium. No one knew what they should do for it, and since I knew that I could not get away because my daughter was in the army and because I would not have left as long as my daughter was in the army I said, listen, I can't leave, you have to come here. So for three days we've been having a love-in, and that was really very, very nice for the family. That really pulled us very much together. I am the oldest sibling and I have a fair responsibility for what happens. And so, for my mother's birthday, I organized all that, three days in Paris, it was really phenomenal. Everybody was there for the workshop, including the sisters from Argentina.

Q: *What do you mean by "workshop"?*

Look, in every family there are things that create friction. This one against that one or with that one, and then this one says this or that. When you are together intensively for three days, things come out into the open, you can work on that and about various things you can, to get over it.

GABRIEL: That birthday party for my mother really was amazing. Except that her purse was ripped off at the airport. But it was a fantastic event. Planned, of course, by our fantastic, general stafflike organizer Esther, with timetable and dress code and [*laughs*] this is the way she is. She does that magnificently because in the final analysis it was great of course that the whole family was there from South America and that we've now reached kind of a new family feeling. There must be someone who does that sort of thing. Esther sees herself a little bit, shall I say, like a family ambassador.

Now while Esther had taken over the organizational matters in our family, my mother has remained the integrative pole. My office is seven minutes away from the house, but I mean I don't live there any more. My mother and her maid are pretty much alone in the house. Of course I am there off and on, and of course my brothers come back to F., but otherwise, my mother does not have much of a social net and did not find much receptiveness after the death. It is because my father really had been living rather reclusively, without a friendship circle, and with little contact with local society. So nothing was left afterward. But she is really not doing badly. Every once in a while she thinks of moving away, maybe to Israel, but otherwise, what can you say, our home where my mother is living is always the great symbolic meeting point of our family, and of course it is a huge house and a huge garden. For a woman alone it is basically absolute madness, but on the other hand it has the symbolic value, and we're always meeting there. Economically, or practically, it is indefensible.

As far as the cousins are concerned, I have next to no contact. I think I am similar to my siblings there. Lilian is in Munich, I see her once every six months; she still works in part here in F. as well, although she lives in Munich. Then there is Jonny, her brother, he is a lawyer in Haifa. I see her father maybe twice a year, and my other uncle, Ignaz, I really only know him from stories. He is supposed to be very bright, but very difficult. My uncle (Jurek) and my father got into a bitter fight with him at the time, in the business. So this image evolved in us, of the dark side; he was always my father's adversary, and they ended up in this fight, and automatically, you side with your own parents and you develop these aggressions. The family's business brought about this atmospheric discord which can no longer be turned off, and I found this discord a very serious issue.

No further step was taken in this respect, too much estrangement had developed. Everyone has their own sphere, is happy with that, no one sees a necessity, and we also really don't like each other that terribly much. To be perfectly honest with you, with my cousins, even when I meet them, they can never become my good friends. It is family, and I accept that, okay, but as we say, you can pick your friends, but not your family. The question is, why does one have that contact? What is decisive — is it the human being, or does one have that contact because as Jews somehow we must stick together?

THE FATHER

He inspired me to think along with him

I was sixteen years old when my father died; when I was four years old — Esther I think had gone to Israel at that time — he had his first operation. He had his first heart attack when I was six years old. There were these ongoing problems in the firm—I of course saw my father suffering all the time, both in terms of health and in terms of his business. I have never known otherwise, I mean, as long as I can remember, my father was always seriously ill.

Problems in the business which you hear about as a child, for that you have to be at least twelve or thirteen years old. Since then, again and again, there were problems in business, sometimes more, sometimes less. But that is how I grew up. Whether this plays any role in my present life—whether certain decisions which I make today or whether some of my character traits are based upon this childhood—that I can only surmise. At the time I still did not have the feeling where I found, okay, I am like that because this is how it has been with my father.

Just don't think because of all that my father would not have had time for me. Even when I think about that now, I always had the feeling that my father was very present in my life. He really did a lot. He got me involved in things, even in my youngest years, and he confronted me with business situations, tried to explain his current situation to me, asked me for advice. At the time I did not realize that; only today can I see that of course the advice of a twelve- or thirteen-year-old [laughs] cannot be taken really seriously. But my father never gave me the feeling that this was total bullshit; he gave me the sense that he was taking it seriously, and so he inspired me to think along with him.

Q: *But being a teenager, didn't you sense the stress, his stays in hospital, the downward slide of the business? All that must have had a considerable effect on you.*

It must have, but I don't know whether I was fully aware of it. It is certainly not easy to grow up with a father who loves you more than anything, and who makes you feel that very much. My father really did an incredible amount, including the matter with the horses. I don't know whether somebody told you that story. At some point, he wanted to buy me a horse. I came—I was looking outside into the garden and was very curious whether there would be a horse, and I was looking outside into the garden, and I see sixteen horses trotting through my parents' garden. All of a sudden, we had a stud farm and huge stables. I really have grown up in a dream world, and lastly I was a really spoiled, pampered kid.

Do you want to hear about the experience with my father that left the most lasting impression? Whenever my father came home from his business, I had to lie with him on the couch [*laughs*]. He simply needed me by his side. I then had to cuddle with him on the couch. He had an enormous love for me, he was really addicted to me. When you are a child, it is a nuisance when the parents want to cuddle with you. So this is the image I still have today, how I am lying on the couch with my father. This was certainly an extraordinarily deep, deep affection that my father had toward me and generally toward his children.

Even now with my thirty-two years [2001] I don't know of anyone who loved his children and who documented this love so deeply as my father did toward us. It is really my father's most characteristic trait, to do basically everything so that his children were happy. The entire firm, this total sacrifice, despite the aggravation, despite his poor health, for him his children were item number one. Toward his children — whether it was the horses, whether it was travel, whether it was a fishing rod which I absolutely had to have on a Sunday afternoon even though the stores were all closed, he somehow got it for us.

THE NAZI IN THE DEPARTMENT STORE

There is such a thing as sympathy with the aggressor

This is how it was in our home and with me and my father. On the outside, though, he really did not have any friends, and this also had to do with the German environment. I believe there is such a thing as sympathy with the aggressor, this kind of love-hate, and at some point my father told the story how he met an old Nazi in a department store, and when he talked about that, you did not find any hatred, more like, "this was a pretty all-right guy, basically, at the time." I believe this is a very particular way to come to grips with such a past, a sympathy with the enemy. We cannot comprehend that, but it must be respected.

ESTHER: Sometimes, my father also spoke of the good Germans. This always made me mad, because I have been much more extreme in my anti-Germanness than he. On occasion, we went on business trips together, I came along because I wanted to buy kitchen equipment for myself and so on. At night, we'd sit in a restaurant, and people started talking about the Holocaust period, and my father would talk to his employees—I thought to myself, I am going to kill you!—about the good Germans who had helped him. I thought, is that possible? Is that what you have to say about the Holocaust? Do you have to say *that* about the Holocaust? Then he also talked about this story that sometime in the sixties or the late fifties, somewhere in a department store, he saw somebody, and he ran after him and wanted to thank him, and that fellow fled or something. And then he saw someone at another point, and he gave him a watch. That is, twice he's seen people, and oddly, he remembered these kinds of things. Despite that, though, we were brought up anti-German.

GABRIEL: To come back to this thing about living in Germany, personally I believe that my father could never really give an answer to that. I believe it is simply a kind of psychological effect that if you survived something like that, you stay where you survived to prove to yourself, "I am still here" or in Yiddish, "mir seinen do"; that is, not to have fled, not to have escaped, not to have left that behind oneself, but to be still standing on the hill, and to be staying there where in the final analysis one had won the struggle, because my father did survive. And what else do I do here with my radio show and the Jewish jokes and my red Ferrari?

LIVING IN GERMANY

I often asked myself the question, why we are here?

ESTHER: My other siblings—excluding Salek, who is also here in Israel—the other three, in my view, they are lost. Unfortunately, they don't see that, but they are lost. Gabriel worries me very, very much. How is that supposed to go on?

GABRIEL: I often asked myself the question, why we are here in Germany of all places? Of course also in consideration of the past. How can somebody who was persecuted in the Third Reich or who suffered so much under the Germans decide to stay in Germany? It is a paradox. I asked myself this question because inside me there was a problem of comprehension, it was schizoid reasoning, although we had it anything but bad here. So my question did not come out of suffering but simply out of a mental schizophrenia. I mean we grew up magnificently, we had . . . neither financial problems nor did we have a bad adolescence, that is, we grew up like in paradise, one has to say that too, and put that into the equation. And Germany also isn't a country where in the country some way, from the viewpoint of politics, one would suffer.

Of course I know that my sister views her own youth quite differently, she hated it here. She probably talked to you about the anti-Semitism, but personally, I never had that experience, even though nowadays I am leading a fairly public life and am relatively well known in the media. And I host as well, I am officially in the media, and I never made a secret out of being Jewish. It is also known, just by the name, that Gabriel Kalman is Jewish, but I never had any official problems there. Here, the city of F. is such a mix between large and small city, and people gossip. Wherever you go, people know "you are Jewish," or you hear that somehow. Whatever I did not succeed with, permits that were not issued, or what was decided somewhere in the backrooms on account of the [Jewish] fact, that I don't know.

Q: *But would you not assume that here and there, in the underground at least, there is still anti-Semitism?*

One simply cannot say that. And let us not go and get paranoid. My mother of course is always very worried and always asks me whether I have any problems, but she herself does not have any. I think twenty years or so ago, a pedestrian said, I believe, "you dirty Jew" [Saujüdin] to her or "you Sarah" or something like that, that was an occurrence twenty years or so ago, it can happen anywhere in the world.

I know, my sister is very different there, she sees anti-Semitism everywhere, she gets it from non-Jewish acquaintances in Israel and this is why she thinks it was the right thing to go away from here. My sister has always been the one who has loved Israel more than anything, who was very Zionist, and really did not want to have anything to do with Germany. She has always been a militant anti-German, and she could never understand why my father stayed here. For her, it was clear from the beginning that Germany could not be her home [*Heimat*], so she left rather early. It is different with Salek, he is not that militant. Although he says that he left for political reasons as well, he really left mostly because of his wife.

Don't ask me now whether I would live in Israel, would want to. Because I absolutely would not.

Q: *Why not? Too hot there?*

No, because I cannot stand the people there. Because for me, they are all idiots. In Israel it is like they are all unfriendly, everybody thinks he is the president of all the countries of the world, and there is no service in the original sense, one cannot subordinate oneself, they have no culture, no politeness, no friendliness, and nothing of what makes a life worth living.

GABRIEL'S JEWISHNESS

*I am not someone who carries his Jewishness very much out
in the open, and I am also not extremely traditional*

As far as my Jewishness is concerned, I have never carried it out in the open, at least in my earlier years. You have to imagine, here in F., there was nothing going on in Jewish terms. Now, with the Russian immigration this might change. I never went to the ZJD and the Jewish summer camps. The reason is that here in F. there is no real Jewish group, and in my youth, I never sought any contact with N. or Munich. Basically, the older generation has been dying off, and nothing new came from the bottom. Also, the young people in part went to Munich, and in part, I had a girlfriend. My first great love was a Jewish girl from F. This was absolutely extraordinary, because we were of the same age and emotionally compatible, like two drops of water in the ocean, but in the meantime, she is happily married in New York. When I was around twenty, there was nothing here in F. to keep anybody, the active young people left, the older people passed away, and at the time it seemed as if at some point everything would be over.

A Jewish atmosphere at home would be important to me. Because it was always very important for my parents. But I am not someone who carries his Jewishness very much out in the open, and I am also not extremely traditional. Mentally, I am Jewish, and I am certainly aware of that. I am not one of those extrovert Jews, but I am still conscious of it, and I stand behind it [1995].

As far as a Jewish domestic atmosphere is concerned, I am still [2001] not married, but I am nevertheless totally relaxed and happy. It is not my idea, having a family and children and finding a suitable wife for that project, but rather, to find a woman with whom I can imagine this state of affairs. You cannot force that to happen. The older I get, I will say one day, okay, now, I'll serve myself, let me make that happen. *Take up one person and make it work.* At some point you have to find somebody where you say, that's it . . . and this I still don't have.

You asked whether a Jewish wife would be important to me. To be honest, I don't care. It would be nice if it turned out that way. But I am too egotistical to be spending my life with somebody who I don't love one hundred percent. If you consider all the variables necessary for me to fall in love, that alone would be difficult. If I reduce that pool even much further and exclude everyone who is not Jewish, then I think things would get very, very difficult.

ESTHER: You have heard already about Gabriel's thirtieth birthday party, with the terrible Hasidic dress code. In the last couple of years, Gabriel has become interested in Judaism — not as religion, but exactly as I have, in the sense of history, and of one's background. He also took books from me and old lithographs. He is simply interested. Of course he does not know anything. He has no idea about Judaism, not even the basics, something went wrong in his upbringing, but it probably has to do with the fact that my father was not there anymore, because he died too early. Gabriel has come closer to Judaism, and maybe it is true that his non-Jewish friends can be more relaxed about it. But just imagine, they were all non-Jewish friends at his party who came with peyes glued on. I am far more burdened with it. I cannot see that as easy as he. And then this invitation! Here is a Jewish birthday party, it said, dress code Jewish Orthodox. I spoke to my friends here in Jerusalem about it. They were all shocked. I thought I would faint when I saw that.

I said, "Gabriel, tell me, have you gone crazy?" He of course thinks I have become psychotic and that I am paranoid. "What you are worried about has long passed, and because of people like you we will never have a normal situation." I told this to the people here, Israelis. They all said he's gone nuts. Now, in hindsight, I understand what he wanted to do. But I don't know whether that could work. Lots and lots of people came to that party, with peyes made from paper and black hats . . . like in costume, you know, funny.

Then he has this radio show, once a week, where they only spoke Yiddish, and Jewish jokes. He found somebody in Munich, and they were telling each other Jewish jokes, in Yiddish, he does not really speak Yiddish, the other guy does. It was a real Yiddish comedy show.

Now in the *Allgemeine jüdische Wochenzeitung* you might have a column with Jewish jokes, but that is a Jewish weekly! There is a difference there, this is not a private radio station in Bavaria. Where are we? In a Jewish paper this may be funny, but we are talking about an entirely different audience. Zero Jews, all non-Jews. And even the Catholic Church got upset about it. This is how far we have come.

Still, Gabriel's message is totally different, hard for us to comprehend; for our generation, it is an interesting new message. Maybe he is ahead of his time. I told him already, maybe you are avant garde, but as long as the perpetrators and the victims are still alive you cannot do that.

GABRIEL: As I said, my radio show is called "Bread and Circuses," from 6:00 to 8:00, same old show.

Q: *Esther told me that together with a friend, kind of in Yiddish, you were telling Jewish jokes there, and that the Catholic Church went against it.*

Yes, we have a lot of jokes about Jews. We always get into trouble because in this comedy show, we constantly make jokes about minorities. We believe every group has the right to be made fun of. It is a form of discrimination if we make fun of everybody, about Austrians, about the Swiss, about Germans, but not about Turks or about Jews. You have to tread carefully, of course, it must never be distasteful. We would never make jokes about the Third Reich or something like that. But Jewish humor, as you well know, was part of the Jewish cultural heritage in Germany.

And the business with the Catholic Church: there is a kind of Pavlovian effect. The moment you mention the word "Jew" on the radio, people jump up, simply because someone says "Jew" on the radio. Immediately, the alarm bells start ringing, without anybody listening carefully to what was said. Of course these jokes relate to certain people with certain characteristics, but this is neither racist nor anti-Semitic.

This surprised me: people did not listen carefully to this. They have this defensiveness that they grew up with, and they say, for God's sake, we cannot start once again making jokes about the Jews. They don't even take note of the next generation and they don't take note of this development. They don't ask, what would integration look like in the future? Certainly, this cannot succeed if we have these taboos and are afraid to even mention a certain group of people and if the word "Jew" sits like a lump in one's throat.

We wanted to be humorous; it was to be a small attempt for groups to come closer together. Once people can laugh about one another, this is a small step. But even that was nipped in the bud, and we got into a lot of trouble because of it. We had long discussions, all the way to the Bavarian Broadcasting Commission, and this went all the way to the highest body, but they muzzled us. This was specifically concerning Jewish jokes. I cannot tell you one of these jokes just like that, but we basically had two characters, two Yiddish-speaking people.

At that time, we had another Jewish coworker in the station, Jean Spanier from Munich. He speaks very good Yiddish, and so we developed this comedy series, where two Jews have a conversation, in Yiddish, and tell old corny jokes and puns. It is a parallel comedy to two Turks who talk in a Turkish neighborhood, in a Turkish-German slang that is very much in vogue in Germany right now. That is, Turks speaking German, and this accent is being made fun of. We have the greatest success with the Turks, they have the best sense of humor. There are of course a bunch of high school teachers who feel morally called upon to condemn that.

So this was one approach, with these two Jewish kids. Then at some point there was this song, this hit — but for you in Toronto this would be hard to follow. We rewrote this hit. In the original, it is, "Waddehad-deduddeda," it is the Cologne dialect and means, "What have you got there?" It is by Stefan Raab, at present a great star in Germany, he participated in the Grand Prix. Now we rewrote that, "What's the Jew missing there?" — alluding to the foreskin, of course. It came to be a great hit. People thought this was very funny, we did as well, of course.

Now this came to be a huge scandal and had to be stopped immediately. We of course did not think there was any problem with it. I had no qualms with it, it does not have to do with the Third Reich, with the recent past, but is simply as if I were to make jokes about the Prussians, that they talk funny or that they are stupid or something. Here now there is an evil prejudice, but one can turn this around, into a punch line, here with two taboos, Jews and sex — this is a heavy-duty satire program, a bit like Howard Stern in the U.S. You need not like it, but it is not unlawful to be saying something like that on the radio.

Add to that the Jewish side. The Jewish community in S. reacted, their president, Frau T., who I much respect and like, reacted. She had actually helped me a lot at a point when we had problems with the broadcasting commission, and when my broadcasting license was in jeopardy. At that time, I was still a shareholder in the station and one of its managers. There she really helped me a lot. But in this matter, she really did not look carefully enough and basically reacted like somebody who judges a book by its cover.

And then, jokes about Jews: are you for it or against it? Here, someone like Frau T., as the representative of the Jewish community in the Bavarian Broadcasting Commission will say, well of course, it is my job to be opposed to something like that. I am sure she was also under pressure from her people and for that reason probably did not bother to look into the details. She cannot explain this to her people in ways that they can understand it. I realize that. Which is why in this case she went against me. It's okay.

Q: *I wanted to ask you something totally different. Esther told me she was absolutely shocked about your birthday party with the Hasidic dress code.*

What? [*laughs*] She's giving away all my secrets. She really is a dud, my dear sister. Of course she is not a dud. But here, the two of us disagree. Now it is true that because I am working in broadcasting and in the communications area, it might have lowered my threshold. At present [2001], radio has become more kind of a hobby for me, I just do it on the side. But I am sure I have a tendency to a certain offensive manner to deal with these things, and as you can see, the reaction is not very positive.

Here's the story. For my thirtieth birthday, we organized a really big party here, in an old movie theater that has been shut down, and the dress code at the time was in fact "Jewish Orthodox" or, alternatively, "sexy." I was obviously very glad that everybody came Jewish Orthodox [*laughs*]. It was real nice, there were over two hundred people at the party, and really very many came with home made peyes, braided from card board and glued on, and with home made kippas, the way they know it.

It was simply funny, I mean, I am a Jewish kid and I stand up for it. I don't ignore it and I carry that out in the open, in a modern way, and I communicate that. I believe that I do more for Judaism, in my small microcosm, making Judaism cool, as opposed to some old-fashioned Orthodox Jews with their ideas. Why can't we have some humor about it? I believe Ephraim Kishon has done more for the Jews than any rabbi. Others in my generation support that completely. Take Jean Spanier for example, the one who did the Jewish jokes program with me, he had a lot of fun with it and he sees it the same way. This is simply a generation that is saying at some point, how will it all continue? Do we on the one hand want to live here in Germany, and on the other, still feel the reproach in us, or do we have to say at some point, we have to go forward and make progress. It is not a question of forgetting. And concerning my sister, I did not understand her entire criticism.

Esther, of course, has a huge aversion against Germany, and this probably explains a lot. She is far more sensitive there. She is correct in many things, the tough reality outside, as far as reactions are concerned. But I have to tell you quite honestly, I have not experienced once any anti-Semitic, racist manifestations here in town. It also happens often that I meet people who would say, oh yes, your father. Our family had a strong presence here in F. and you can actually say, it was a great history. There were the many kitchen appliances stores in F. and the region, there was the big sawmill, where the kitchen furnishings were manufactured. Many employees still live here from that time, and, well, the bankruptcy was in the media as well.

So we cannot speak about anti-Semitism here, even though I carry my Jewishness officially out in the open. How much further can you take this as with the Kalman family which is already known in town as, lastly, Jews, and then with the most popular radio program in which you represent Jewishness? It is nice, actually: people call us during the show, live, and say, Shalom, and when we had Jewish weeks, people could haggle about winning prizes. We were cooking cholent together, and there was folklore music, it was very Jewish.

I have to explain this. In our radio show we sometimes have what we call a "Jewish week" because when there is a holiday in Bavaria or in Germany, on that day, the show is canceled. That is, our show, in a series of five weekly shows, is cut to one day less, which is why we say, this is the Jewish week, because it is "cut," or circumcised [*laughs*]. And this is when people can "jew," or haggle for prizes, and we play Jewish songs, like "Wenn ich einmal reich wär" and all the programming items that we have in the show we reorient toward Judaism then. In these "Jewish" weeks, we have also experienced that people call us in the middle of the show, and they don't say hello, but Shalom, it is really on a very sympathetic level where you can say, it is really cool, it does not trigger a new anti-Semitism, as one might expect — that some sort of psychos would call in and let loose with some anti-Semitic remarks. That was my sister's objection: that all we are doing is provoking people with it, and to stir them up. That is exactly what does not happen. My approach is de-tabooization.

I hope I could help you with that. And when the book is out, will I get a copy?

2

Ignaz

and Dina

Ignaz

DINA'S FATHER

1922   born in Slawkusz

1941   transported by Wehrmacht to Hermann-Göring-Werke
        (forced labor)

1945   liberation in Buchenwald (April 11)

1947   starts auto repair shop with brother Albert

1950   leaves for Brooklyn, New York, near sister Gertrud

1951   returns to F.

1956   marries Fela

1975   leaves the Kalman firm

Very early on, Dina, with whom this project really began, suggested that I go and visit her father and ask him to tell me about his life. At that time, she herself had not been able to speak to him about it. Subsequently I decided to go to F. to visit and speak to him.

Years after meeting Dina, and when Dina started living with Johannes, I asked myself, what are we to make of Ignaz's radical rejection of a future son-in-law? Often, especially in traditional milieux, potential spouses are looked upon with reserve and skepticism, and socially inappropriate candidates face resistance from parents and family. Undoubtedly, this aspect plays a role in Dina's case as well. Yet Ignaz and his wife, as we have seen, are not that traditional or religious to go to such lengths and to keep their only daughter from their door, nor, as we have seen, are the families of his brothers that uncompromising. I believe therefore that this explanation does not suffice, that there is more to this rejection: What are we to make of the fact that Dina, who loves her father, wants to come to F. to meet him, and that her father, who also loves her, wants her to come to F., and yet both can never meet — or when they do meet she feels like "jumping out of the window" — that they cannot share common space?

I would argue that there is another more important reason. In one of their better moments, on his visit to H., in 1993, Dina asked her father to speak about what he remembered about his life and his ordeal. It was important for Dina to have her father's story in order to pass it down to her children. Ignaz had never spoken about his experiences in detail before. Dina sent me a copy of this report, which she wrote down, with a note to me, "What my father has told there is not exactly a lot" — Viel ist es ja nicht, was mein Vater da erzählt hat. In that half-hour interview, of no more than ten pages in transcript, Ignaz talks — emotionless, as Dina put it — about his ordeal, beginning with the order to get ready for a forced labor camp, on "April 1, 1941," when he was called to the Slawkusz synagogue for the transport.

The report speaks of good and bad guards in the labor camp, of his hunger and his seven week march from the camp in Silesia to Buchenwald. In its last sections, it speaks of the time after liberation and what he saw as the "two most important things in my life," which fall into the time after liberation: a big packet of gold he received in the black market coffee trade, transactions that took place between the Königsplatz and the Möhlstrasse in Munich, and a trade in "dollars and cigarettes" in front of the synagogue in F. The "most important things" in his life, then, occurred before he met his wife, before the birth of his daughter, or the rise and fall of the family firm, Kalman Haushaltsgeräte.

I would argue that Ignaz never fully left that space in front of the synagogue in F., an epiphany of the synagogue in Slawkusz, where he was waiting for the transport to the camps. He also never left the Königsplatz and the Möhlstrasse in Munich, sites of the black market after the war. This is where his life truly began. For him, Poland and the camps were prehistory. At the time of the black market and the German economic miracle, Ignaz, in enemy territory, could experience the type of economic success he could not have dreamt of back home in Poland. He has become frozen in that postwar past, has long since become out of reach, disconnected from his present environment, encapsuled in the time-space of the camps and of the postwar period. Both of these, like Poland earlier, were hostile environments, and Germany then was indeed divided in many pieces.

Here is a man we can no longer communicate with; as Dina put it, "My father basically does not have a language." His struggle with his daughter is that he wants to drag her out of an imagined environment of deadly danger, back into his own time capsule, back into a time-space which neither Dina nor anyone else could ever share.

When I met Ignaz in F., announced as a friend of Dina's, he picked me up from the train station in a big beige Mercedes. He drove me to his large house somewhat removed from other houses in the area and on an open field; a house with an inhospitable feel to it, a large living room, sparsely, almost negligently furnished with little more than oriental rugs, and at its center, a big television with a big chair on which he rolled and rotated back and forth. My interview with Ignaz did not amount to much. He in essence refused to be interviewed and told me to interview "the important people." His experiences and recollections, he said, were of no use to me. It was at the time of German unification, and I asked him what he thought of it. He told me that Germany should never be united; after all that had happened, Germany should remain divided, it should be divided even further, divided into quarters, into eighths, into sixteenths. When I mentioned this to Dina, she commented, "So what's he doing here then? Why then does he raise a child here? If he thinks like that, why does he raise a child here? I am asking you, what's the logic behind it? Money you can make everywhere. If someone is as clever as he is about making money, then you can make money everywhere. He could have gone to Israel, he could have stayed in New York, he had infinite possibilities. You did not need to stay here."

I asked Ignaz for an interview a second time, a few years later, but his position had not changed. I suggested to him, would it not be good if his granddaughter would know about her family's history, about her great-grandparents and about her grandfather as well. He refused and told me he knew nothing, that he forgot it all. In what follows, we find some fragments of his story.

FRAGMENTS OF HIS STORY

*Day in and day out I was in front of the synagogue
and traded dollars and cigarettes*

IGNAZ: On April 1, 1941, I was called to the synagogue, it was in Slaw-kusz, and from there I was deported in a covered truck of the Wehrmacht. All I had with me were the clothes that I was wearing; I was there with others from Slawkusz. We were not crammed together. Soldiers of the Wehrmacht were guarding us with their guns.

The Labor Camp

First I came to Sackenheim, to the Hermann Göring Werke, coal refineries. We built a factory there and roads and did other types of land-development work; this went on for about half a year. After that I arrived in Brande, in an RAB camp. RAB stands for Reichsautobahn, the national highway system. For the autobahn section between Gleiwitz and Breslau, I cleared the forest, pulled out roots, and built bridges. I never went back there. Every night, they gave us one ration of bread, less than a pound, 400 grams to be precise, we got some margarine and sometimes a portion of marmalade for the following day. We were always hungry. Some people died from hunger, but not in masses.

From there, we marched to the next RAB camp, totally without *Selektion*. We slept there in bunk beds with straw mattresses. A few days later, Jews from a neighboring camp came to that second RAB camp with a column. Some of them were from Slawkusz as well, and they told me that my brother Albert was in that other camp, and they also told Albert about me. Through an exchange, I could meet with Albert. After some time, by sheer coincidence, I was moved over to the camp where Albert was. From there, we were sent to Freiwaldau, to the roof tile factory of the Butz brothers of Poland, and Albert and I were together there for one or two years.

Potatoes

One day, I was ordered to night shift. The advantage was that we only went to work around one or two in the afternoon. You could sleep longer that way and did not have to show up for roll call. Instead, they took us sometimes to peel potatoes, and so we had access to the potato cellar. It meant you could "organize" potatoes, and carry them on your body. I was never caught, but one of the inmates discovered my storage hideout and stole everything. At the brick ovens, you could put the potatoes into the fire. From there we took them, hidden on our bodies, back to the barracks, and that is how I could help Albert. The others worked from seven in the morning to six at night, with an hour at lunch time. This was in accordance with the German labor conditions. Being privileged like that helped to survive.

Caretaker

I heard how the camp eldest told the leader of the column, "I need a kid." The camp eldest was the head of operations and a Jew from Breslau, and the column leader was a Jew as well. Reflexively I said, "It is me." And even though I did not have any privileges, the column leader told me, "Okay so you go." So I came to be the caretaker of the Jewish head of operations, his name was Bubi Rinner. It was my job to clean the office, just like a cleaning woman. I did that well and thoroughly. On the second day, the head of operations asked me, "What's your name?" I told him my name and he said, "Okay, Kalman, you'll stay with me." It was like being voted mayor by the people. On the third day, he said, "Go off and take a bath and into the supply room and to the barber."

DINA: Were you shaved?

IGNAZ: Yes.

DINA: So how did you take that?

IGNAZ: Compared to the general situation in the camp, that really did not matter any more. So I had become part of the camp administration. It meant that from now on I stayed inside the camp, and I realized that I had greater chances to survive. Work was easier, and I did not have to go to the roll call. Hunger was still bad, but psychologically I was in better shape.

The Good SS Man

Later I was shifted elsewhere and had to guard the gate. The guard detachment were people from the Luftwaffe [air force] who for whatever reason were taken off air force duty. I cannot complain about their behavior. My main job was to open and shut the gate and to watch at the window in case the ss camp leader was showing up. Then I had to stand to attention, had to open and shut the gate, and do likewise when he returned. This was the first time that I had to deal with the ss at the rank of an Oberscharführer. His deputy was an Unterscharführer. We always called him "Uschi." He was a good guy, but the Oberscharführer was a real bastard. But from what I heard after the war, the two were God like compared to the ones in other camps. For that Uschi I was a witness in 1948 at the police head office in F. The criminal investigations unit took my testimony.

Death March

When it turned out that the Russians had crossed the Vistula River, the camp was evacuated, and we were sent on a march. This was in early February of 1945, and we were marching about six or seven weeks from Kittlitz-Streben to Buchenwald. We started with about 500 people, about 400 arrived in Buchenwald. The people who died on the way died from illness, from the cold, or from weakness. Here I have to say that although the Oberscharführer had been very strict in the camp, on the march he was exemplary. Again compared to other camp leaders, as we heard later on.

So on the first day, two people got shot because they did not want to march. Then he took the weakest prisoners on a light trailer with rubber tires where we had our tools as well. The other prisoners pushed that trailer, and we took turns. The destination was not known to us at the time. Dead prisoners were buried along the way. Some days later, the Oberscharführer organized peasants with tractors who pulled the trailer from one village to the next. It was my impression that this procedure was his own free decision, it was not an order from above, and to bring as many people to Buchenwald alive as was possible.

On one of the stopovers we were in a barn. Apparently we did not have anything to eat for some time, and Uschi came by and was ambushed with "food—we are hungry." He left without saying a word. Two hours later he came back with steaming potatoes. We pigged out.

Liberation

We stayed for two days. We were supposed to march on. It got to be seven, then eight, nine, and ten o'clock. Nothing happened. In between there were announcements over the loudspeakers about air alarms. Around eleven or twelve, we heard shooting and we saw how American planes circled over the camp area. The shooting lasted only for half an hour and suddenly, the Americans were in the camp. Blacks, whites as well, and tanks. The guards ran off; the towers had been shot at as well.

DINA: How did you know that it was all over?

IGNAZ: The loudspeakers probably were saying in all languages, "liberation." That was on April 11, 1945. Then we were free. There was food. We were still in prisoners' clothing. A couple of days later they brought up the people from Weimar to show us to them. Mountains of corpses.

DINA: Do you really remember that?

IGNAZ: I don't know whether I have that from my own memory. Occasionally, we went into the town to see life once again.

DINA: Weren't you afraid, being among Germans like that?

IGNAZ: No, American soldiers were everywhere. We had a little bit of money. No idea what we bought with it.

The Most Important Events in My Life

At Königsplatz in Munich, the black market, around 1946, a man offered me two pieces of gold. I bought them from him. Then he asked me whether I could get him coffee. I got that for him and sold it almost for what I bought it. Then he told me that next week he would have gold again. I sold him coffee. One day, and I don't know how, he came with a really big package of gold pieces and gold bars. I told him to go to the M. family. He waited there for me and entrusted the whole package to me. I don't remember whether I paid right away or a week later. I made a lot of money selling all that in the Möhlstrasse in Munich.

One day, a German came to the gate of the Jewish community center to sell cigarettes. That day, somehow, the price of cigarettes had dropped and no one wanted any. I got into his car and asked him, where are these cigarettes from, and who are you. He answered me, he was the head of the PX [U.S. military store]. I could get coupons in the black market, and we agreed that I would give the coupons to him, while he would get cigarettes from the PX. For each coupon a dollar, and he would get cigarettes for that from the PX. He was the PX head somewhere in the Württemberg area. We made a deal to meet halfway in a parking lot in order to reload the goods. This went on for a longer period of time. One day the man was arrested. We heard about that from his wife. We were afraid we would get betrayed, and I thought about fleeing.

Day in and day out I was in front of the synagogue and traded dollars and cigarettes.

Dina

FROM GERMANY TO

ISRAEL AND BACK

1957   born in Zurich

1962   Dina's family moves into large renovated house

1973   joins Zionist Youth movement (ZJD)

1975   father quits family business

1977   Abitur; leaves for Israel

1984   marries Mark in Israel

1985   Avital (Tali) is born

1988   returns with Mark to Germany, to H.

1990   civil divorce in H.

1990   enrolls in Middle Eastern Studies and Hebrew

1991   Mark gives Dina religious divorce ("get"); since 1991 Dina
        works as translator and interpreter

1993   four-week exploratory return visit to Israel

1994   meets Johannes

1998   Clifford is born

Dina plays a particularly important role for this book because she was the one who, in 1990, gave me access to and awakened my interest in the Kalman family. I have had many conversations with Dina about her family and over the years have conducted several interviews with her in her home. She usually did more than one thing at a time, looking after Clifford or speaking to her daughter Avital, while cooking delicious suppers at the same time. Nothing would distract her from the forceful-ness of what she had to say.

When I met Dina at a party in H. in 1990, a lively, outgoing, sharply dressed and attractive woman, she was still strongly oriented toward Israel and full of plans for what she could do when she went back there, where she might find a job and who could be of help. In H., she had some Israeli and other Jewish friends, a number of Americans, but men from the Mediterranean were more her type, she said later on. Other than a few women from day care, her contacts with Germans were few and she stayed away from German men. She would hang out in a cafe downstairs run by a Turkish man.

She felt herself to be entirely Israeli and definitely wanted to return there. In her apartment on Bogenstrasse we would listen to the latest Israeli music cassettes; my own interest in Israeli singers dates from that time. She was always au courant with the music and theater scene there, and even her name on the doorbell downstairs was in both Hebrew and German. In the future, when she would move back to Israel, her good friends and contacts in Israel would help in various ways, she believed. I doubt that she was really at home in H. at that time. The watershed toward a reorientation, her ex-husband Mark believes, came to be the Gulf War in 1990. I agree. At first, however, Dina became totally caught up in the panic-ridden atmosphere then prevailing in Israel. For me at that time, it became difficult to even phone Dina and speak to her from North America, where I was at the time. She seemed in constant telephone contact with Israeli friends, and all other concerns in her life were moved to the background. Later on, Israel turned into a less attractive option to return to, and North America, for a time at least, seemed to provide an alternative.

THE GHETTO WITHIN THE GHETTO

*If you are equally good, you are not good enough,
because you are Jewish*

DINA: Until I was about fifteen I led a sheltered life away from other children. At first, before elementary school, I did not go to the kindergarten because my mother did not deem this to be necessary. So I sat at home, barely had company, and never saw other kids. By the time I was five, we had moved to a new home. I got to know the boy from next door who was one year younger than I. That was my first friendship ever. Before that, I only knew my cousins, the only kids with whom I had contact.

Later, I could not go to school because I had not turned six yet. They could not accept that I could already write and read and that I was intelligent; they did not want that. At that time, as a consolation, my mother sent me for a year to kindergarten. For me, this was an entirely dramatic experience. At that point, I could not tie my own shoes, nor could I eat without help, or clean or tidy up or anything else, because I was such a spoiled brat that I was still being spoon-fed. I was only allowed to eat with a bib, could not make my bed, nothing. At the kindergarten, I refused to sleep there at noon, and all sorts of things like that.

Even when I was already out of elementary school, and when I went to a private high school where my cousins went as well, or later to the Gymnasium, I was still kept away from other kids. I was always driven to and from school, under the very cute pretext that the way to school would be shorter and I would get home more quickly, and would not need to get up earlier in the morning and so on. Usually, my mother drove me, and occasionally my father. He would drive from the firm past the school to pick me up, and from there to lunch at home. Then he would go back to the office and I was ordered to do my homework.

Most of our vacations, religious holidays, even weekends were spent in Switzerland. My mother did not feel comfortable in F. and kept half her life in Zurich. I was born in Zurich, my mother still had her doctors there and of course her mother, my grandmother, was there, too. My mother really used every opportunity to go back to Switzerland to see her parents. During summer vacations we went for a month to Italy, and subsequently for an additional two weeks to my grandparents. This happened regularly, every year, for fourteen years or so. Every Rosh Hashanah and Yom Kippur, every Pessach and Pentecost, on any conceivable possible vacation, we were there. Even on long weekends.

My grandmother's home was a kosher household and when I was still little, I was superkosher. So kosher. Outside the home we ate everything, but at home, it was supposedly kosher. How kosher it really was, I cannot say. But I remember a couple of nice stories. My grandmother in Zurich always bought live chickens on Thursday and had them slaughtered by the shoichet in the market—he always came to the market—and she plucked the feathers and all. She made it all kosher. It was great, superceremonial. I was always there for it, I was enthusiastic about it. It was great, the smell and all, and she cleaned the chicken, she filled the neck with something, and cooked it in the soup and with the unlaid eggs. There were egg yolks of all sizes, all the way to the very smallest one. This was my favorite ingredient in the soup.

F. with its uprooted Jews could not be compared to the stability of Jewish life in Zurich, and a real Jewish life could not be maintained there. At one point, I told my grandmother that my mom also buys chickens in the market, but these chickens are very clean. So inadvertently, I gave away that my mother had been buying perfectly ordinary meat in the market. All hell broke loose, because she had thought that my mother kept a superkosher household as well. Subsequently, we ordered stuff from the kosher butcher in Munich, but apparently she was uneasy about it. Much later, this was relaxed and on a birthday, for example, we might have shrimps at home, and there was bacon, except the problem was, it could not be eaten on bread with butter, because which set of plates should we use then, because until this day, we have separate meat and dairy dishes at home. Until today, this story about kashrut I find extremely impressive.

You have heard about the quarrels among the three brothers. This had clear repercussions for my family and me, also in relation to this small Jewish community in F. Everyone knew everyone else, and when I was little, everything was still okay. Once my father was booted out of the firm, Jewish community life in F. split between those who supported Albert, and those who supported my father, and those were very few. All of this touched me insofar as all these contacts collapsed when my father was thrown out of the firm. At that point, my mother did not go to synagogue anymore, because she felt ashamed, my father still went, sort of, even though he was ashamed as well, I think you can imagine this. So there was not a single person in F. who could have helped him with money or otherwise. In Munich, he went begging in the lodge, hoping that someone would help him to make ends meet and survive.

So in my childhood, the only meaningful contact I had was with some of my cousins, especially with Salek, who was three days older than me, and, more ambivalently, with Esther, who was four years older. In some ways, Esther was also a role model for some time. But I felt isolated, and my isolation was exacerbated by my mother putting a great deal of pressure on me, especially about doing my homework, in addition to the usual nouveau riche silliness, ballet, piano, and so on, something that was motivated by this ghetto mentality: you have to be better in school than the Germans, so that you can go on to university and get a job later on; if you are equally good, you are not good enough, because you are Jewish. But I also enjoyed doing ballet and playing the piano. It was nice, great, I liked it.

The only thing, perhaps, that stuck out from this ghetto existence — or maybe it was just another part of it — was the environment of the U.S. army in Bavaria. My mother was in the Lions Club, and my father played bridge in the officers' club. So I got to know a few people, the families, and a rabbi who before that had been a rabbi in Vietnam, pretty nice people. So I always had contact to Americans, via my parents.

Q: *Were these Americans not exclusively Jewish, though?*

No, not exclusively. But we did have more contact, then, with Jewish people who either came to the synagogue in F. or who invited us to their services — this was very, very nice because it was their form and an entirely different world. Especially during the time when their rabbi was still there, we got to know Jewish people there. Later on, around the time of my Abitur, I got to know primarily American blacks, and I was in touch with them, really neat types, musicians and so on, and while they were in the army, they were something special. Incredibly gifted jazz freaks, I simply found that fascinating, I went with them to dances and so on. My parents knew nothing of all that; had they known that I was cavorting with blacks, things would have gotten even worse.

What all of us, I think, experienced, was this contradiction between our parents' social climbing on one hand, and their ghetto mentality on the other. My cousin Esther and I were facing a similar predicament there. She and I were in the same ballet school, and she got into problems because Albert, her father, did not want her to perform, and her mother said, yes she can, why not — this was a pretty strange story. I really liked going there, until I turned fourteen, then I had to stop because of the ballet shoes, my mother did not want that. We also had dance lessons, they were run in the framework of the Gymnasium. What else? Of course I was not allowed to go to parties, and while after the dance lessons I was still allowed to go downstairs into the disco, I was picked up right from there and was not allowed to go out. So my situation was pretty similar to that of Esther.

Even within the Jewish environment this was not much different, and only when I got a bit older, and through my cousin Salek's intervention with my parents, was I allowed to join the ZJD. Here, I met other

Jewish kids my age, and went on a trip to Munich here and one to Berlin there. But this was very limited. For example, I was not allowed to go to machanot during the summer. Still, weekends I was allowed to go to Munich and on Saturday afternoon they had peula, but there the trouble started, because I wanted to stay for the entire weekend and on Sundays go for brunch at the Mövenpick. The Munich crowd was always considered a bit like higher society, in the ZJD as well, and they were respected by other people, those in Cologne for example and from Düsseldorf, but they also were so nouveau riche and such braggarts. So we did this, we were fifteen and we went to the Mövenpick and made trouble there, it was also pretty funny. And I wanted to stay in Munich for the weekend, and there was a huge fuss at home, and where are you staying there, who are these people, I was staying with a girl, and her parents had to call, it was horrific, until finally, I got permission.

I also remember that for one bar mitzvah I went to Frankfurt and I went out with the others, to discos and so on, until three or four in the morning, I mean that is an obvious thing to do when your parents are not around. When I came back home, the first thing that happened was that I was being slapped, and being accused that I was whoring around in Frankfurt. I had no idea what they meant. I did not know what I was supposed to have done, and of course like all the others I was kissing around, but, God, it is normal, we were teenagers.

My mother had no friends, Jewish or non-Jewish, and had nothing real else to do, so she focused her entire attention on me; my mother looked at me as the equivalent of the firm: my father had the firm, and she had me. So she sabotaged my relations with girlfriends from school, she was hellishly jealous about every girlfriend I had: I was not being driven to them, and where I was not driven to, I was not allowed to go in the first place. Going by streetcar or bus was taboo.

One girlfriend she had a special dislike for. So she invented this story that she allegedly had heard in the market — imagine, in the market! — that my friend takes drugs. That was absolutely false, and I told this girlfriend everything, it was heart-rending, I told her that despite of everything, I wanted to keep her friendship, with tears in my eyes, and to hell with my mother. I was devastated that my mother wanted to wreck this relationship, it was my first truly serious relationship with another girl, I was seventeen then. I always had difficulties with girl-friends because my mother meddled in it a lot.

But my mother was not only jealous about my relations with girls, she even kept me away from my father. I had to be in bed at seven, even when I was twelve already. Dinner at six, bathing at six-thirty, in bed at seven, lights out. My father never came home before seven-thirty or so, only rarely would I see him, then I had to go to bed right away. I had next to no opportunity to talk to my father, except maybe on a Sunday morning, which was our only time together. Typically, I would pull him out of bed around nine in the morning, pretty cruel of me, and I would bother him, why don't you come, come on let's go. And my mother would continue sleeping until eleven or eleven-thirty, and I had these few hours. With him.

We would go to the zoo then, or on a walk sometimes, sometimes we would simply lie in my bed and he would tell me stories, from his family at home, and here I also found out that his parents were murdered in a concentration camp. This was our only time together, where my mother could not disturb us.

THE FAMILY RUIN

Alone against the rest of the world

Already by the mid-sixties, the relations between my father and my two uncles had become ever more fractious. There were now three competing wives and there was a hierarchy between the three brothers which however was always contested, especially between my uncle Albert and my father, and much of that was traced back to their childhood. It is my theory that for his entire life, my father was in competition with my uncle Albert, because Albert was the firstborn son, and many of the stories I remember my father telling me about this childhood, on Sunday mornings, when I had him all to myself — these stories always had to do with things that my father got some way or other, things that Albert already had, and that he did not. This might have been a bicycle — once, for example, he stole my uncle's bicycle from the basement and got into an accident and was punished for it. Or: my father did not have ice skates, and so he got some skates somehow and hid them in the doghouse, and when they were found, there was trouble. Albert, of course, did have skates. Such stories I remember from my childhood, stories he told me about his parental home. In all these stories the competition with Albert came up. For him, I believe, it was a formative story that he did not receive what he would have wanted, that he was envious toward his brother.

There was so much fighting that at one point the three brothers agreed on an arbitration panel, but that was botched from the outset. The arbitration panel was that everyone brought his own private representative, his father-in-law, into the firm. Now because my father could not bring his father-in-law into this, simply because he was not versed in that sort of thing, my father decided to bring my mother into this. But he always got upset because he felt that she was trying to flatter them, that she was working more on their behalf and that she was not loyal enough toward him. Eventually, this was being dealt with in court, and the fact that my father was expelled by a court order from the business was the greatest insult that he ever experienced, and this is why he no longer speaks to them.

Because of all that, my relationship with most of my cousins is not good either, the bad feelings are still there. Some years ago, I was visiting with my aunt Eva, and Berthold was there as well. And he started to argue with me about what kind of asshole my father really is and so on. So I told him, Berthold, I don't want to hear about it. I especially do not want to hear from him when he talks to me in that tone of voice.

When my father was fired from the firm, he received a monthly indemnity of three thousand five hundred marks and later of five thousand marks. A ludicrous amount, for his situation. At some point, while I was living in Israel, my aunt Eva came to Israel and was looking for me and eventually she found me and saw that I was not getting any money from my parents, so she deducted some money from the indemnity they were getting and transferred this money into my account instead. It was some story like this, and my parents were mad at me and mad at her. It was always sheer hell.

So figure this: I had few friends in school and I was effectively kept away from my relatives. And there were always conflicts. It was always on and off. There were times when I was told, there is no contact with the family, but do greet them, you are allowed to greet. And I did not know then, should I be greeting or not? Because my mother at times did not greet, in synagogue for example, then they would greet again, and the competition between the three wives was tremendous.

When my father was booted out of the firm, it meant for me also a significant decline in my standard of living. Esther, for example, was being driven back and forth by a chauffeur whereas I had to be driven by my parents, mostly my father. I was the "poor little cousin," and when I left for Israel, my father even pressured me into lending him money from my savings account. When I finally arrived in Israel, I was made to feel that Esther, already settled there, was part of the "better society" and that I was excluded. She is also not the same type as me. We are not on the same wavelength. She thought that she was God knows what. You have seen her and you know how she presents herself. This is a woman who had been living a life in Israel where I could not compete. She had money from back home. Every bathroom tile in her apartment in Israel, every wall and curtain and floorboard, it was all being brought in from F., from Germany. Workers arrived in Israel from the firm, they were being flown there and they installed everything, the kitchen cabinets, cabinets this and closets that. Do you think I could compare myself to her? During that time in Israel, I worked as a receptionist! And why should she respect me? I was below her dignity, and so it has remained, do you understand?

Now that my father was no longer involved in the business, he spent more time at home and he also spent more time with me. My mother felt very threatened by that; eventually it brought about a series of mental breakdowns. The jealousy was incredible between us, she saw me as a competitor to an unimaginable degree and to the point where her gynecologist in Zurich told her — I found out about that much later on — that she was jealous about me, and she almost jumped at him then. But it was probably true. That, taken together with her strategy of keeping me away from my father. I mean he was attached to me, I was his only daughter and he would have liked to have more children, but she did not want any, or — well, I don't know what was going on between the two, it is all in the dark, but he surely did not have a happy marriage with her.

The school years between 1972 and 1977, when I left for Israel were hard, very hard years. Basically, I was trapped: I was cut off from the other Kalmans, I could not have friends at school, and then these difficult parents. The conflicts with my mother began when I was about fifteen and a half or sixteen, they were extreme. I could not stand it anymore. My mother had a couple of suicide attempts behind her and after that she was totally crazy. She went to a psychiatric clinic for six months and when she returned, she said, "It is either her or me." So I moved out, it was February, I could not stand it any more. I worked in a bar and at the same time I prepared for Abitur.

Everything came together during these years: my father was booted out of the firm, spending more time at home, the atmosphere at home deteriorated, and I eventually had to leave. It was very, very difficult to resist; I was alone. I was alone against the rest of the world, and for so many years, when Tali was still little, I was still alone against the rest of the world.

IN THE PROMISED LAND OF EQUALITY

I was right in the middle of this Israeli life

One of the few extracurricular activities that I was permitted to have was a Judaism class, and later, as I told you, via Salek I ended up in the ZJD, and for the first time, I went on a trip with the ZJD to H. Salek had spoken to my parents and convinced them to let me go, so at last I could be in touch with a Jewish environment and become more familiar with Zionism. The upshot of that was that in July 1977, I finished my Abitur, I got my report card, and on August 15, got onto a boat to Israel and arrived in Haifa on August 19. With my small car and all of the money I had saved up.

Since my father did not have any money at the time, I could not study. I worked as an au pair girl, as a receptionist, at a travel agency, and as a salesgirl in a boutique. Then I took a course in graphic design and an ulpan. My basic rule was: no immigrants, no olim, no foreigners, hang out only with Israelis. I wanted to adapt, I wanted to belong, more than anything else in the world. Very quickly, I learned Hebrew and within two months already, I could make my own way really well.

My father made several attempts to get me back to Germany, and in 1979, during a vacation in Germany, my parents bribed me with an apartment in Munich and sufficient money to study there. So they registered me, and ten days later—I could not sleep at all, day or night, because this idea drove me completely nuts—I flew back to Israel to pack my things, to sell everything and to return to Germany. And I sat in the plane, and I looked down onto the Tel Aviv coastline and started to cry because I realized that I could not get away from there. I can't, I have fought for this for so long, I will go on fighting, I will stay. I will not go back to Germany. What am I supposed to do there? Am I crazy?

Am I insane? Now that I have achieved a reasonable command of the language, no way. So I flew right back, I saw the coastline again and said to myself, I am not leaving from here, I am going to fight tooth and nail until I succeed. I registered for this three-year evening course, four hours twice a week, in graphic design that was offered as an extension course by the Technion in Tel Aviv. I took the test and everything, but I did not call back home and did not say anything, I did not dare, and after two weeks, my father called and asked, well, what is going on? I told him, I am not coming. He was totally devastated, my mother flew into a rage, and then he said, well, at least come home for Rosh Hashanah. So I flew back and went to F., for another three weeks. Then I returned and started to take this evening course, for three years.

I really was hellbent on integrating into Israeli society, and four or five years later I was Israeli. I was right in the middle of this Israeli life, in contrast to these rich new immigrants who came from Germany. I felt comfortable among the Israelis, because it was not important there who I was and where I came from — well, okay, they realized that I was not Israeli-born, but not because I might have had a German accent, but because I had an accent somehow. In some ways, I was more Israeli than the Israelis themselves. Often, I was told, are you crazy? Why did you come to Israel, what's the point, you've got it so comfortable in Germany, what do you need this country for? When I told them, because I am a Zionist, they laughed at me. For these people, I was an oddity. I was an oddity.

I was also different from the other olim, including such olim as my cousin Esther. I was literally shocked when I came to their homes. I remember this young woman from Frankfurt who had moved to a new apartment building near city hall in Tel Aviv. It was a new building, superluxury. I came into this apartment, and it was furnished like any Jewish nouveau riche apartment in Germany. And that in a country of all places where you have dust. Wall-to-wall carpeting backwards and forwards, shaggy furniture, only air conditioning, windows never opened; I found this gruesome. Gruesome. But somewhere, I admit it was attractive as well, it was home and not home at the same time.

For my Israeli life, on the other hand, it was not important where I came from and who I was. I was one of them, I had as much or as little money as they did, and I only had Israeli friends, no foreigners, not people like Esther and nothing. I did not want that. It would only have gotten on my nerves. Everything would have been different if I had been raised in America or Israel in the first place. But when you raise a child in F., without Jews, then you cannot expect that this child would want to be without company. And the company that my father had to offer — no thank you, I don't like these nouveau riche pigs. They are too dumb for me, I am not interested. They are all so hollow, you cannot talk with them. Look at these people, they are running around H. as well, the likes of Skyjak and company. Who needs these people? This is not my social ambience, really not. I cannot deal with them. When I only see them, with their tassels and their whole pretensions, I start shuddering. All they can talk about is, have you already seen the new collection by Cartier?, have you bought yourself this or that already?

I did not want to have anything to do with the German olim; every once in a while I saw them again, like those from Cologne, like Grischa Aloscha and Frankie, Schloime Lastman and all these people; but I did not want to deal with them. When my aunt Eva came to visit from Germany, she always invited me to dinner. Or for breakfast in the hotel. I was in the Arcadia Hotel then, where in earlier days I had gone with my parents, and where I simply signed for everything without an idea how expensive it was, how expensive such a vacation really was. Now I went there to meet my aunt, I was the poor little mouse to whom my aunt gave five hundred marks. Thank you, aunt, thank you, I am so incredibly thankful and so on, it was horrible. It was great and horrible at the same time, I suffered and was delighted to be able to smell this atmosphere again which I had as a child, and still, it was terrible. For me it was terrible.

As I said, it was an atmosphere which I experienced as a child, and I did not want to have anything to do with it now. It was the same with the German olim whom I met. I did not want to deal with them, I came into their homes, and they had the same sort of things that were sitting around with the others in F. before — you know, the typical bamboo shelf with the books, the typical books you read when you are on the left and intellectual. I did not want to see that, I did not want to see these homes, I cannot tell you why, this is simply how it was. My attitude toward these people was a strange mixture, and I did in fact have some friends within that German Jewish milieu. In the graphic design course that I enrolled in, for example, I met a woman from Frankfurt. We were friends for a long time, I had seen her once before at the immigration office, and when I came to her apartment for the first time, I was shocked — the same wall-to-wall carpet and bamboo shelf chic that I told you about. But this just in brackets. She was from Germany, but our German was pretty odd, because they did not say, of course, let's go to the sea, but, let's go to the Yam, and we're not going to the swimming pool, but to the brecha. Are you coming with me to the brecha? This was our speaking German, just like the old Yeckes in Israel, we talked the same way.

Yet overall, the German olim were a wealthy community of their own, I was not at their level, I did not share their lifestyle, and I did not want to share their lifestyle. They were constantly together. Roberto Meyersohn and the old Buchlers with — no, not Ingeborg, Vivian, I think. What a puffball she was, and constantly together. How much contact they actually had with Israelis, I don't know. But if you had seen them, they were living like in a commune, and then set themselves up in a house commune style — I did not want that, I also never was accepted by them, I was not popular there. I was from F., from the provinces, I did not belong to them.

On the other hand, after five years, I was Israeli. I had a passport and everything, and the German olim were still busy studying. They could come and go or not go, their situation was entirely different. It was the same with Esther; for the longest time she had a license plate from F., she was still a tourist, whereas I was right in the midst of this Israeli life; a niche of superwealthy people and having brunches together — for me these were unimaginable categories. Unimaginable.

MARK, THE INTELLECTUAL

If you don't read at least one book a week, then you can forget it

Soon after I came to Israel, I dated a few people and then for a year and a half, I had a relationship with a man who was a bit younger than me, he was in the army at the time, but it was quite nice. Eventually, I met Mark Ziegellaub, who became my husband; we were introduced to one another through a mutual friend. Like Aurel, Esther's husband, Mark as well came from Czernovitz in Rumania; the families actually had known each other. Mark's parents spoke German fluently. In 1976, Mark completed his army service, then began to study theater at the university until 1981, without, however, finishing. He wrote a few screenplays and plays and also did some directing.

Through Mark, I got in touch with a very different world. At home, I had suffered on account of the fact that I had grown up without real intellectual stimuli. It is true, my mother came from a home where culture and classical music and opera and so on were encouraged, but it did not matter much in our house. It was also probably more important that my father had no intellectual interests. In fact, my father did not even have a language.

You see, my father had only two years of schooling, because after that, he got trachoma, and he had to leave school, because that is highly infectious. So he had to be absent from school for an entire year, and then he did not want to go back because he was older than the other kids, and so he worked in my grandparents' store. Today, he regrets that, that he has not had any education and no school. He barely even speaks Polish; very little at least. In fact, you could say that he does not even speak Yiddish well, that is, he speaks it, but he cannot express himself in a more sophisticated manner. He simply does not have that intellectual level. He never read. In his entire life, my father read one single book, *The Struggle for Europe*. This book he can cite from memory forward and backward, but other than that, he has never read anything. He reads the newspaper, but that is all.

This explains why in F., I really had no relationship to reading and to books and it might explain, in part, my poor grades in German. Also, one of my teachers did not think that my family fit the image of the German cultured middle class. So, because of that teacher, I was impaired as far as German books were concerned. With books in Hebrew, I had the feeling I'll never manage, it is taking me too long — that is, I read very well, even today, but there is still this psychological barrier in that I think it is taking longer. This is not true at all, has not been true for a long time, but Hebrew I cannot just skim, I really have to read it. And English books in Israel? What kind of books could you get there except bestsellers? But I did not go for bestsellers, it was not my thing, and so I did not read at all.

Even worse, the German olim whom I met in Israel, they classed me with the people from Munich, that is, with the people who have more in their wallet than in their brains. And since I had not been to university — remember, when we first met, remember my inferiority complex — that since I had not been to university, therefore I was also not intellectual. I am not at their level, and I'll never get there. All that changed only when I was back in Germany and started going back to university a bit; at that point, this got a bit more relaxed. But before that, still in Israel, it was awful for me: all the others were studying, they were not even olim chadashim, they were just students, whereas I, after four or five years, I had become an Israeli.

It was only through Mark that I really entered this intellectual world, and the world of artists. That was wonderful, so wonderful. And Mark, when I met him, he told me, listen, lady, if you don't read at least one book a week, then you can forget it and we won't have a relationship. Wow. So I started reading again. I read his books. He really had fabulous books. And I started reading a lot, in English, in Hebrew, and all kinds of things. Here I began to immerse myself into intellectual matters again.

Shortly after I had met Mark and had moved in with him, my maternal grandmother died, and I flew back to Switzerland for the funeral. My mother was supposed to pick me up at the airport, but when she saw me, she fainted and collapsed. In this weak moment, when they could not defend themselves well, the funeral and all the family turmoil that went with it, I told my parents that I was living with somebody. They did not accept it of course, but they still sent me money; I went back to Israel and was living my life, except they did not find this acceptable, me living together with a man like that. In 1984 I applied for a job, and I also got married then, on the fifth of April. That same year, Mark had won a prize for alternative theater.

FAMILY WARS

*We were a family with power games that were
running within well-worn tracks*

Making my parents accept Mark was an ordeal that lasted for two years, really until Avital was born, and my parents used their money in order to keep me dependent on them. You haven't got the story yet how I came home to my parents with Mark. It was in January 1984. Before that, I told them I wanted to get married, and my parents told me, you cannot marry him, we don't even know him. First of all come home. I said, I don't know whether he can make it, he does not have any days off. It went back and forth, we will pay your tickets, we'll pay for everything, just take a two-week vacation and come home. So we went home. We arrived there, they pretended that there was nothing unusual. Finally, on Friday night at dinner we raised the issue of marriage, and we wanted to raise our glasses in relation to that decision, with my parents. But my father said, "Hold it, you cannot do it like that." "What do you mean, we cannot do it like that? Mark and I, we want to" — "Hold it, you can't do it like that. What do you mean you want to get married? Who are you, sir? Who are you, what do you have, what do you have to offer? [*laughs*] Who is your family?" — and all these questions. Mark said that he is divorced, whooom, another fuse went off with my father. "What's your job?" "I write plays." The end of the story was, "Who do you think you are, to marry my daughter." [*laughs*]

Whoosh, that was it, I wanted to crawl inside the floor, something horrible happened to me, terrible. I knew it would get to be horrible, but I never imagined it would get quite that bad. You are not experienced with that sort of thing, I stepped into this situation pretty innocently. Well, it turned into a huge circus, and "it does not work that way, we'll have to think about it," and my father said that he did not have the money for a wedding right now, and my mother said that it did not work because she was still in mourning and God knows what, they came up with every conceivable excuse why we could not get married. It was a huge circus. It got worse and worse, day after day. It got to the point where Mark said to me, okay, he was going to pack my things, and I could decide whether I want to stay here and meet him in Israel later, alternatively we could stay for a couple of days in N. or in Munich — we had a restricted fourteen-day ticket — and go back to Tel Aviv together. The money for the ticket which they had promised to me was always on the table in the living room, but I did not get it.

So we stood there, penniless, and so I decided, I would go with Mark. My mother was shocked and screamed at my father, "You better make sure that they will stay," and my father yelled, the way he likes to yell, "She can go to hell, if she wants to go, let her go." She said, "You can't do that, stop them," and this went on until we were downstairs at the entrance. We went to the next phone booth, about two hundred meters away, and called a taxi to go to the train station. I was so confused that I did not even realize that the taxi driver took a big detour because I know the shortest way to the train station perfectly well. All of that did not matter to me anymore, at that moment, I was no longer of sound mind.

So we took a room in N. for a few days, and on the last day there, I called my parents to invite them to dinner. And what was their answer? "It is not appropriate that a daughter invites her parents to dinner. We will not come." That was it. We returned to Israel. A week later, a letter arrived in Israel. Special delivery, express, a madness. "Do not marry this man. We have already committed too many mistakes in terms of family politics." The background was that my mother had visited us in Tel Aviv half a year earlier, during summer vacation. So she had already gotten to know him. In this letter, this was declared to have been a mistake, because it sort of legitimized that I was living common law with a man.

As you can see, this family is a war of all against all: I recognize perfectly well that my father did not do all that completely on his own and that they were fighting with one another and that they both had their individual fight against me — but they also conducted a joint war against me, and there was also, my father and I against my mother. And there is she, except there is no war of her and me against him. That does not happen.

Today, I am no longer willing to blame him or to blame her with regard to the one or the other stage in my life. Now, after these many years, I am of the view that my parents were a team that was perfectly in tune with each other. We were a family with power games that were running within well-worn tracks. Only now they have been transformed because of my genuine development, and only now it has become apparent how rotten these structures are and how simple they really are. I was the one who has caused this entire landslide, this collapse. I am responsible because I have pulled myself out of this, and because I said, I don't play with you anymore.

After this, my parents made a second attempt to stop the marriage; they invited me to come back to F., unaccompanied by Mark. I responded by writing them a twelve-page letter. In this letter, where I wrote my heart out, I declared my independence, I told them I have the right to lead my own life, and that I would follow through with my wedding plans. My father made clear again that he would not come to the wedding and he stopped talking to me. My mother in turn all of a sudden started being friendlier. Once every two months, she would call me when my father was not at home, because he was not supposed to know about it; all of a sudden, she was my friend. Because now that he was mad at me she could afford being my friend. How are you my sweetheart, back and forth like that. That stopped in the very moment when I told her that I was pregnant, so first of all, oh my God. My father did not even say *mazel tov* — or maybe he did, I don't remember. I believe only from that moment on it was clear to my parents that I would stay with this man and that they would have to accept that. Incidentally, years earlier, my cousin Jerry in America had a similar experience with his parents.

My mother arrived four days after Avital's birth, they both came. We were supposed to rent an apartment for them. Then they wanted to be driven back and forth every day. Going by taxi was not an option. There were arguments because Mark did not always feel like driving them back and forth. The fights started right on the first evening because I served a vegetable soup. In fact, I had hoped they would invite us out. My mother eventually was prepared to buy a few baby clothes, but then she already felt almost sorry about the money. They always hung out in our living room, people came to visit and to congratulate, bringing presents, having a cup of coffee of course, you know how it is in Israel, with cake and so on. My mother sat in the corner and made a big face. I had to run back and forth and make coffee for everyone, you can imagine, I was pretty exhausted. Mark was totally fed up with my parents, so much so that he smashed a chair. I called his sister and told her to come right away, I was so frightened.

MARRIAGE BREAKDOWN, RETURN TO GERMANY

I really was not in the mood anymore, with all the anger in my gut

MARK: There was also a very difficult situation, that is, a family situation; we no longer got along well after the birth of our daughter Avital.

DINA: To me at first, Mark represented a combination of a European intellectual tradition and of Israeli culture. There was some of that. But soon, especially after Avital was born, too much of it turned out to be Israeli macho culture, and our relationship deteriorated. Although Mark worked at home, he did not help around the house and he did not tell me where he went in the evening. I find it normal that when you live with somebody, you know where he is going or when he will be back. Then I would know, am I eating with him or by myself. Basics like that. This was a lousy relationship, and he pushed me down, put me down. I let it happen, I was dumb enough then, because he was more important to me than anything else, he was the only thing I had, except my parents, and my parents I did not have anymore then. When I asked Mark where he went at night, he felt like he was being interrogated, but I sensed that something was not right and that he might be out with other women.

Mark was totally egotistical. He went on vacations by himself and he spent any extra money we had, from a lottery win, for example, on his own trips and obviously on his affairs with other women. I was nursing the baby, and I worked and was nursing, fourteen hours per day, because Mark did not earn any money and I could not imagine going back to my father and asking for more money. I worked like crazy. The marriage broke down because he started having affairs and because I really was not in the mood anymore, with all the anger in my gut, to sleep with him. I was tired and I was already happy if once every three days I could get into the shower. This was awful of course, and then he started having affairs, it went on for half a year and there I first wanted to get a divorce. What he did, it was a question of judgment. A woman who does not sleep with her husband has her reasons. I did not do that for kicks, I was also missing something.

So I considered a divorce. In 1988, Mark was on vacation, Esther had found me a lawyer, very expensive. My father told me not to get divorced, with a small child. When Mark came back from his vacation, he begged me to reconsider and to give the relationship a new try. But this lasted only a short time and at some point it was again like before. After his earlier success, Mark's career did not go any further and he thought we should try to change the environment. I did not want to. He worked on me for a couple of years, until I got to the point where I said, for one or two years, okay.

MARK: So in 1988, we emigrated, that is, we left, the idea was not to emigrate, but to change the ambience, the atmosphere a bit. Tapetenwechsel. It was my idea and my venture, not Dina's. She wanted to stay, not to leave, but I was at that time more like, I have to get out, from all points of view, professionally, I had just experienced a flop in the theater, my piece did not go well and the prospects, for the moment, were not overly favorable. The political atmosphere was also extremely depressing. That climate killed me, all of this was a bit too much, and I thought, let's go to Europe for one or two years, let's recharge batteries, and then back. It took a while to convince her of that.

In terms of our own family, it was a difficult time. This also brought me to say, let's go away for a bit, maybe it will be good for us, maybe not. So we were aware that a trip like that could bring us together or take us apart, and then really take us apart. This is what happened. It was all or nothing.

DINA: Mark was fed up with Israel. It all did not work out well for him, he had the feeling he was locked up there, this pressure, and life's stress. This idea came up, therefore, we'll leave here, we'll get rid of all of the stress, he'll be a human being again, because it just kills him so much that he cannot be a human being as long as he is there. I thought about it back and forth and then said to myself, well, it cannot get any worse, it'll either bring us back together or it will break completely. The next question was, where shall we go? He always wanted to go to London, and I said, no, what should I do in London, I hate London. I think it is a terrible city, I don't like that atmosphere at all. So we compromised on H., and that is what we did.

For me, it was a real sacrifice. I had decided to start a new life in Israel, and now, I had to start from the beginning again, I arrived here and again I was a nobody, a nothing, a nonentity. But I can tell you, it is good that our relationship broke apart completely here. I would not have gotten through it in Israel. Here I succeeded, thanks to German girlfriends who were incredibly self-assertive as women. They gave me such incredible support. I sent Avital to the kindergarten and found my first woman friends there, they supported me so much. An extraordinary human accomplishment. They have done everything conceivable for me.

So within five or six months in H., our relationship had fallen apart completely, and now it was Mark who wanted to return to Israel; in fact, he made preparations to rent an apartment for us "two girls" in Tel Aviv. But at this point, I did not want to go back; all the changes were not good for Avital and I felt more comfortable in the German environment, because in Israel, they look down on women from broken marriages. They look at you in a funny way, suspiciously, and as a single mother you have difficulties in any case. Men, especially divorced men with children, think that you would just go to bed with them, because after all, she needs it, so you have to take her, and she will not find another real partner in the first place. All of that I found very difficult to handle, and in the meantime I feel at home in H. The break with Israel took a longer time. Mark, who had gone to Israel briefly hoping to lure us back, came back to H. to be near Avital. I was now seeking a divorce, we divorced in 1990 and had the *get* in 1991 — Mark gave me trouble with this at first.

MARK: The Gulf War brought about a lot of rethinking. Since then, she is not that enthused about Israel anymore. Same with me, though, because when I had understood from family and friends — we were in Israel after the war and before that, we had constantly been on the phone from H. — when I had understood what sort of hysteria this was, I thought to myself, no, one doesn't have to inflict that on Avital.

DINA: After the Gulf War period, it was the time before I met Johannes, I had another real letdown. It was a guy from America, an American Jew who had money like hay, the ideal man to show off with, from the looks of it, a man presentable to my father; except that I know today, and I recognized it already then, that no matter whom I would have brought home, he would not accept anyone, it would not have mattered at all.

Finally in 1993, I went back to Israel for four weeks with Avital and two weeks on my own to see how feasible it would be to return there. I tried to find out how it is, buying an apartment, how much you get as a single mother, and so on. So I investigated all that, my father told me, you check it out, we'll do that, I'll buy you an apartment [*laughs*], to this day I do not get anything from him — it does not matter. I ran from one bank to the other, I went to the immigration office, I checked out schools, and everything. But when Avital was back in Germany and when I was two weeks on my own, I reconsidered this very carefully. I went to the movies by myself and the sort of things that I am doing here by myself as well. When I noticed how people were staring at me, and I realized that people were wondering, who is she waiting for, and in the end they realized she was waiting for nobody, she is going to the movie on her own, it was a strange sensation.

Of course I had acquaintances from before with whom I could have gone to the movies, but I did not want to go with them. I just wanted to see how it feels, being alone. My old acquaintances, they are all married and have children, not like me. It also ate me up in a certain way that exactly the people who at the time had their first children together with us, in the meantime have moved from their three- into a five-room apartment, they expanded their living space onto the roof, now they have two or three children and still in the same marriage, happy or not so happy, but they manage somehow; whereas in my case, all is wrecked. That bothered me quite a bit. Despite difficulties, they continued to build their lives together, whereas I kept going back to point zero. I still had nothing, and would have had to move, several times over. That alone would have bothered me.

Finally I returned from Israel and wanted to see how it all resonated with Avital, going back to Israel and so on. Avital told me, "If Daddy does not go back, then I don't want to go there either." So I understood, in addition to all my other concerns, that to pull her out of there, this would be inhuman. I would have been glad to be free of him. Far away. But for her, it would have been inhuman. So I said, that is it, I am in H., I will stay in H., finished.

With that visit in particular, it occurred to me that I was not at home in Israel either, because for the Israelis, I was in fact from Germany. All of a sudden, after twenty years of being Jewish, I was a German in Israel. It was a terrible experience. I thought that once I get there, I will have finally arrived. But it was not like that, suddenly I was a German. Jewish, to be sure, but the difficulty was also with my name, because my name is Dina, which is a name used often by converts. So I got the question quite often, have you always been Jewish or did you convert? I found that insulting. God, I was Jewish in Germany for over twenty years and I wanted to be left in peace with all these classifications — and now, everything is starting from the beginning.

The sense of rootlessness that I picked up in my childhood at home, it resurfaced here. It is this having to grow up without roots, insofar as people told me, you don't belong here, but I do grow up here, but this is not your home, you are not like the others, they will never accept you. That is, I was not at home here because my parents told me that I cannot be at home here.

AT HOME IN H.

I have understood that I belong here as well

You were saying about me that I don't leave decisions up to chance and that I have always made up my mind first about what I wanted to do with my life and then built suitable relationships around it. Now, at any rate, the time had come to settle down in H. That decision I made, totally determined, really once and for all. I started renovating my apartment. Then I started furnishing it, it was in the Bogenstrasse, I wanted to feel comfortable.

When I first met you, Michal, I felt, much like you then, very uncomfortable in Germany and marginalized. But the Dina of that time and the Dina of today, that is not the same Dina any more. The mid-1990s was a time of deep transformations, also in my identity. Of course it has changed and did not change at the same time. What has changed is that I have understood that I belong here as well, that because of my background, I am simply at home here. Whether people like this about me or not, it does not matter. It is my mother tongue, it is the language in which I can certainly express myself best, Avital's home is here, and the most important thing is that with what I am doing and what I can do, and what I have in terms of social contacts, I can feel comfortable here.

There was also this issue of thinking about returning to Israel at a point at which I had slowly been getting going a career here. Another rupture, starting from scratch again; that would have been yet another hurdle for me. The desire was there, to be sure; but only once I had made myself aware that as a woman, in terms of a career, and as a mother there would be too many obstacles, only then did I decide, okay so let it be, and now you'll stay here, you do things here and really make a go of it. That is what I have done. Professionally, I have invested massively, I got certified as an interpreter, and I got all of that circus behind me.

The fact that I met Johannes has played an important role in my settling in here, of course. I had known Johannes for a long time, I met him as a friend of my cousin Motti, they were students together at the architecture faculty at the university. It is a relationship that developed over a very long period of time. He was somebody whom I came to know again and again, and I have taken a fair amount of initiative. The relationship developed slowly, and on a pretty sound basis. I got to know him at parties and did small talk with him. At some point, it was in 1994, we decided to go out on a date because I thought it was silly just to be seeing each other at parties all the time. We were getting along so well, so I thought we could go out on a date.

This was not just an ordinary date, it was also a test in a way. What happened with me there, why I did it, because it came from me, I just don't know, but we made a date to see *Schindler's List*. That was of course the film at the time where afterward you know exactly who you are dealing with. So we talked about the fact that this film had just started. "Have you seen it?" "No. Have you seen it?" I said no. Then we decided that we should go there together. In fact, I had no one else with whom I would have wanted to go there.

Then there was the postponement of the date. He called and said, oh, listen, I got the weeks mixed up, I cannot do it that day. So we had to move it. At that point I got into a panic. I thought, what am I doing here, I am going into this film with a German guy, and I don't know what I should expect and how I will be touched by it. Maybe I will cry terribly. That will make a great impression on a first date. Or maybe I will be really angry. After the movie, I was silent first of all, both of us walked around in silence, in the night, and I did not know what I should say and where I should start to be saying something.

Then we sat down in a pub, we talked a bit about the film and I became aware about the way he is thinking about this entire history and about his, his . . . He was terribly afraid that I, as an Israeli, would be tearing him to pieces. He had always thought that I was one of these Israeli women, tough fighter and so on. Which is why, at parties, he was afraid to approach me, I seem to have given this impression of a fighter even though I was not even in the army.

During this early time with Johannes, in 1992, I had also begun a therapy, it was with a female Jewish psychologist. This was really great. She was first-rate, a great woman, and only thanks to her and with her help did I get through. I stopped the therapy in 1995 with my birthday and at a point when my relationship with Johannes had become solid.

So both of us gloriously passed the *Schindler* test, we started dating, going to movies and to the theater, and all of this slowly, very, very slowly. With caution on his part and mine. As it was being built, I could see step by step that this is doing good things to me, and with my therapy I was advanced enough that I permitted that—to let things happen that are good for me.

As this relationship was evolving I was aware of two things, first, that my father would disapprove of it totally, and also, that my Jewish environment would disapprove. But my therapy was advanced enough that I could recognize a few things. I said to myself, I don't care, as long as things go well with Johannes and as long as he recognizes my Jewishness. He has accepted what I am leading here as a Jewish life, he does everything together with me, comes to shul with me on the High Holidays; that is, we are doing Kabbalat Shabbat, we have holiday meals, we celebrate Hanukkah and Pessach, real celebrations just like I did before, nothing has changed in this respect, and Johannes enjoys doing that with me and is learning more and knows ever more and is very open to it.

Sure, in theory a relationship with a Jewish man might be preferable, but they are all too screwed up, and Johannes is accepting my Jewishness, which is centrally important. Avital loves him more than anything, so what else would I want? Nothing. So I said, fuck it. That's it, what can I do, there are only so many men, and of these to find someone who is not yet married, whom I like and who likes me, where everything is perfect, maybe he exists, maybe he does not; I certainly have not gotten to know him, and I have only tortured myself. The Jewish men with whom I have tried to start something, they are all too difficult, and why would I need that. I am screwed up enough myself, and with Johannes, I found it a relief, in a way, as a recovery.

Of course, Johannes has problems as well. Everybody does. But his problems are different. He is simply touched by very different things. At the beginning of our relationship — it was fifty years after Auschwitz and so on and there were lots of films at that time — Johannes said that is not the kind of thing that he is much occupied with, and I said, well, okay, it is simply not what he is occupied with.

JOHANNES: If I may interject, I felt under pressure, it happened to be fifty years after the end of the war, and there were a thousand films, and I simply did not have that daily reflection and debate on this topic, so I felt a little under pressure, suddenly . . .

DINA: . . . to have to do that . . .

JOHANNES: . . . to have to do that, and so massively.

JÜDISCHE GEMEINDE H.: UNEASY INTEGRATION

For the High Holidays, I buy the synagogue tickets

DINA: Originally, when I arrived in H., and outside the day-care environment, my contacts were primarily with other Jews; and this was in relation to Gemeinde activities and also in terms of my friends outside the Gemeinde; most of these people were Jewish as well. Over time, though, many of these friendships disappeared. In the early 1990s, I was particularly close with Irit, we were both in Jewish Studies at the university together, it was quite nice, we developed a kind-hearted competitiveness, because we were both top students. We also had things in common: we did not start university right after Gymnasium, and we both had problems with our parents. Irit's parents who are Israeli had problems with her Jewish commitment and put her down a lot, considering her a failure.

Today, I have Jewish friends here and there, but not only Jewish friends. Irit and I are no longer friends. She is together with Schloime now and did not want to hear about my problems anymore. Before that, we were kind of each others' wailing wall, but later, "I cannot hear anymore how miserable you are, I am sick and tired of it." She was with Schloime, and all of a sudden, everything was wonderful. Before that, we were often out together, as a threesome, really good friends. But later, they took me with them, graciously, and looked each other into the eyes, and I was sitting there and did not know what I should do with myself. So I said, I don't need that, and so it ended. Some time ago at Rosh Hashana, surprisingly, the first time after all these years, they were wishing me Shana Tova again. Other than that, in terms of Jewish friends, there is not much. There is Macki and Jusha, they separated, but I am still in touch with both. You don't know them, they are from Stuttgart. Then there is a couple from Avital's school, Russians, but I really don't have the time, I have so much going on in my life.

Then I taught Hebrew at the Jüdische Volkshochschule, but I did not get along well with Elinor Lewandowski, the director. She obviously felt that I was too fresh, she did not have the independence to say to me, you may be pretty obstinate, but we need nonconformists like you; you are a damn good teacher with real Israeli experience. Our relationship turned for the worse when a student complained to Elinor about allegedly rude treatment by me. I did, in fact, yell at the student, it was an older German woman, because she did not know the Hebrew alphabet even after an entire trimester, and it slowed the rest of the class down. Elinor and I got into an argument, and this was the end of my teaching career with the Gemeinde. They also did not ask me to help them organize Jewish cultural programming; I was simply not well connected enough, even though I completed my M.A. with high distinction. There was an event at one point hosting former H. Jews who had fled Nazism and I was asked to act as interpreter, but this assignment did not have anything to do with the Jüdische Gemeinde. I have nothing else to do with the Gemeinde, except that Avital goes to the Jewish school, and for the High Holidays, I buy the synagogue tickets and go with Avital and now also with Johannes to synagogue. Only on the High Holidays. Not during the year.

I used to be friends with my cousin Motti for some time, but we don't see each other anymore. As you know, Motti and Johannes were good friends while they were students, but Motti stopped all contact when Johannes started going out with me. Concerning me, he once complained that I did not take his partner Cornelia seriously, that I did not accept her or something. It is not true. Since she is my cousin's partner, I would always accept her, I always treated her decently. But he has reproached me, I would not accept her because she is not Jewish. That is a projection, of course.

He told me once that it bothers him that Cornelia does not want to convert or to raise their children as Jews, that is why he is madly envious that my children are Jewish, no matter what their name would be. He told me that years ago, before I was with Johannes. It is also true, of course, that Johannes is interested in Judaism. But my father, interestingly enough, is of the view that it is fine for Motti, for example, to be with a non-Jewish woman, because he is a man. But I, who will have Jewish children, am not allowed.

THE LONG ARM OF THE FATHER

But with him, it would really hurt

When I was in New York and visiting my aunt Gertrud in Brooklyn—I had a really good talk with her, by the way—I managed to retrieve a bunch of photos of my father, it was very important to me. On my father's eyebrow there is a big scar from a car accident in 1947, when cobblestones flew against his windshield, and one of these hit him at the eye. They sewed it up badly, and now it is crooked. Just look at this photo here, it was taken before the accident, he is so young and has such incredibly good looks, with his eyebrow intact. I am so glad Gertrud gave me these photos.

The problem with my father has always been that he does not accept me the way I am. He disapproves of my circle of friends, and he has always disapproved of any man I was with. At the same time, he was trying to keep me dependent through his financial support. He did not accept my husband Mark, and it was obvious that he would not accept Johannes. Today, I am really aware, I have really recognized that no matter which man I am with, my father would never accept anyone, and frankly, I don't give a damn anymore. My relationship with Johannes in a way became possible only because I have achieved financial independence. I have an awful lot of work now. I am working like a dog, and, things work out okay. Suddenly. Marvelously. Ever since I am no longer taking any money from my father. I thought it would never work. But in the very moment where I no longer took my father's money, things started working out, and of course, these two things are connected somehow.

I decided to give up my father's money also sort of in preparation for the moment where I would tell him that I am living with a non-Jew. I could not deal with the fact that I am taking his money and at the same time, am living this secret life with Johannes. They did not know anything. Then I wrote them a letter for Rosh Hashana, and that was my goal for Rosh Hashana, not to take any more money from my parents. It was a long letter, thanking them for supporting me for so many years, and that now I could deal with it myself, and that I would want to do it myself. It really was a very long letter about why I did not want to take this money any longer, and I really thanked them cordially, and I really meant it. I explained to them why I had needed all that money in the past, that special circumstance, living alone with a child, going back to university, and all these things.

Then, he sent me the money nevertheless, and I returned it. Coldly returned it. It was enough money to be living from without lifting a finger. So I renounced quite a bit there. But it was important to me, because I knew and I realized that if I did not do that, I will never gain my freedom. I never thought I could actually do that. It was so unimaginable to me, just as if you would tell me now, we can fly to Mars in ten years.

Two months after Johannes and I had moved in together, I wrote yet another letter to explain to my parents why I had moved. I wrote that I now have this man and that I am living with him, that was a bitter letter. I wrote that letter over several weeks, and at the end I threw it all overboard and wrote another one in one night. I started in the evening at nine and was finished at seven in the morning. I broke into tears, I was totally finished. It was the strangest feeling. It was as if I was all of a sudden in a different skin, it was an insane experience. I wrote the letter, I cried and then left for my appointment with my therapist and talked it over with her as well. That week, or the ten days after that, I had the feeling I was running more slowly, everything was slower, suddenly I seemed to have an entirely different rhythm. I threw something overboard, I was suddenly in a new skin, everything went more slowly.

I had packed everything into that letter. Everything that was so difficult for me in the past years and why it was so difficult, to be living by myself, raising Avital by myself, that I did not have their support, and still I thanked them for their support as far as money was concerned, that I do recognize that value. I wrote them everything, and about everything; why I am together with this man and what he means to me. Afterward, I felt so totally free, I was suddenly myself, in net weight. Nothing is driving me, nothing is pushing me anymore. I was not even afraid anymore now about what would happen once he got the letter, for example. It was all over. I was [*takes a deep breath*], I could take a deep breath.

My father called and told me that while he was neither in favor nor against it, "just come home first, and we'll discuss it." I refused, saying that everything that I have to say is in this letter, you can read it a hundred times until you understand it totally and finally. Everything is in there that I had to say; I can't tell you more if I came down to F. "Come anyway," he said, "No," I said, "But come anyway," and back and forth it went. Not long after that, my father went on a visit to his sister Gertrud in Brooklyn, it was on the occasion of one of Jerry's son's bar mitzvahs. I had sent him a videocassette of *Schindler's List* and then called to congratulate him for his birthday. He was hugely delighted. When he was back in F., he called me and complained about his health, and I suddenly realized that I will not have my father forever. So this dawned on me, in a more concrete manner, and I began to worry. I told Johannes about it and he said, what if something is going to happen now, and I realized, it would be really hurtful to me if something happened. With my mother, it would not hurt me, but with him, it would really hurt.

Johannes told me then, "You know what, let's go and visit him." I said, "Do you know what you are talking about? Do you know what is awaiting you there?" He said, "We'll manage, come on, let's go." So we thought about it back and forth, until I said, why not? We asked Avital,

"Oh, yes, great, to see Grandpa again" — she does not speak about Grandma, because Grandma is not interested in her. That was it, and I said, okay, I will call and tell him we are coming. I called, it was evening and said, we wanted to come to F. Also from the vantage point that I had not been at home for about four or five years. I always thought he would be really happy.

So I called. "What do you mean, we?" — "Johannes, Tali, and I." "Well, I don't know, I'll have to talk to Mummy first. Call me again in ten minutes." I knew exactly that he would say, "Who is we?" I waited for ten minutes, called again, and he said, "No, it does not work." "What do you mean, it does not work?" "Mummy does not want that." "What do you mean, Mummy does not want that?" "She does not want a goy comes into the house." "What's that supposed to mean, I am coming anyway." "You can't come with him. I can't explain that to you. She does not want that. We can't do it. Apart from that, I don't have my teeth, they are in repair, so it does not work." I answered, "Excuses. Do you really need excuses? Why don't you say plainly what you want, you don't want me; it is not only Mummy, it is you, too. Let me talk to her, I want to hear this from her directly."

She comes to the phone, I want to hear this from her. "Yes, please?" I said, "Do you have something to say to me?" She answered, "A goy is not coming into this house here." I said, "What is that supposed to mean, a goy does not come into this house?" "Well that kind of future son-in-law does not come into my house, a goy." I said, "Excuse me, does that mean that I am persona non grata if I come with him?" "A goy does not come into my house." "Am I persona non grata?" "A goy does not come into my house." This went back and forth about ten times, exactly these two sentences, like a broken record.

So I said, okay and she put my father on the phone again. I said, "Now listen, don't call me again, don't ask me one more time to come home, this is finished. If I cannot come and the man whom I love and who loves me cannot come and your grandchild cannot come, into this home, then it is not a home anymore." I said, "Really, you need not call again and ask me to come. Save yourself the effort." That was it and I hung up.

That was not the end of the story, though. On the next day, I received a call from my aunt Eva, from the other side of F. Apparently, he had called her and had asked her to get in touch with me to tell me to come home. She told him, "Forget that, if she cannot come with

Johannes, then she will not come by herself." She also quoted from the Talmud that you are not allowed to close the door to your children. And he cried and screamed, "What am I going to do now," and Eva said, "If you behave like that, you will lose your child." She said, "If I did not allow my sons to bring their girlfriends home to me, then of course I would lose my sons as well. Berthold has an Italian girlfriend, and Gaby has a non-Jewish girlfriend as well, and they come home to me." From what Eva was saying, the Italian is there with him on the holidays, which is why Eva tolerates her. She does not ask for more. All of that is what Eva said to my father.

My aunt also told me, "Don't go there, it is sheer hell, you won't be able to stand it, and your friend will be so shocked, he might even leave you. It is traumatic when you go there, and you'll be sick for a month thereafter." That is what she advised me, don't go back to that house. This was my gut feeling as well. I can't go there, it is going to make me sick. The last time I was there was five years ago. If, at the time, Avital had not been with me in the room and if I had not seen very clearly, this child is my child and she needs me now, then I would have jumped out of the window. I fled after nine days although I had planned on staying for two weeks. At the time, I had thought, I am going there for two weeks to make them happy. It was a disaster. My father was upset, he drove me to the airport, in silence, and pushed five thousand marks into my hand. You shall have that. Money. It has always been like that. Money.

Johannes

Rautenstrauch

A GOY IN THE HOUSE

1962	born in P.
1981	Abitur
1981–83	technical training with Nixdorf Computer
1990	graduation as architect
1994	relationship with Dina
1997	wedding
1998	birth of Clifford

Johannes and I first met when Dina invited me to their apartment in H.; at the time of our first meeting, the two were not yet married. Johannes, originally from the Rhineland, has something of the proverbial "Rhenish cheerfulness"—he is open, articulate, and easy to connect with. I spoke with Johannes again long after his and Dina's son Clifford was born: that interview took place in their kitchen, with Clifford running back and forth trying to get his father's attention (and dessert from the nearby refrigerator).

A YOUTH IN P.

I had the feeling my life sucks

JOHANNES: Let me start with the hard data, including my name. I was born in 1962 at the time of the Liborius festival and my name is therefore Johannes Liborius Rautenstrauch. Liborius is a very rare name. He is a patron saint, amusingly enough, of the urologists. My father, born in 1918, was a urologist. An explicitly Christian name, just like Johannes. The city of P., moreover, where I grew up, also has Liborius as its patron saint. Anyone who hears that my name is Liborius grins. My mother, born in 1925, is, like my father, a physician as well, but she never practiced. Both parents are arch-Cologneans, but in the late fifties they moved from Cologne to P. because my father found a job there. He died in 1983, during the Cologne carnival. Later, my mother returned to Cologne, she is a Cologne patriot.

Another piece of hard data is that I have nine siblings. Each one of us was a bit like a badge of honor for my mother. I am the seventh. In terms of age, there were two groups, first numbers one to six and then numbers seven to ten. The ten children were born within fourteen years, the last two were twins; that is, there was a child one year after the other, including two miscarriages. Most of my siblings are academics. My oldest sister has a diploma in education, then there is a physician, a special education teacher, then there is a well-known filmmaker, then my brother, the physician who works near Munich, then there is a psychologist, then me, then a sister who is also a physician, then there are Georgia and Ursula; Georgia lives in the U.S., she is married to a Jew, by the way, a chef; and Ursula is a nurse who lives near P. My sister Hermine, the film director, and I are exceptions, we are more artistically inclined.

At first, I went, perfectly normally, to school in P. and passed my Abitur in 1981. I liked sports the best, but when I was younger, I liked Latin very much and, until grade ten, I was very good at it. I liked it because through Latin I could be in contact with my father, and that motivated me a lot. Before me, two brothers learned Latin with him, and so it motivated me very much as well. I studied with my father two, three, even four times a week, for twenty minutes each. This was practically the only time in my life when I was alone with my father, the only opportunity where he would spend some time with me. I learned everything by heart and I always won vocabulary contests and I knew everything. I liked the idea of contests, and training, practicing, achieving results.

My father was a very conservative man, a strict Catholic, and we prayed a lot. Religious holidays were celebrated intensively, and were of great significance. Christmas was the feast of all feasts, emotionally highly loaded. Every Sunday, we went to church. When I was little, we prayed every morning at seven, later on then at eight. Every Sunday. This was a central concern and an untouchable order. The older we were, let's say, from thirteen, fourteen, or fifteen, the more we experienced it as coercion. My father was rather authoritarian and, at the same time, the hypersensitive type. And, as often with authoritarian types, he was one who could not articulate his sensitivity and his feelings, and who perhaps tried to compensate for his timidity by means of authority — that strictness and those strict Catholic imperatives. None of us still practices that today. Not one. None of us would have lived by these precepts only one day after leaving this system. The only thing that is left is to celebrate Christmas a bit. Here in our house we don't do that, and I can do well without it. It is good for me. It is like changing one's skin without replacing one authoritarian system with another one.

My mother supported that system completely, in her own way. She had studied, she is a physician, has an MD degree. Titles are everything to her, and having the degree of professor is the greatest. She is politically inclined and is a high-ranking lay Catholic. She was a vice president of the family league of the German Catholics; she knew every archbishop, every suffragan bishop, with contacts all the way to Rome of course and to the top functionaries of the lay Catholics. She was the ideal of a Catholic woman. As a lay politician of the church, she moved to the very top. She had top contacts in the CDU, she received the German order of merit, has given lectures, and so on and so forth. At the same time, ten children.

Later on, I had a huge fight with my family. I was in a deep crisis, did not want to have anything more to do with my mother, and we did not speak to each other for two years. Only very late did I start to think about my life. I believe the relationship to my mother was a very close one. Everybody says that I was my mother's most desired child. My sense is that this overly close relationship started very early, perhaps even before I could develop my own consciousness. This was being dragged even into the time of my first jobs.

Let me go back to the time after Abitur. I did not really know what I wanted to do. My dream of becoming an actor was one that I dreamt for me alone. So I ended up going into an apprenticeship as an industrial economist, in 1981, with Nixdorf Computer, where my mother had connections. I had ambivalent feelings about that. I actually got along quite well with the people there. I also learned a lot. The training was superb, but I also felt like I was in a straitjacket. I really did not know what I wanted.

Then I thought about what I might like to do, and architecture seemed a good mix of my artistic and the economic sense. During my apprenticeship, I also wrote a play that was performed in youth centers and so on, but then I realized that the theater was probably not the right thing for me, and so I stopped doing this. Then I applied to H. University and studied there until 1990, including my diploma and my internship, seven years altogether. I felt very comfortable here in H. At first I lived by myself and later then in a house with others.

After the architecture diploma, I went to Cambridge, where I applied to the School of Architecture. It was really difficult getting accepted there. I prepared my application really well, I prepared a portfolio, including an essay about synagogues in H. I went there and I could have stayed for a year, but after three months, I had enough. It was at the time that I had begun to question my life completely. Before, I had lived one day to the next, but then I got into this existential crisis. What shall I do, why study architecture? Didn't I want to be an artist, an actor? I was in a total existential crisis, I felt absolutely rotten, then I heard from my siblings that my mother was suffering and that she was very ill. I told them that I didn't want to have anything to do with her anymore. It is difficult to explain now. While I was studying architecture, I went into therapy in order to work through that. It is difficult for me to describe that exactly. Then I led some sort of dual life, on one hand a regular job and a cv — excepting Cambridge — without blemishes, but on the other hand, I could not find a proper foothold any more. I had the feeling my life sucks, and during the first two years of study, I dabbled along without really knowing what I wanted to do.

WITH MOTTI KALMAN

We really were buddies without words

During that time, or rather already during the time of my studies, I got to know Motti, Dina's cousin. Especially during the period where we prepared for our diploma, we become closer to each other. At the time, he fancied himself a bit of an artist. He always twisted his hair with his fingers, and I always had the impression that he was pretentious. In the early days of studying architecture, I actually found him odd, and I could never have imagined that I could ever have an intensive friendship with him. It was surprising, therefore, that when we began work-

ing on our diploma projects, we started talking and that we were notic-
ing that we fit together somehow. That was the time when I was not
feeling very well, but we got along incredibly well, and very soon, we
were very close to each other.

That initial period between Motti and myself was actually really
fabulous. He was an incredibly nice guy and also very hospitable. Eve-
nings we would often work alongside each other for long stretches,
then we went swimming. So we had a very beautiful time. We really
were buddies without words. He was very warm with a big heart, and I
believe I was nice to him as well. I am also always someone who often
has a best friend with whom I can have exchanges and who is very close
to me. For many years, we were close friends. He gave parties, birth-
days and so on, and at one of these birthday parties, I also got to know
Dina. I kept meeting Dina at Motti's place again and again, and we
always had good chats together.

Now Dina was a very important caesura in our relationship. With
Dina entering my life, my life changed. Until then, Motti and I were, if
you like, fellow sufferers. While we did our different jobs, on a strange
level we were soulmates. It might have had to do with both our mother-
son relationships, or perhaps also that melancholy inclination which I
had at the time. On the other hand, during my friendship with Motti, I
had the feeling my muddle would never end, would get worse even, and
that was one reason why our paths separated.

At the time when Dina came into the picture, Motti and I no longer
had that same personal theme. For Motti it was certainly an irritant
that through Dina I suddenly gained insight into his family. For me, all
of that was not that dramatic, I know complex family systems. But for
Motti it was irritating, because now I could look into something about
which before I had no idea, something that was never a topic between
us. The Jewish/non-Jewish theme was never an issue between us. We
had never even talked about it. I knew somehow about it, but for my relationship with him it was without significance. I cannot remember that
very well now, but at the time I did not know that he was Jewish. It was
totally unknown to me. For months and years this had no significance.

I also would not know what in his apartment would have signaled
to me that he was Jewish and I non-Jewish. It was a nonissue. I also
knew nothing about his family, his mother in Auschwitz, nothing, nothing at all. The issue of Jew and non-Jew only got to be a topic when I
met Dina. Somewhere I noticed something then, but for our relation-

ship it was not significant. Also, Motti's girlfriend Cornelia was always very nice to me, always approached me and embraced me. I think she liked me very much. The fact that I was now together with Motti's cousin was an incredible caesura for them. It was a particular spark, everything like a small sensation that they could not have imagined. I might also have been an intruder into the family. Perhaps that was a problem as well.

Later on, too, I could not be a bridge between Motti and Dina. The problems between Dina and Motti, on account of the problems between their parents, were too great, and so this became a path of separation. Motti is where he is and stays where he is. Dina is already somewhere else; the two of them have separated and I am going with Dina, and we are going someplace else. It fell apart. We did not talk any more. He could not deal with it.

DINA

She was like an anchor in my life

At that point I met Dina, who was in the final stages of dealing with her inner debate about her Jewishness, about her identity, about family, Auschwitz; a stage where she problematized these issues constantly, where she struggled with herself, where everything was stirred up in her. That is where I stepped in, in that final stage of her inner debate. The question is, was there a decisive criterion for us to be possibly living together? It was a stage where I was still so confused. At home, we had an authoritarian family situation. Now, being on my own, that authority had disappeared and I was totally disoriented. For me it was decisive that Dina is someone I can hold on to. I felt so totally unsteady, and she was so clear. She could formulate things so well, and at first, I was pretty speechless.

She was also prepared to focus on and deal with me very intensively. Being with her I had the sense I was finding my way to myself, that I was getting a sense of orientation. So I realized that either I say, this here is the way I have to go, or else I will not find any ground under my feet at all. There was an element there of conscious decision: either I am going to let myself get involved in a relationship with this woman, or I will not get out of my mess at all. For years now I had been wading through this chaos that had been stirring me up, because of my family situation, my relationship with my mother, and the therapy. Here, Dina stepped in, stepped before me with this energy and this warmth. She was like an anchor in my life. Had she not been so amazingly prepared to deal with me, I don't know where I might have been stranded.

Of course there is the question of what role Jewishness has played in our relationship. Initially, it did in fact play a role, but never a basic one. We always met as two human beings. We had this date for *Schindler's List* and talked about it for a long time thereafter; it was important for Dina. My family background, as far as I was concerned, was not important for Dina — that I am a German and a non-Jew and she, Jewish. At least it was not its core; somehow it was not relevant. It is not really our topic. For us, our love was decisive, that we can relate to each other as human beings, and so we have built up an extraordinary intensity and depth.

So the Jewish theme is not the decisive one between us. Of course it is very important, but it is not decisive for the core of our relationship. I had no problem at all accepting it, and I really wanted to go with Dina to Jewish events. Quite to the contrary, to be going with her to synagogue reminded me of going to church and it has touched me emotionally very much. I really did participate there with awe and intensity. I went along.

My family reacted to Dina without much comment; there were no questions or discussions. It was clear anyhow that my mother would not ask. This separation from me and the years in which we did not have anything to do with each other were so harsh, so severe. She cannot intervene in my life anymore. She is rather more reserved and positive because she is glad that I resumed some contact with her in the first place. It would have been fatal had she made it difficult for us. But she did not. There is, of course, a certain curiosity there in my family, also a certain shyness, reserve; it was something new for my family. But they do like Dina, my siblings like her.

DINA: Did you tell Michal the thing with your mother, that it was not so important to her whether the child or the children are Jewish as long as they have any religion? [*laughs*]

JOHANNES: Did my mother say that?

At home, we no longer meet as family and Dina and I also did not have a get together with my family before our wedding. But we did visit various siblings. Big family gatherings are not so important to me. Only in my later adolescence did I become concerned about dislodging myself and finding myself, to find my identity, away from my mother, away from my family; I did not want to have anything to do with my siblings. My siblings and I meet, and it is quite a bit of fun, but then I am also very glad when I have left again. I don't feel comfortable there, I slide into old gears, into old sentiments which I no longer have in my life, and that is why I don't like it.

DINA'S PARENTS

A goy does not come into my house

Now a word about Dina's family, more precisely, her parents. When Dina and I first met, her father's maxim was, "a goy does not come into my house." At first, we lived sort of secretly. It was the time when Dina was in therapy and when she tried to detach herself from her parental home, the time of letters to her parents — she still read them to me — a time when she took very decisive steps for her life. Dina has the fascinating ability to work on something in order to achieve clarity, and once she has made a decision, to really stay with that decision and to orient herself on it. I found that fascinating. I tried that in my own therapy, but it never really worked.

The matter with her parents was of course scurrilous, because we lived in hiding. I moved in with her fairly quickly, but her parents knew nothing about me and I was not allowed to go to the telephone. Dina was working on detaching herself, and it took a while before she could muster the courage to tell her parents without having the feeling that she would be falling again into a hole. Losing the financial support and so on. In that situation, Dina did quite well in terms of her work and she had the feeling, I don't need them anymore, I am making my own money. So, with a great deal of energy she opposed herself to her parents and their pincerlike hold. At some point, she told them I exist and it became clear then that we would get married. Dina, I understand, has described these events in detail to you. In short, they knew about me, and soon thereafter, we met for the first time in F. I was very nervous and really curious how this would work out. I had heard the most terrible stories, the crazy mother, sheer terror, and I was worried. Well, and then there was her father who would pick us up at the station, such a small, shaky, brittle, elderly little man. I walked toward him, and the first thing he did was kiss me on my cheek.

I was so happy, so relaxed. In place of the horror that I heard so much about — first thing such a welcome! I experienced that in a very intensive way. Dina as well was so happy. A ton fell off us, and her mother was basically pretty nice as well. All told, I had imagined the two of them to be much worse. The house was reasonably neat, there was of course a bit of a facade. They made a real effort. Tension erupted as well, of course, between Dina and her parents, odd attacklike conflicts, suddenly, for no reason. But I concentrated very intensely for three days; I observed very carefully how they behave, and then I followed my intuition as to how I should behave in turn. I focused intensely on these two people.

I knew what kind of catastrophe it had been with Mark, Dina's first husband, how he entangled himself into conflicts with them, how Mark and Dina took off and how Dina's mother yelled after them. Her father is also a very instinctual person; he rejected Mark from the beginning, and obviously — I could see that from his gesture at the station — he did not reject me. He accepts me, they've accepted me as their son-in-law. I am their son-in-law. Husband of their daughter.

It was clear to me, I did not want any altercation with them. I am here with Dina and will do everything to support her, even on this very difficult visit. I was highly focused and cognizant about what I did and I was extremely politically sensitive, too. Dina once told me that I can deal so well with her mother because I sensed exactly what it would take to keep this woman happy; how to relate to this person so that she remains comfortable and does not feel she is being challenged. For Dina, this was sensational, how I could move in this thicket without tension. She was immensely happy.

It is actually not that hard for me to do. I am fairly good at focusing on other people, and making them feel at ease. I am simply trying, when we are visiting there, not to add to Dina's troubles, and to give her support instead. She needs that security, and the assurance that she does not have to worry because of me. The issue of Jewishness, by the way, was not raised at all during our visit.

For Dina and me it turned out to be real happiness and for Dina the recovery of a certain domestic peace, in contrast to her wedding with Mark, a situation where they did not come to attend the wedding. Here now, there was a bit of healing. Her parents as well have returned into a normal life to some extent. Things that were previously shattered, fizzled out. A new son-in-law, a wedding, my daughter is married, we will go there and we will go back, she is taken care of, so there is a family. A certain order has come about when previously, there was disorder. With a non-Jew to be sure, but there are no problems with that.

DINA: Did you tell Michal the thing with the uncles who you did not invite to our wedding? And about that contrast with the ten siblings on your side, and the single person on the other side?

JOHANNES: No, I did not talk about that. Here it is. For the wedding we thought about where to go for the ceremony and whom to invite. We decided on an old castle, Schloss Carbow, near Lübeck, not too far from H. It is in Mecklenburg. Really a great place. I could have invited a couple of uncles and aunts there and I told Dina how old they are and what they did and — this I did not tell her — that my grandfather really was a super Nazi. He was a bank director in the Third Reich, of the Deutsche Bank, and apparently there are photos in the great conference hall, only military, with my grandfather in the middle and a bust of Adolf Hitler behind him. This kind of odds and ends we had in our family — this undercurrent of Nazism, particularly also on my mother's side — in 1938–39, for vacation, they still drove to Italy in an open-top Mercedes.

So we thought, whom are we going to invite. Dina had problems with all of them, and it is true, they were soldiers, or how should I put it, such honorable old people from the Wehrmacht. So she was not keen on having them, and so we decided not to invite any of my relatives except my immediate family. No uncles, no aunts, nobody. She also wanted to invite a few people, but they could not come and it was clear to us that I could not move in there with a whole clan, and she on the other hand completely without. She was not to have the feeling to be practically without family.

With my mother and the two in-laws, it went relatively smoothly. My mother has strong political inclinations, she adjusts and makes for good weather, even if good weather is not what is called for; both sides played the game of nice in-laws, and they got along quite well. We had the impression they were comfortable and enjoyed themselves. A great accomplishment by any circumstances.

WITH DINA IN THE JEWISH WORLD

I am a bit worried about the bar mitzvah,
because I don't have a clue

We had Jewish friends — but more so when Dina was still by herself — Schloime and Irit, for example. I got to know them and others as well, but that was it. We have few Jewish friends, not even through Avital's or Clifford's schools. Sometimes I think about that, and am concerned about it, that I have the feeling I should do more, get more involved about the Jewish things. I know it would be nice for Dina, but I also know how difficult it is because of the type of Jewish community life here.

I do have a bit of a funny feeling when I think about Clifford. Since he is a Jew, he will go to a Jewish school and so on, and everything he brings home from there and what he learns I will accept with the greatest goodwill and I will encourage him to learn still more. Dina told you about the Hanukkah book, the story that fascinated Clifford so much. So I am pretty sure he will pick up more than what might be assumed. I can see that is in him, and that he will teach me. That is how it will be, that's what I feel.

I am a bit worried about the bar mitzvah, because I don't have a clue. Sometimes I have the feeling that I should get more involved. I am not setting a good example with respect to that. I should get more involved in the traditions, but I don't take the time for it; Dina is the one who is in charge of these matters. I am only an observer. I like to get involved in it, but do not play an active part. Maybe it is a problem that I don't have the kind of energy and that I don't appropriate these things for myself, and sometimes I have a really bad conscience.

I am sure there are things that I am not occupying myself with, and if I did do it with Clifford, then more like out of fun. I don't have the feeling that I really have to appropriate this myself. A friend of mine, a non-Jew, even wants to convert. He is engaged to a Jewish woman and is interested in Jewish matters, and sometimes I am thinking, God, shouldn't I do this as well? Am I not now a bad father for Clifford, for Dina, and for Avital? I don't think I am a shining example of the husband of a Jewish woman.

I should be more engaged. I believe that Dina is regretting it a bit. I am sure she would like it if I could muster this as well, that involvement, husband, wife, and children, family life, and the Jewish environment. As interesting as it is to go to synagogue, it is a little bit odd, because I don't really belong. Then it is a funny feeling, because I am the father of a Jew. Then I see how these Jewish kids come into the synagogue, running around the benches and yelling, totally normal, and nobody realizes that I am not Jewish. Perhaps I fit in reasonably well. Everyone says that when I put on a kippah and a nice suit, I sit there almost like a genuine Ashkenaz, almost like genuine. If I knew a bit of Hebrew and a couple of formulas, I could, well, I could pretend to be a Jew. It would not be a problem at all. But I don't have that in stock. I feel a bit odd, out of place, and I don't really belong.

Q: *How is it with the other grandmother now? What will happen when Clifford comes to your mother and when he sees all these Catholic things, a line of tradition to which he belongs as well, with his aunts and uncles?*

JOHANNES: That is not important. First of all, we have never gone to visit her. Until now I have not been in the mood. So it does not play a role. About this line of tradition, I will tell Clifford about it. I don't know what is going to happen. This is an unknown for me. In the realm of his possibilities he will simply grow up Jewish. I rely on Dina there, so that he gets enough Jewish identity. I will give all possible support, but in specific terms, concretely, I will not be able to be of much help. As far as Clifford is concerned, I go along with everything and am supporting it, except that realistically, I cannot be a teacher to him. Dina will be his teacher. I simply don't have it in me, I am not a Jewish father.

DINA: But you are a good father, that's more important than a Jewish father, you know. You should not have a bad conscience because of it.

ISRAEL, JEWISH MILIEU

As a Jewish woman, she feels she's being taken good care of by me as a non-Jew

Of course, ever since I have known Dina, I am far more interested in the Israeli situation and in all these topics. In the first two years of our relationship this was very, very intensive. Then I also began to see far more consciously films about the Nazi period. We talked a lot about it and twice on TV there was an intensive occupation with this topic, but that is finished now. There are basically no new insights. At first there was this Holocaust phase, then there was the Israel phase, and at the moment it does not play a role. Ever since Netanyahu I was not that interested in Israel anymore, we were simply so disappointed about that development, disillusioned. For the moment, it does not play an important part for us.

I've also been in Israel with Dina, and I felt comfortable there. This is a country with such warmth, unlike any other I know. Maybe I am naive here. I have no aversion at all and no conflict, I appreciate it without heroizing it. In that sense, the Jewish/non-Jewish question is not raised for me at all. My relationship to Judaism is primarily my relationship to Dina. When I am in Israel, I feel comfortable, and if somebody wears a kippah there, then it is fine with me, it is not an issue for me. And, what can I say, I would not even know what I should do in order to make myself into a Jew. I also don't have that urge now to become something that I am not yet, to omit something of what I am. To convert, I don't know, I don't have that inside me. I don't want to convert, that's it.

Then there is the question about the Jewish milieu. This is all so terribly relative. Here in H. I am not in a Jewish milieu. So let us look at Israel. Is that a Jewish milieu there? It is a normal life, simply Shabbat in place of Sunday. Is that not more the question of a sense of life, or does it always have to be occupied with particular rituals and ominous prophecies?

On the holidays, for example Pessach, Dina cooks and we take a walk. We invite people, Jews and non-Jews, and have a huge party and a huge meal, singing together and so on. Hanukkah, for Clifford, is a really important event. Why, I don't know. There is no disagreement between me and Dina. As a Jewish woman, she feels she's being taken good care of by me as a non-Jew. Anything else is of no interest to me.

3

Jerry

Guterman

Jerry

and the Fossils

1948   born in Landsberg DP camp

1949   parents move to Brooklyn, New York

1966   admitted to MIT

1970   admitted to University of Pennsylvania; graduate studies in economics

1974   Ph.D.

1979   position at the Federal Reserve Bank

1981   position at Lehman Morgan

1984   chief financial officer, Chemical Bank

It was difficult at first to locate Jerry. Earlier, I had interviewed his mother, Gertrud, in Brooklyn. She was then in her early eighties. She was not in good health and could not remember many things. She and her husband Leon live in a somewhat rundown, lower-middle-class area. We sat in her extremely modest kitchen in the dark apartment. The living room seemed not to have been lived in for a long time; much, including the kitchen table, was covered with transparent plastic sheets. Later in the afternoon, her husband came back from synagogue, barely took notice of me, and, yelling and gesturing wildly, made it clear that what his wife was doing with me was pointless. I was hoping to get Jerry's phone number from Gertrud, but despite several efforts in this direction, she did not want to give it to me, because, as she said, he is very, very busy. I received Jerry's phone number through another family member and interviewed him on the occasion of a later visit to New York.

Jerry lives with his family in one of the best areas of New Jersey, in a sprawling house on a hilltop. I remember a huge, ultramodern kitchen, filled mostly with magazines and books. One of his sons was doing his homework there. In the living room, a desk filled with a large number of

framed family photos, including those of Jerry's wife's father, amid his children and a large number of grandchildren. A photo of Jerry's parents was nowhere to be seen, however. Nothing particularly caught my eye — it seemed an all-American upper-middle-class home with the furbishings and artwork that could normally be found in numerous other American upper-middle-class homes — with one exception: a glass vitrine in one corner. Jerry explained that his hobby is collecting fossils from many famous locations around the world, including one not too far from where he was born, in Franconia. Why this interest in fossils? These fossils, after all, are suspended in time and removed from place, far enough in the past not to furnish any coordinates of orientation. Perhaps his hobby is linked to his own self-definition. At the end of his interview he states that he can fit into many environments.

Jerry is also active in the Jewish Federation of New Jersey, and he has led an active campaign in support of Israel under the Sharon government.

JERRY: I was born in Landsberg in Bavaria, which was a DP camp. When I was just a year old, my parents moved to the United States, so I have no memories of Germany, and I rarely spoke to my parents about that period. It would come up only infrequently, maybe a couple of times when I may have asked. They were not anxious to speak about it. And as far as the Holocaust is concerned, they said almost nothing whatsoever. Since you did this interview with my mother, you probably know more about it than I. I'd love to listen to that sometime.

The only thing my mother expressed a couple of times, and what was obviously a very painful experience, was that one of her sisters died after the camps were liberated, before they moved out of the camps. You had mentioned to me that this was in Bergen-Belsen, and that she talked about that to you a lot as well. What she told me was that apparently this was a sister she looked up to, who took care of her and the others. But after having taken care of my mother, her sister then passed away after the liberation, which obviously was very painful to my mother. She has not spoken to me much of that, partly because when the subject came up I did not press her; because she was upset and it's something that got me upset.

GERTRUD KALMAN: I was in Groß-Rosen concentration camp. I was just passing by and then I went to Bergen-Belsen, end of '44 to end of

'45. I was liberated April 15th or 14th. It was downgraded for me, for myself, because I had to see [*sobs*] my sister Gitla pass away six days before the liberation. So I was there with her [*cries*] . . . but the English army, they took me to Buchenwald. In Buchenwald I met my brothers. I don't remember exactly how this happened, but that's what happened. I was there a couple of months, then I went to, what's the name of the city? Landsberg, right. I was in Landsberg and I met my husband, right on the train I met my husband. My brothers lived together with me. They were going out practically every day, dealing in S. We all lived together. That's what happened. We got married in 1946, and my husband was dealing a little bit of gold, with this, with that, and that's it, waiting to go to the United States. I stayed in Landsberg from '45 to '48. It was considered a camp, or something like that. I don't remember. Tried to forget the whole thing, like a dream. We stayed there till my husband got an invitation to come to the United States. That affidavit. His aunt was there. So we came here.

JERRY: We also never really talked about her other siblings who perished. I don't know much about them. Several years ago, I did ask to set up a family tree and that provided the excuse to ask some questions. But aside from getting names I got little else. In some cases I got some birth years, but the dates were obviously guesses, specifically for her parents, but for the brothers and sisters I think I have the years.

I know we have a relative in Toronto, Rita Volkov. I have not seen her in a number of years. I think she came to my wedding. We invited her to our childrens' bar mitzvahs, but I don't think she attended any. The subject came up again recently, because we were talking about an invitation for our older son's wedding. I chatted with my mother about her recently. My mother had not spoken to her in a long time, and it was not very important to her whether we invited her or not. I don't even know her exact relationship to us. All I know is that she is some sort of cousin, or didn't you tell me she is a half-sister of my grandfather's?

I knew that back in Poland before the war, my mother worked in the family tobacco store. I heard a number of times the story of them burying the flints during the Occupation. Flints were very precious at the time, and then they went back after the war to dig them up and they got some money that way. There are also a number of versions as to who went there to pick them up. I am not sure which is the correct version. My father always complained and kept on telling me that he was the person who went back. But it does not make any sense that my father should go back, because he did not know Slawkusz and did not know where the stuff was. So someone must have gone back with him.

I have never been in Slawkusz myself, I was just once in Poland, in Warsaw, for a day or two on business. I have also not thought a great deal about going there and taking a look. It is obvious to me that it is difficult for my parents to talk about it, and that's made it very difficult for me to read about it, to see movies about it. For example, when that Spielberg movie came out . . . I haven't seen it. My wife has seen it and she thinks it would be a good thing for me to see it. I can't bring myself to go and see it. I know the period was very difficult and very upsetting to my parents. And I am very reluctant to ask them questions that would force them to talk about it. An interesting possibility is that they might talk to our children about it. But it is relatively difficult for us to visit because — you know, you have met my father.

MY FATHER

He's perfectly happy to explain economics to me and he has
no interest whatsoever in hearing what I have to say

My father is an extremely difficult individual to talk to and it's very difficult for me to deal with him because on the one hand he's very proud of what I've accomplished, and on the other hand, he is very jealous of what I've accomplished because he seems to feel that under different circumstances he could have accomplished it too. You know, he dismisses the fact that I went to MIT and that I have a Ph.D. He tells me, I have book learning but don't have common sense. That's the way he presents it. Yet I can also tell you that the day I was accepted to MIT I came home and he was smiling from one ear to the other ear and he was clearly very proud. Not that he could acknowledge it.

So my father wants to be recognized for being successful, and his great success is that he made quite a bit of money. What is really odd is — I have never told him this — that he has made a great deal of money despite himself, not because of any special expertise. He was very fortunate in that he put money into the stock market shortly after coming to the U.S. and was very focused on the stock market and every penny that he could he put into it. As little money as he made as a factory worker, he didn't spend it. And so, over the last fifty years that's been a wonderful place to invest. And as a result, he is a reasonably wealthy man, not hugely wealthy, but he has more than enough money.

He did a certain amount of speculation, he was always looking for different investments. I know how he analyzes stocks and I can tell you with a great deal of confidence that it is not an advantage. That did not help him. What really helped was that he was always investing. There is a whole literature on this in terms of what is called efficient markets; if you have a diversified portfolio then you have at least earned the market rate of return. Well, the market rate of return over the past fifty years has been very good and compounding is a very powerful force. So even if you start out with a very small amount of money, if you continually add to it, and you reinvest all of the proceeds, and you reinvest all of the dividends and just let it keep on compounding, it ends up quite a tidy sum. And that's where my father is.

Apart from investing, they own the building they live in. There are three apartments and they live in one. In addition to the two other apartments that they rent, they also rent out the garage and the driveway. So that house today generates more than enough income for them to live off. They have paid off the mortgage completely so the only expense they have is the cost of oil and gas and property taxes and insurances and things like that. But otherwise, they spend very little money. So the rent that they take in on that house means that everything that they earn on their portfolio gets reinvested.

With all that, my father is unable to spend money. There is one and only one thing that he is able to bring himself to spend money on, and that is me. I am the only thing that he is comfortable spending money on. And he won't let me spend money for him either. And at this stage of their lives, every year they give me money.

In that way, he is similar to Albert and maybe Ignaz, because my father's whole world focuses around his very, very limited family. When I say limited, I mean three people, as in my mother and me. With his cousin, the one who helped arrange his papers for immigration, I don't remember much about that relationship and there was no contact with that family. They were older. My father did have a brother who lived in Brooklyn and he had left Poland before the Nazis took control. He went through Russia and eventually went to Brazil and married there. But my father and his brother did not get along that great. His son, my cousin, never went to college, he is a salesman, so he and I did not have much in common and it was not a close relationship.

My mother, in turn, does not have friends either, but she would do quite a lot for others. She feels very close to Ignaz and she also feels somewhat close to Jurek. She did not go to Albert's funeral, but she was already pretty old and my father didn't want her to go. But she was upset that she did not go. My father, on the other hand, was jealous of my mother's brothers. After all, they were very successful because of this kitchen business and my father could have been part of that; he had a sense of entitlement and felt that he missed something large and resented my mother's brothers as a result. When Ignaz sent money to my mother, my father felt this was only fair because they'd made a lot of money and my mother had not gone back to become a partner in the business. He resented Albert because Albert appeared to discourage that or did not send any money; did not have him share in the benefits of that business.

I think the reason my father is so difficult has something to do with the Holocaust, but I am not sure what. My father is disturbed in some important ways. I am not a psychologist and I'm not sure why, but I think he has probably become more resentful as he gets older. He has more than enough money to be able to live quite well. He just cannot bring himself to do it. I think he is socially retarded and I attribute that, a substantial part at least, to the Holocaust. He has difficulty dealing with anybody else. He has a very high opinion of his own abilities and he explains things to other people who don't need things explained to them. He's perfectly happy to explain economics to me and he has no interest whatsoever in hearing what I have to say about anything, including economics.

Some of it is typical for a European immigrant, but I have a lot of friends whose parents are from immigrant backgrounds and who are much more adapted than my parents are. Part of that is because of his age when he came to the United States, part of it because he immediately went to a factory to be able to support his family. He didn't have the opportunity to get any more education to be able to do anything else.

SCHOOLING

My wife has joked that I sort of raised myself

At the time when I grew up, they did not own the house, I grew up in an apartment just a few blocks away. It was a small apartment. It was only four rooms, two bedrooms, a living room, and a kitchen. I had my own room. We had a cousin on my father's side who lived upstairs. He was the one who told my parents about the apartment. I first went to a public kindergarten and apparently asked why we didn't have a Christmas tree, and shortly thereafter found myself in a yeshiva. I went to yeshiva for eight years. We studied Jewish subjects all morning and in the afternoon we studied secular subjects. We were not particularly religious at home. My parents kept kosher, and it was my mother's initiative to keep the holidays and so on. My father at the time was even less religious than my mother. She was urging me to go to services, but neither of them went. When I was a child and went to services on Shabbat, my parents didn't go, I didn't go with my father. I went to the place where I was a student at the yeshiva.

When I graduated, there were a number of high school options: a local high school that I would go to just because I lived in that area. Yeshivas were a possibility, and another possibility was a very competitive magnet high school in Manhattan. You had to take a test to get into that school, and of the yeshivas that were available, one was a more secular, a less Hasidic type of yeshiva that I preferred to go to. But the principal of the yeshiva that I was graduating from wanted me to go to a more religious, almost rabbinical type of yeshiva. I was not interested in that but for some reason did not get into the more secular yeshiva. Instead, I got into the more religious yeshiva and we always thought that the rabbi had manipulated that. I also got accepted to the special high school in Manhattan, a secular, very academically oriented school and decided that was where I wanted to go. It was my decision, and I have joked and my wife has joked that I sort of raised myself. It was not something my parents could help me with and I just said one day, I am going to go to this high school and they said, fine.

So every morning I took the subway. It was an hour's commute each way. But it was an exceptional school, Stuyvesant, not just one of the best high schools in New York City, but one of the best schools in the country. The year I graduated, there were twenty of us who applied to MIT and eighteen were accepted. So that gives you a flavor of how strong the school was. It was a wonderful school and a wonderful challenge for me. In yeshiva, I was not the most well-behaved student, probably because I was bored. But once I got into Stuyvesant, that completely disappeared overnight as an issue. I did very well at Stuyvesant.

A CAREER

I am very goal-oriented and wanted to move as
quickly as possible through the system

When the time came, my mother did not want me to apply to college outside the New York area. In the National Merit exams, there was a place to indicate what colleges I was interested in and I put down MIT as one of my top choices. But my mother asked me not to apply to schools outside New York City; they wanted me to live at home. So I never applied. But then I got a letter from MIT indicating that they had received information from the PSATs that I had done extremely well, and that they had discovered that I had not even written and asked for an application to MIT. So they were hoping that I would apply.

With that kind of a letter coming from MIT, it was difficult for my mother to say, don't apply. I sent in the application and my mother hoped that I would not get in. All of the acceptances came out on the same day so I knew which day it would be. I called home and my mother had already received the letter and opened it, so I discovered that I had been accepted. When I came home that day, it was very interesting because my mother didn't mention it, and I waited for my father to come home, and he came home with a smile from one ear to the other ear but he didn't say anything.

And the three of us sat down for dinner, and we ate dinner, and no one talked. In my parents' household, that's an amazing occurrence, that no one spoke over dinner. It's the only time I can remember. After dinner was over, my father looked at me and said, "Well, I guess you'll be going to MIT." And I said, "Yes." And the subject didn't come up for two weeks. Two weeks later, my mother came over to me and she said, "Tell you what, if you don't go to MIT I'll buy you a car." And in the right flavor of what I was like at that age, I told her, "And if I go to MIT, you'll give me a car in two years anyway, so I'm going to MIT." And that was it. I arrived in September of '66 and left in May '70.

I was accepted in economics at the University of Pennsylvania and started there in September 1970. My specialty was macroeconomics and as subspecialties, finance and international economics. I got my degree in the minimum period of time, in 1974, I am very goal-oriented and wanted to move as quickly as possible through the system. As one of the better students, I was encouraged to go into academia and actually received a few academic offers, right in the middle of the recession at the time. I had started doing academic research and wrote a series of papers, had a number of papers published over a number of years. I ended up accepting a one-year visiting position at Northwestern rather than a tenured professorship at Penn State or another one at the University of Maryland. Northwestern was considered top ten in academics.

But even at that point, I was a little bit sour on academia, in part because of the politics and the rivalries between different schools of thought in economics. Maybe I was somewhat naive, but I was very disappointed. Having decided that if I had to put up with so much politics, I might as well get paid for it. I had already been speculating in the market and making some money and I enjoyed that and decided that the better thing for me to do was to give up academia and go to Wall Street. Because of my research and publication record, I ended up at the Federal Reserve and that was a perfect springboard to the Street. In fact, I got a call from a headhunter at Wall Street within a week or two of going there. In April of 1981, I took a job with Morgan Lehman, was there for three years, then was hired at Manufacturers Trust, survived the merger with Metro Bank and was put in charge of the combined operation, as chief financial officer. A couple of years later, the place was getting increasingly political. I had made a lot of money both in the market and from my position, so I decided to leave and start a hedge fund, together with Henry Kaufman.

The timing for the hedge fund was terrible. Lots of things were happening in the world and Henry became very frightened and decided to pull out. I had to decide whether to close the hedge fund or bear the cost myself; so I decided to close it and then started the Guterman Asset Management firm that I am still involved with today. So this is principally what I am involved with although I have also become very active in real estate, something my uncle Jurek proposed to me five or ten years ago, to get involved with real estate in Boston, together with another cousin, on Jurek's wife's side of the family, Zysman, who had studied at Brandeis just like my oldest son.

THE FAMILY

Ignaz was the character that he is

The first time I met my German relatives would have been when I was five years old, 1953. Periodically, my mother would go back to visit, for the whole summer. The story is told that when I came back to New York in '53 after spending a summer in Germany, that I had forgotten how to speak English, that I could speak only German and one of my friends claimed that he had to teach me English all over. I know we stayed in my uncle Albert's hotel, and returned when my uncle Ignaz got married. I don't remember which weddings I went to. I remember I definitely went to Jurek's wedding, that was in '59. And at that point Esther was around and she was someone that I could sort of play with. She was five years younger.

At that time, we were closest to Ignaz, at least my mother was, and he was the one who visited us here a couple of times. I remember that I was still a child at the time, but Ignaz, in typical fashion, flew in from Europe and he told my mother he was coming one day and he arrived the day before because he didn't want her to worry, and I was outside the house playing ball with friends and Ignaz was across the street and I saw him come to the house. I was just very excited to see him and I ran across the street to jump into his arms. Meantime a car was coming down the street and almost hit me, because I was so excited.

Ignaz has always been the most scatterbrained of all of the siblings. He would come up with all kinds of business ideas. Some of them sounded like the wildest speculation, but he was the one who really established the family wealth. Now it is true that in Albert's family they believe that Albert was the important figure. But my understanding is that Ignaz came up with the idea to buy American war surplus. Albert may have managed the business better, but Ignaz had the idea to sell the American war surplus to Germans and they made a lot of money doing that. There are many, many arguments about who was responsible for the whole thing. Ultimately, it broke the family apart, with each one trying to lay the blame. There was a great deal of competition between the brothers; Albert was clearly trying to control the business. Ignaz was the character that he is. So the business relationships were clearly a big problem for the relationships.

One of the reasons my parents favored Ignaz was that he wanted to encourage my mother to move back to join the business. It was Ignaz who sent my mother money, because my parents were comparatively poor, and they appreciated that; my uncles were clearly well-to-do and my parents had very, very little. But I am closest to Jurek because he is from my standpoint the most cosmopolitan. He is the one who's easiest to talk to and I never got to know Albert that well before he died. It is also much easier to stay with Jurek, he's easy to talk to. Before, when we went to Germany, we stayed with Ignaz.

COUSINS

Dina was the only one who had any interest
in communicating with me

As far as my cousins are concerned, I used to be closest to Dina. With Albert's kids, we were never close. Esther, people said, was quite arrogant, quite difficult, and I don't think Albert was particularly warm. My parents seemed to find him threatening. But Ignaz was always trying to include my parents and would have accepted my mother into the business, but Albert appeared to want to exclude them. Albert excluded everybody and his kids also stayed separate from the others, and that's not inconsistent with my recent exchange of e-mail messages with Esther, who does acknowledge that she was never close to any of her cousins, only to her own brothers. Dina was excluded by everybody. She had a difficult childhood. Jurek's kids, all three of them, had each other and so they were not very close to Albert's kids.

From my perspective, until recently, Dina was the only one who had any interest in communicating with me and I was very concerned about her welfare. At one point I invited her to live here, to emigrate to the United States. This was after she had divorced her husband and she was very concerned about having enough money to live. I said, look, I can afford it, why don't you come live with me. You can live in my house, and you can do whatever you need to do to get American citizenship so that you'll be able to work. But she didn't want to do that.

She was in New York at some point because she had started a relationship with somebody, so she visited us a couple of times and stayed in our house and lived at our house for at least a few weeks at a time. She and I were the only two who were only children and didn't have the benefit of brothers and sisters in the family relationship. I offered that to her and for a while I think we had something like that. When she met her current husband and that became very serious, I think she was looking to me for approval. She was very upset that I gave her only limited approval, that I didn't give her wholehearted approval. This was when I visited her in H., a couple of years ago. And she stopped responding to my faxes. It was in June '97.

Q: *She told me she felt that you were being somewhat arrogant and looking down on her then, that you did not try to understand the situation she was in. In the past, she had always looked up to you, you were important to her.*

JERRY: I think she was looking for me to give approval of this German guy and I was not entirely happy that he was not Jewish, that he was German. I did meet the guy and he seemed like a perfectly nice guy. Keep in mind that I really didn't have an opportunity to spend a lot of time with him. I understood that she badly needed to get married, that she was very lonely. That was one of the reasons why I had encouraged her to come to the U.S., indeed we had open discussions about this, that if she should come here there would be many opportunities to meet Jewish guys; that kind of opportunity simply didn't exist in Germany. I was very disappointed that Dina cut herself off from me despite my efforts to try to stay in touch. My wife and I talked about inviting her to David's wedding and we don't even know how to get in touch with her except through her parents.

Oddly enough, partly as a result of your involvement with our family, I got a call from Esther in Israel. At that point she thought that one of her daughters was going to be coming to New York and her excuse was that she just wanted to have a phone number in case her daughter had any problems, and then we started to talk and started e-mailing back and forth. I never visited her in Israel. I was in Israel for Jonny's wedding, in '88. I know that he is considered a high-powered lawyer. Jonny was here on vacation once with his wife and kids. They were only here for a week and they called us and we all had dinner. When I was in Israel I did not have any contact with Salek and Esther.

The one cousin I am probably closest to now is Motti. He's been here a couple of times, for his photography project, and he's brought Cornelia a couple of times, so we've met her. He is really very warm. It is easy for me to talk to him and it's very easy for him to talk with me. Ronnie, on the other hand, went to New York, where he was as a resident for his medical training. He was there for roughly six months and he called a week before he left and so we saw him one time just before he left. And that's a good flavor of the effort on the part of Albert's kids. Lilian was much younger and was involved with her sports equipment store, so I did not see much of her. But recently we exchanged some e-mails and I have seen her when I have gone to Munich. If it were a little more convenient it would be very easy to have a closer relationship with her.

So it wasn't a very close relationship, neither with the relatives on my father's nor on my mother's side. The family that I have become most close to is my wife's side of the family. There I am very much accepted and very, very comfortable. My parents are difficult even now for me to deal with. My wife says that for my parents, the only thing that she ever did right was to have three sons. She wasn't particularly well accepted by my mother and it is hard to imagine my mother accepting almost any girl I brought back.

My wife's family are German Jews who arrived a number of generations earlier, and are very well established. I joke that I married Jewish bluebloods. My wife's maternal grandfather was the vice mayor of New York City under LaGuardia and he had a heart attack and died in office. And on the other side, my father-in-law's father was a big macher [bigwig] in Cincinnati, was president not only of a synagogue but of a Jewish organization and was involved in trying to get the U.S. government to pay attention to what the Nazis were doing in Germany.

Religiously, they were not only Reform, but ultra-Reform in Cincinnati. The question then was, how would we arrange ourselves? We ended up in the middle, Conservative. My wife says that I am a chameleon, because I can be in an Orthodox, Eastern European shul and fit in and two hours later I can be in a country club, very modern, Jewish Reform and even fit in there too. I can fit into all of those environments.

4

Jurek's

Family

Jurek

1928   Jurek born in Slawkusz

1945   liberation in Buchenwald (April 11)

1949   sells textiles, later in business with his brothers

1959   marries Rayna Zisman (b. 1935)

1978   Jurek leaves the Kalman firm

1995   Jurek, Rayna, and Motti visit Slawkusz and Auschwitz

Albert Kalman had passed away long before this project began; Ignaz did not speak to me about his experiences in the camps and after 1945, and Gertrud in Brooklyn, partly on account of her age, did not recollect much and had difficulty communicating coherently about it. In the end, of all four siblings, Jurek was the only authentic voice to speak to me more in detail about the past. As we shall see, Jurek's attempts, as a young teen, to save his parents' lives played a major role in his story; Jurek also kept returning again and again to how a German police officer had saved his life. I spoke to Jurek a number of times on visits to his spacious suburban bungalow-style home; I remember in particular the marble, the cheerful pastel colors, and the indoor plants. His wife Rayna was never far away and contributed actively to our conversations.

HERR OPPERMANN

He spoke better Yiddish than I, and he knew more about Jewish rituals and customs than I did

JUREK: In September 1939, the Germans marched into Poland. I was eleven years old, almost done with elementary school. Then there was war and no more school. About a year and a half later, there was a ghetto. In the meantime, my eldest brother, Albert, and my brother Ignaz were, as they say, drafted, like being drafted into the military. You have to know that this town, Slawkusz, was incorporated into the German Reich, and we had basically German police, German currency, German goods, everything was German. My brothers were ordered to appear before a board where they were examined, and then they were drafted into the labor service [Arbeitsdienst]. They were sent into a camp and from then, they were behind barbed wire. At the beginning, they were in two different camps and I don't know just when they came together. They were involved in work details building the Autobahn; the work details were moved around, and that is how they eventually came together. They were then together for the entire time until the end of the war.

I was the youngest, that is, I was the eldest son left at home. I had two younger brothers; we were eight children at home. My sisters were there as well, but they were sisters. My father, God bless him, could not even hammer a nail into the wall. It was not just because he was a merchant; he simply was not good in practical things. So I basically was the man of the house. I was the man in the house and hid my sisters and my family. I built bunkers, hiding places in the house in the ghetto. My two sisters, Gertrud and Gitla, they worked in a shop for the German Wehrmacht, the shops were well known, the so-called Rössner shops. Rössner saved many Jews, just like Schindler, and he had permission to open these types of shops and he recruited Jews.

One day, the shop was surrounded and everyone was taken away. At that moment we knew that for Jews, Slawkusz was erased from the map. Perhaps four or six months later, Jews were evacuated from the town. For that purpose — because we saw this coming — I built a bunker in the cellar and another one under the roof. When the evacuation began, this must have been in 1942, my family was hiding in the two bunkers. At some point, I had to get down from under the roof to the cellar to let people know that we would stay. At that moment, police came inside the house and they saw me. They were specialists. They knew what they were doing. They asked me where the rest of my family was, and I told them everybody had left already. Then they took me to the collection point [Sammelplatz] and I was sent to Mengele, who you probably have heard of, and he made the selection right then and there. I was maybe twelve or thirteen years old then [*sic*], but I knew what was happening.

I also noticed that a smaller group was separated, I don't know, for social reasons maybe, and these chosen, I assumed, would be taken away for cleanup operations, and I figured they would not be the ones to go to Auschwitz. I was part of the larger group, I was still a child. By accident, near where I stood, there appeared a police officer whom we knew, I believe, since 1940. His name was Herr Oppermann. An Austrian, from Vienna. He spoke better Yiddish than I and many others, and he knew more about Jewish rituals and customs and laws than I did. He associated with all our Jews. When our grandfather still had the butcher shop, Oppermann used to watch out so that the shoichet could slaughter undisturbed — they slaughtered illegally and Oppermann got some bribe or something for helping out. Imagine, he told the shoichet, Adam, "Go and do the slaughtering now, but you are not supposed to be afraid, because if you are afraid and you tremble, it is not going to be kosher." He knew that. Imagine the craziness. I did not know this story, people talked about it in our place. What kind of fellow is he, how does he get this kind of an idea? Normally, among Christians, shechita is described as an enormous, how shall I say, cruelty to animals. And he did that quite frequently. The same man knew my grandparents and all of us. He played cards with my blessed father, downstairs in the house where we were living. Of course, it was normal that he got paid because of the business with the meat. We also sold tobacco, and with the new German administration, all the German officials, be they from revenue, or from the employment office, they bought from us. They knew we were Jews, and so this Oppermann was a customer of ours as well.

Now back to the Sammelplatz. I was standing there, near Herr Oppermann, and I spoke to him and said, "Herr Oppermann, you know, I have two brothers and two sisters in the camp. I want to go to the camp with my brothers and sisters." He knew us well, and he knew all about my siblings. He played cards with my aunt, even though this was strictly forbidden. He also knew all the hideouts and escape routes. After a lot of talking back and forth, and pestering him and convincing, he told me, "Okay you go over to the other side." I said, "But I can't just go over there like that, with all the guards." Then he stamped with his foot on the ground and pushed me and said sternly, "You are going right now. Tell them you went peeing. That you went to the bathroom." I went straight across the soccer field.

Imagine me little pinsele running all the way across this soccer field. With all the guards around, I run over to this small group. But these people got afraid because I was there, and they were the chosen, and they, understandably, did not want me in the group. But I pretended to be dumb, and stood on my toes, to look taller. In short, the big transport was taken away, and I was with the small, chosen group. This is how I came to the transit camp at Sosnovitz, where people were distributed to the labor camps. If he had not stamped his foot! This moment it was either "hop or top" and this is how I survived.

After the war, there was a Jewish students' dance in Munich. This might have been around 1953. There I met a friend, Marian Bankier, and he asked me how I survived. So I told him the story, including the story with Oppermann. He says to me: "Oppermann? But he lives in Vienna!" So I say to Marian, "I am going to Vienna, let's go see Oppermann together." We met there, we go to Oppermann's flat, and Oppermann was paralyzed. Like a column of stone, a column of salt, of stone. This fellow was huge, 1.90 meters. This encounter was something else. I began to tell my story, and he sits there like a piece of stone. I drew sketches for him, also about the slaughtering, and where we lived, and that he played cards with my father. We had the tobacco store, and through the cigarettes, we came to know him. How was it possible, I cannot understand until this day, that he was so knowledgeable about Jewish laws.

He knew exactly who I was. He would have recognized me in the middle of the night, my voice; he knew all of us. He was simply afraid, and not without reason, except for me. I tortured myself with sketches, explanations, lectures, and memories. I was so excited, I was sweating, totally wet, but it did not do me any good. I told him I am here with good intentions, I want to help you, I can help you. I tried to soften up the column of stone, without success. I would have stood up for him in court, I would have given him a Persilschein [exculpatory affadavit], any support imaginable. But nothing. Not a single word, zero. I left his flat without even so much as one word. Nothing.

Listen, between us, I don't know whether there was anyone in Slawkusz who could have proven that he shot anyone. I don't know that, but I know that he was no angel. Except, the reason that he refused to acknowledge his identity and his connection to me I could only explain with his fear that he probably had done more sinister things than what I know.

THE FEUERSTEINE (FLINT STONES)

We took all the stones with us

One item that was very expensive in Poland was flint stones for lighters. The state monopoly covered matches and flint stones. In order to sell matches, they made the flint stones incredibly expensive, and only rich people who wanted to show off—like today with, say, a Philippe Patek or another wristwatch—would have a lighter. Now when the Germans arrived, we bought flint stones by the kilo for dirt cheap Reichsmark. They cost only pennies. We had this idea that since we could not buy dollars or gold, we would invest everything in flint stones. When we had to leave the house for the ghetto, we took all the stones with us; we could only take a fraction, of course, of what we had in the house, but the flint stones we took with us, as a reserve. Where we lived in the ghetto, I buried them in the cellar. No one knew about that, just me. Of those who survived, Albert and Ignaz by that time had already been sent to the labor camp, and Gertrud was away working in the shop, and no one else survived. I was the only one left who knew about the flint stones.

Right after the war, when we were in the DP camp in Landsberg, I told my sister that I had buried the stones and she and Leon, my brother-in-law, went back to Poland, to dig up part of the things that I had buried. This was not jewelry or gold or diamonds, it was just the flint stones. They sold them right on the spot in Poland, because they were not widely available then. Nevertheless, they sold them for a pittance. So my sister came back with a suitcase of Reichsmark, which was our starting capital.

RAYNA: [*laughs*]

JUREK: You are laughing, that's really nice.

RAYNA: Yes, I am laughing.

JUREK: This was our starting capital, and many people had far less than what we had.

LIBERATION

They opened the gates, and we were basically free

There were constant transports from all the other camps into Buchenwald, and people were sent off from there as well. And my brothers and
Herr Schenfeld and the whole crew arrived in Buchenwald, from the
death marches. Buchenwald was supposed to be an interim stop. They
were supposed to go on. By coincidence, one of my brothers asked
somebody in Buchenwald whether I was there by any chance. Imagine,
in this tohu wa bohu [chaos] they asked after somebody in particular.
The fellow whom he asked knew that I was there, that I was in that
particular barracks further down. My brother asked whether this fellow could not go down and try to find me and bring me up to him. That
is what happened.

I said to my brothers, stop right there, come down with me to the
children's camp. Since people were constantly chased out of the main
camp, onto death marches, you cannot imagine. The ss took one block
after the other, calling them up onto a transport. We in the children's
block were privileged, because we were not being called up yet. Also,
people felt that the days were numbered. All the nervousness . . . it is
hard to explain this to anyone. In all the goings-on in camp life you can
sense whether it is quietness or restlessness. Food came either at two
o'clock or at five in the morning or at three o'clock at night, or the food
crew got robbed on the way, case closed, we did not get any food. All of
that happened.

So I took my brothers immediately out of there, brought them into
the childrens' block, and we hid, in the sewers, under the roof and here
and there. They beat us and chased us out of there and finally, we ended
up on the Appellplatz [collection point] as well, where people were
taken onto transports. But the children's block was not taken away but
left right there in a pile. We were lying down there, and I covered my
brothers with blankets so no one would find out that they were adults.
Transports left until five or six o'clock in the evening of April 10th.
Then they locked the door, and whoever was left, who was ill or
couldn't walk, were all taken, including the children, and locked up in
the camp jail. We stayed in that jail overnight, and in the morning, there
was the order: everybody get ready to go on a transport. We were all

ready and standing there in rows of maybe four, guards to the left and to the right of us. Everyone got a piece of artificial honey, and the bread for it we were supposed to get later at the gate.

It must have been around eight or nine, and suddenly, a tank alarm saved us, the alarm that enemy tanks were nearby. The guards were in total frenzy [heller Aufregung], the gate was shut immediately, and we went right back into the jail, and the jail locked. Then total silence. I did not see any more guards. It was like that until three or four in the afternoon, and then we heard machine gun salvos, and you could see that they ricocheted off the guard towers. Then there were vehicles coming not far away, but they were not the vehicles of the German Wehrmacht. You could also see immediately that the guards ran away, followed by a huge explosion outside, an antitank grenade as we found out later, directed against the Americans, and after that, absolute silence. A couple of hours later, we saw that the Americans were there, in the camp, and a lot of shouting and you could hear shooting. The guards from the guard towers fled.

In short, we spent another night in the jail, even though the Americans were already there. On the following day, the jail was opened, and at night we still had heard massive shooting. We were horribly afraid, afraid that the Germans might come back again and wipe out everything. But seemingly, with God's help, nothing further happened, and the next day, they opened the gates, and we were basically free. It was a relief, it was the end. But it was not a feeling of cheerful joy. We embraced each other. We were glad, but we knew that we could not be happy. We knew that. My brothers were taken away early and they did not know any details about the family. So how can you be happy.

This was the story of the 11th of April. Later on, we were loaded onto trucks, all kinds of people including Russian Jews who had fled from the Soviet army. Eventually we landed in a DP camp, in Landsberg/Lech, into barracks there; we had one room of about thirty square meters, for at least three families, separated from one another by sheets and closets: my brothers and I, and my sister Gertrud and another family and later Leon Guterman, Gertrud's future husband, but he did not belong to the family then as yet.

Jonny

A CAREER IN ISRAEL

1960   born in F.
1978   father leaves the firm
1979   Abitur, leaves for Israel
1980   studies law at Hebrew University
1988   married, and lives in Haifa
1989   birth of son
1992   birth of daughter
1997   birth of son

Among all the Kalmans, Jonny was the only difficult person for me to interview. He agreed more reluctantly, and his siblings and cousins were not surprised. They said he is quite reserved and I should not take it personally. My impression was they were letting me know that he is somewhat difficult to figure out at times. After many attempts to try to speak to him, both on a visit to Haifa and in Germany, he finally agreed to speak with me on the telephone for about half an hour after I had tracked him down in Germany. At the time he and his wife were on one of their regular, once or twice a year, visits with their children in Munich, and in the home of his parents. As in the case of Albert's and Eva's children, there is a division of roles between Jonny, Lilian, and Motti as well.

JONNY: I live in Haifa, and am specialized in trade and bankruptcy law. I got married in 1988. My wife's parents are from Germany, but she does not speak any German and neither do our two children. It is a bit difficult sometimes because on visits to Germany, it is difficult for them to communicate with my parents. My mother speaks Hebrew, though.

   I am the eldest in our family. I was born in 1960, which was within a year that my parents got married. I went to school in F., both to elementary school and Gymnasium, and basically, I did not have any negative experiences there. My main interest in school was math, and there is an affinity to studying law because logical thinking is involved in both fields. People knew, of course, who I was. Every teacher knew that I am Jewish. And of course, when there was a discussion on religion and on Judaism or on Israel and so on, then every teacher knew that I am a Jew, and every student knew that I am a Jew, everybody. And I knew that these discussions concerned me differently from all the others. But that is not anti-Semitism.

When I say I did not have any negative experiences, it does not mean it was all positive in F. You have to put that differently, it was neither, nor: it was simply neutral. It was not really positive because in my opinion, you cannot be Jewish in F. in any way. I may have participated in the one or other demonstrations against neo-Nazis, but as far as other encounters with the non-Jewish environment go, I just don't remember right now. I had relatively little that tied me to Germany, and that was very consciously so on my part. The only other Jewish person in the school was my brother Motti.

Q: *Really? Motti told me that there were about five Jewish students in school with him.*

Maybe. I don't remember. I had relatively few friends from school and was maybe somewhat more withdrawn. When I lived in F., my only friends at the time were in the Zionist Youth movement. I really had relatively few friends in school.

Today I have no friends here, but I am in touch with Alex, a friend formerly from F. who made aliyah together with me, and who later went back to Germany and now lives with his wife in Berlin. My wife and I are friendly with a non-Jewish couple from F. whom I met through Alex. In fact, when we are done with this interview, my wife and I will go and visit him and his wife. When I was young, the only meaningful relationships were with my friends from the Zionist Youth movement here in F. We were the ones who, basically, started it and the group only kept going until the time we left for Israel.

We were not religious at home, but Israel played a really big role for my family. When there were news reports about Israel, it was most important and was gobbled up, and as I said, I had the youth group. Munich, the next big city, was not all that attractive to me. True, this was a larger Jewish community, but as far as the Zionist youth is concerned, I had more friends elsewhere. I did not know anyone in Munich whom I would have particularly liked. Jewish society in Munich was very materialist oriented, and when I was seventeen or eighteen this did not appeal to me at all.

I could not relate to the Jewish community in F. I hated the Gemeinde, we did not get along with the community leadership, and that also had to do with the Kalman family, but it had reverberations back on us. The Gemeinde had nothing to offer to the youth, nothing at all, absolutely nothing. There were also not many Jews there our age, maybe three or four or five Jews in our cohort. And that community leadership was really hated. You have heard about that already, Mr. S., for reasons which I cannot call rational, reasons that have to do with our parents, not with me, I did not know that man at the time. It was the general atmosphere, very much against him, and the Gemeinde had nothing to offer to the youth, and perhaps it could not offer much, with so few kids, but the fact was, it did not offer anything.

As a town in Germany, F. was unpleasant, and there was no Jewish life, neither in F. nor in Germany at large. And then the Kalman family, my uncles, all the trouble there. Sometimes, we would meet Dina's father, for example, in front of the synagogue, and sometimes my father and he would shake hands, and sometimes not. In 1978 my father was forced out of the firm, and I left for Israel a year later.

LEAVING FOR ISRAEL

Today, Germany is the last country that I would want to live in

I left for Israel basically because I wanted to get out of Germany. To be staying in Israel was not definite, no final decision at the time. It evolved over the course of several years, but the decision to leave Germany was something clear to me and that I wanted to try.

LILIAN: Well, whether it was for political reasons, I don't know. Jonny did his ulpan, and I think he simply liked it so much in Israel that he decided to stay. Perhaps, staying in Germany might have been too easy for him. Maybe he needed a challenge. Because here he could have received a scholarship and everything, but he probably was looking for a different challenge. And of course, his best friends left for Israel together with him. This may have been another motivating factor. Perhaps he also wanted to get away from home.

JONNY: Getting out of Germany and trying something new, that is what I wanted to do.

Q: *So you are really happy now that you decided to move to Israel?*

Yes, but it is also because I am doing well and because I like it. Apart from the objective problems which every Israeli has, I cannot complain.

I forgot to mention one thing. I have to clarify something. If there was little that kept me tied to Germany in 1979, then today Germany is the last country that I would want to live in. I see the neo-Nazis here being stronger than in earlier years. I have the feeling that I am getting much more direct contact with anti-Semitism than in the old days when I was living here. I have seen the opinion surveys and the election results. Not directly. I don't know it from direct contact. I am not out there on the street. I don't know the general atmosphere. And I am very skeptical concerning Germany's new power in Europe after unification. The strong national sentiment together with unification — I find that pretty repulsive.

RITA VOLKOV: Jurek's family, I feel is like my family, you understand, I do anything. So I love them very dearly. I was in Israel, I said to Jurek, give me the telephone number of your son. He has a son in Israel. I'll call him. I want to see him. I called him maybe five times and I said, would you like to come over, I am staying in this and this hotel, I just want to meet you. I don't need nothing from you or anybody. So he came, he did me a big favor. So I said, do you know who I am? So he says no, I don't know. Well, I am your grandfather's sister. He looked at me, he couldn't . . . but I'm your father's aunt and I'm visiting here with my granddaughter so I wanted to meet you. So he came, he was with me for two minutes and then he left.

AN OBSERVER: I grew up in Cologne, and I knew Jonny through the get-togethers of the ZJD. I made aliyah a year after he did. What he has been too modest to tell you is that he's made a spectacular career for himself in Israel; he is one of the outstanding lawyers in his field, and you can even see him occasionally on Israeli TV. He has a fabulous office in Tel Aviv. So he is a real success story as far as this Jewish emigration from Germany goes.

For him and a bunch of us, leaving Germany was the obvious thing to do, also a question of values. He and I and others made a clean break, unlike these guys who left Germany with great fanfare for Israel, with banner headlines in German papers saying, "Germany is not my country." In reality, they were too comfortable in Germany, too cowardly to really try making a living here in Israel. I am thinking in particular of people like M. B., a real slut, worse than the lowest prostitute. They pretended to be living here, but never made a serious attempt to learn Hebrew. Instead, from an Israeli address, they wrote for German publications and told the Germans how terrible they are, and later, about how crazy Israelis are. For that, they are bought by anti-Semitic German publishers, move back to Germany, and for 25,000 marks a month lash out against German leftists or other easy targets, or go on personal vendettas, especially against former friends or associates, never against the people with power. It is a jungle. Real opportunists.

Q: *How can you be so dismissive? B. H. and Eva or even Motyk B. have some very poignant things to say about Germany in their articles and novels, including about the left. Lots of people in Germany love their work.*

First of all, especially B. H.'s writing is getting more pale and more tedious by the minute; she's beating the same old dead horse and is full of herself at the same time. She and some others have this s/m relationship with the Germans, kind of a Miss Severitas with a whip. That is why the Germans love them. When you write your book, you should write about that. We loathe these guys.

Lilian

1964   born in Munich
1983   Abitur at economics high school
1986   graduates from college for commerce and management
1987   marries Henry
1989   birth of daughter Gila
1991   birth of twin sons
1993   growth of neo-Nazism; Lilian and husband buy house in the
        United States

Lilian had heard about me through her parents and, unlike Jonny but much like Motti, was most generous about giving me the time for the interview. Somewhat in contrast to her brothers, she appears very down-to-earth, less complex perhaps, someone who enjoys being with people and most of all being with her family and her close friends. Lilian, like Motti and Jonny, was born in Munich, not in F., largely on account of her mother's parents, who lived in Munich and who could give her mother support during her pregnancies. Like the other Kalman cousins, she was raised, however, in F. At the age of eighteen and a half, she graduated from a Fachoberschule für Wirtschaft, a high school for trade and commerce in F. after transferring from the private Gymnasium for girls that her cousins Esther and Dina had attended earlier. In 1986 she received her degree from a college for commerce and management in Munich.

LILIAN: In my Gymnasium and in F. in general, everyone knew, with the surname Kalman, that I am Jewish, and my overall experience in school was very pleasant, really great. I mean, they simply knew the Kalman family, and I never had any problems. My fellow students always knew that I am Jewish; instead of me getting into problems because of it, they were very interested. I have to add, I never, ever had any clashes in that direction.

In my parents' neighborhood in F. where I grew up, there was Gisela, a non-Jewish girl. She is a very, very close friend to this day and it has touched our family environments. We used to decorate the Christmas tree together. I got the Easter eggs, and until recently — she now lives in Würzburg — I am sending her matzo. For Pessach. We still do this. I get the Easter eggs for my children. I have decorated the Christmas tree with her and the manger, and in our house, she ate the gefilte fish.

For Gisela's family, our friendship had further repercussions, because Gisela's parents became active in the local Christian-Jewish friendship society, and Gisela herself had gotten interested in Jewish things, she took an internship at Hadassah hospital in Jerusalem. She also met her boyfriend there, and her colleagues at the hospital gave her a Jewish name, Yael. When my daughter Gila was born, in honor of Gisela, we named her with her Hebrew name Yael. I completely forgot to mention that I have a second very close non-Jewish girlfriend who I met when I was in college. She is working in my business as an accountant, and believe it or not, this boss-employee and friendship relation is working superbly. I should say, my husband as well is very much integrated into the non-Jewish environment here, with his sports activities and our business.

PARENTS AND FAMILY

The nicest thing about living alone was to go home on weekends

I have always been the type that enjoys dealing with people, working in retail. I liked doing that even when I was working with my father in the business, and I was working there often during my vacation. I had a knack for it. Of my siblings, I am the only one who was interested in that.

I never really left this area here. I was too cowardly to get to know the world or to try my luck elsewhere, maybe because I always had a very, very good relationship with my parents. I really have to say that. I was very closely tied to my parents. And at the time when I was a student and living in the Olympic Village in Munich, in a student apartment, the nicest thing about living alone was to go home on weekends.

MOTTI: I see a clear role division among us siblings. My sister is living here in a very clear framework, in a Jewish context. In my view, it is the attempt to continue the life of our parents more or less in the way in which she has gotten to know it. To put it negatively, she is simply more in the ghetto. But I would not say she is religious. I don't consider her as being religious, strictly speaking.

LILIAN: You had mentioned my parents' history and together we went through my father's side of the family. I vaguely knew that my father had four other siblings who did not survive, but he never talked about it, he never spoke of them. I do think there is a crack there. My parents simply are not like other parents. There are things that cannot be discussed, or that you are afraid to talk about. There are also health matters that other people probably have not had to deal with, for example, now with my mother perhaps less than with my in-laws. There are predispositions there that have effects on children.

For me personally, there was a crack when I saw my father having difficulties with his brothers in the firm, and when he was out, in 1978. At that time, I helped out in the office, opening letters and so on. I mean, how old was I, ten or twelve? I was not allowed to do anything bigger than that, except to send telexes and to work at the telephone reception, but it was fun at the time. I was about fourteen when Dad was out. I don't remember too much about it. I only know that at the time, I suffered quite a bit. Also, as long as I was still working in the firm, I always had the notion in the back of my head, this is what you are going to do later, and with this conflict, the dream of a future also went down the drain.

It was a real shock somehow, also because Dad was suddenly out in a void. I did feel that as a child, and that some things were really changing then because in part he spent more time at home. But then, I also had the feeling that in terms of his health, it was good for him that he was out of there. Of all the cousins, I am the second youngest, and as the youngest, they tried to keep me out of the troubles; not to be transferring family matters onto the children. At home, they never slandered, were never abusive or so about Albert.

I saw Albert a lot when I was helping out in the firm as an adolescent. We got along well and, with Eva, I have maintained a good relationship throughout, getting together on occasion, and when I was little, we often went to a cafe together. We had similar interests. I have very nice memories, and I could always complain about my parents when I was with her.

Today, I am occasionally in touch with all my cousins, except Dina. It is a loose relationship. In earlier years, we'd meet in shul or when there were family events, but there was no real relationship. I am not in close contact with any of my cousins. In recent years, I have established contact with Gabriel, but only if one of us needs something from the other. In that case we phone each other. The contacts only began to start again when Berthold recently celebrated his fortieth birthday and there was a party. I was invited as well, and I went, and since my husband was out of town, I made a date with Gaby so he could take me with him. He had to pass by my place, this is how it happened. When he needs something from me, he'd call, and if I need something, I will call. My relationship with my mother's family is much closer. They are a very large family from Israel and Germany all the way to Canada. Often, we meet for my mother's father's yahrzeit in Israel.

SIBLING RELATIONS

For Jonny, I was always the little dumb one, in quotation marks

Over many years, I was closer to Motti, and this started in school. We had similar academic problems. Both of us weren't the greatest champions. Later on, Jonny was away in Israel, and Motti was closer by, especially with his visits from university back home. Jonny, on the other hand, was the elder brother whom I admired even if he was far away. He was the one smart enough to take on the greater challenges, and for Jonny, I was always the little dumb one, in quotation marks. Then we had our children roughly around the same time. His son is six weeks younger than my daughter, and his daughter is a couple of months younger than my boys.

From that moment on, when he expected a child and I expected a child, we came to be extraordinarily close, with phone calls back and forth. Now when I had finished Abitur, when I graduated from the economics college, I was always still the little dumb one, but now, we are at the same level. Before, Jonny simply also had other interests, and right now, we are pretty close. Recently, we spent Pessach in America together, which happened by chance. He went to the family of his wife, and we drove to Leibl's uncle; that is, we went to Disney World, but they live in Miami, and we visited them. We also lived with them. And as Jonny and I talked one day on the phone I told him, we are going to Miami. He said, we are going as well. So I said, let's try to coordinate that. And so we were together for four days, the four days before Pessach. Just this year when we were in Israel we met of course, at Pentecost, when we were all there. That is, with my grandma, and because we were invited to a big wedding, and because it is yahrzeit, everything came together so nicely, and — what normally I would not have done — we lived for a week in Haifa, because of Jonny and his family. We saw each other every day. That was really great.

THE JEWISH COMMUNITY

It really does not concern Israel, but the point is,
to be doing something actively for WIZO

Like my brothers, I got involved in the ZJD and the machanot. My brothers were madrichim at the time and when I was very young, this convinced my parents that I could come along. It really was a great time. I was still very young when I went for the first time. I was about ten, and from then on every year until sixteen, seventeen, as far as it went. There was no other programming from then on because in F. there were only very few younger Jews my age, and I lost track of people. But the one or other contact from the summer camp has been going on until today, and especially when I meet people at weddings or other occasions, the old ZJD acquaintances suddenly pop up again, acquaintances that were dormant for years. But in Jonny's case, the influence of the ZJD was definitely more profound than with me.

My primary involvement today is with WIZO AVIV, the junior women's section of the womens' Zionist organization. I am active in their various programs such as the annual benefit secondhand clothing sales, summer barbecues, and the like. My being involved with WIZO does not mean that I would want to move to Israel; the Israeli mentality is not my cup of tea, but the one does not exclude the other, and I also like the local WIZO's nonsectarian approach. I have taken a look at the

WIZO projects in Israel. I went to see the Beit Heuss, the mothers' recuperation home in Herzlia, and WIZO works on behalf of women of all religions. The kindergartens are open to children of all religions, and I think that is the right thing to do.

So these are not narrowly Israel-oriented projects, and I think that is good. That is the reason I am involved, and now, we'll be adding women's shelters. You might say that some of our local WIZO activities do not concern Israel at all; they are general Jewish community activities and one activity merges with the other. I mean, we also did cosmetics, everything. We also did an evening on fitness which was particularly successful.

Since my two boys went to the Jewish kindergarten and my daughter Gila went to the Jewish elementary school, I came to be involved in the Elternbeirat [parent-teacher association]. So via my activities in the schools, I got connected to the Jewish community by default, joint meetings with the Jewish community council and so on. The children bring back a great deal of Jewish heritage, and if we did not have the children, I don't know whether gradually, our Jewishness would not have diminished a bit. I am not at all religious, but I am definitely traditional, and especially through the children.

Through the WIZO we also often have various discussions concerning historical topics. In part family and child-rearing issues as well. What I am slipping into, slowly, and in part through the children, relates to that Lubavitcher Rebbe, who is relatively active in Munich, and things are being raised there that I was not that much concerned with before. It's got to do with kashrut, the commandments, now again because of the death of my girlfriend's mother, the shiva and all that. These are things that pop up when you are at these meetings, and they do interest me. But that does not mean that I am getting more religious; it does not mean that I will change, personally, because of it, just that I am more interested than in earlier years. Take the barbecue we had last weekend. It will have to be kosher—what can you have, what can you not have, and why can't you do this or that. This gets me more interested than in my earlier years.

Q: *Your brother Jonny says Germany is the last country that he would want to live in.*

What can I say? The fact that I am living here, it might have to do with the accident of my marriage. Now if I had not met my husband, who knows where I would have ended up. I see this as an accident, to be honest, and also because we have the company here.

THE GERMAN ENVIRONMENT

I simply live here, but I don't feel German

We were talking about the crucifixes in Bavarian classrooms and generally about the situation for Jews here in Germany. Well, when I had to register my daughter for an entrance test, I came into the classroom, and there was a big crucifix. I had never seen it as consciously as in that particular moment, when I came into this classroom. I had decided that anyhow, she would go to the Jewish school. And when these right-wing movements started rising here so massively in the early 1990s, my husband and I really did orient ourselves in the direction of America, and we bought a house there. Now we'll be selling it again, but it does not matter. We also thought about, just in case, if we'd really see that we did not want to be here anymore, where shall we go. Now both of us don't want to go to Israel. It is not my mentality, I like the American mentality better. And then my husband—this must also be one of these cracks that we have got—first you have to look for a place where you can live, it is an old Jewish story.

Q: *Now your brother Motti, I asked him whether he would see himself as a "stranger in one's own land." He turned it around, and said, more like "at home in a foreign land." How do you see yourself?*

I actually agree with both formulations. It begins, I think, when they play the German national anthem. It does not mean anything to me. It does not concern me. That is a typical example. With German nationality I've got nothing going. I simply live here, but I don't feel German. No, I would not identify myself with the German virtues.

Q: *And what about your German friend, Gisela? Does she feel herself to be German?*

I don't believe so, Gisela feels that way even more strongly than I do.

Motti

THE SCULPTOR-REMEMBERER

1961   born in Munich
1982   in Israel, in kibbutz with girlfriend
        maternal grandfather (Zysman) dies, buried in Israel
        Lebanon War
1989   in Zurich for one year
1992   meets Cornelia
1994   involvement with Benevolencja Sarajevo
1996   trip with parents to Poland
1999   travel to the United States; photography project on Jewish life

I met Motti for my interview in his apartment, a large, sprawling Wilhelminian apartment in a multicultural neighborhood of H. inhabited mostly by students, older German working-class families, and Turks. The apartment had sparse modern furnishings, perhaps the way we would imagine a sculptor's apartment should look, with the occasional antique piece of furniture here and there. Motti wears longish black hair, befitting a sculptor, baggy linen-type pants and jacket. He was hesitant and pensive in his responses to my questions — obviously a problem for the impatient interviewer. Motti sees a clear division of roles between himself and his two siblings and stresses the way in which he is different from them.

MOTTI: I don't know, perhaps this had to do with my need to be different from my brother. I figure, families distribute roles within them. In our family, the roles have been very, very clearly distributed: my brother, who took the Zionist route; my sister, who, what shall I say, is living here in a very clear framework of a Jewish context; it is in my view the attempt to continue the life of our parents roughly in the way in which she had come to know it. And I, who, well, I don't know, I am looking for a third route. What I am trying to do is very difficult, it is only evolving and uncharted, not my siblings' clear framework.

My story is not all that different from that of my siblings. Like them, I was born in Munich, in 1961, I grew up in F. with all the other Kalmans, I went to the same schools, to the same Jewish youth group, and I stayed in F. until Abitur. After Abitur, I spent two or three years in which I did not quite know what I wanted. I went to Israel and lived on a kibbutz with my non-Jewish girlfriend, then back to Germany. I tried out a number of things, working in a hospital, working on a farm, doing very different sorts of things. Then I decided to study architecture. This was a rather complex and cumbersome process, but in the end, I got admitted to the program in H.

OBSERVER: I think going to H. had to do with some other things as well. Motti's former girlfriend, Irit, formerly a close friend also of Dina's, was from H., and he visited her there often.

MOTTI: Let me go back to F. for a minute. As I mentioned, just as for my siblings and some of my cousins, the ZJD in F. was very important for me. I would bet that in the interviews, neither my siblings nor my cousins had much to say to you about their bar mitzvahs or their rabbis or religious instruction, but a lot about the ZJD. In F., the Jewish community was very small, with totally uninspiring Hebrew teachers and so on. There was also no religious orientation in that community; that is, there was really only one family that was truly religiously oriented, and that was the S. family. The remainder were either oriented toward Zionist Youth or else they were on the path to assimilation.

With our parents, we did not normally go to synagogue except on the High Holidays. As far as I am concerned, it was not so much my environment that made me Jewish and which defined Jewishness for me; it really was distinctively my family that defined me as a Jew. For me, this community would never really have been of any significance if there had not also been the Zionist Youth group. With this youth group, I did a lot. I was really active there, basically this started when I turned twelve or thirteen. All I did during winter breaks and summers was to go on machanot, and I became a madrich and so on.

Also, through the ZJD, you could build friendships with Jews elsewhere in Germany. In this way, you were not dependent on those few

Jews in F. We in F. were in contact with kids in Munich, but through the ZJD, we were also in touch with people, say, in Cologne, Düsseldorf, and Frankfurt. My girlfriend was in H. I was sixteen, seventeen at the time, she was two or three years younger than me. We really were a young couple all in love. This was my entire life at the time, the Zionist Youth.

Incidentally, the reason why my parents moved from F. to Munich must have had to do with that as well, because there was nothing going on in F., as far as the Jewish community was concerned. So they moved to Munich, even though most of their business activities are still located in F.

But then, at the same time, there was that life in school. I developed important friendships there, with non-Jewish classmates, friendships that have lasted until today. I experienced almost no open anti-Semitism. It is more like everyone knew that I am a Jew. And as soon as a Jewish topic came up in class, they simply looked at me, so I had to react. Someone only had to mention the word "Jew" or any Jewish topic, and they expected a reaction from me. Or at least I thought that; it seemed they did, they looked at how I was reacting. I was the one who was really being addressed. And in school, we were five Jews at the most, the majority were Kalmans.

AFTER ABITUR

There was a void which developed because the ZJD was not there anymore

As I mentioned, after Abitur I spent time in different places, from an Israeli kibbutz to a German farm, working in a hospital and also getting into different relationships. I think there was a void which developed because the ZJD was not there anymore and because I was not all that interested in religiously Jewish matters. Because of that, the contact with Jewish people diminished, and this continued until I came to H. Here in H., I resumed contact with friends whom I still knew, and because of that, my Jewish life became more active again, but not in an organized way. I did not have anything to do with the Jewish Student Association, but I am in touch with the Jewish community on holidays or, let's say, when there is a Jewish bazaar or the like.

There was also a group that called itself the Kritischen Juden, like the Jüdische Gruppen elsewhere in Germany. I had heard of one of the figures there, A. G., who had also been living in Israel, an older guy who was active in progressive causes like the Liga für Menschenrechte. I knew him because we were both involved with Benevolencija Sarajevo. But that group of critical Jews . . . I was there once, but these people were too old for me, the socializing aspect is important to me, and so I did not feel too comfortable there, and also I did not know anyone there.

BENEVOLENCIJA SARAJEVO

It is a reversal of history, because this time it is the Jews who are helping Christians and Moslems to survive

In 1995, I came to be involved with Benevolencija Sarajevo. Otherwise I am not politically active. I am not a member of a party, not politically involved. Benevolencija is the philanthropic organization of the Jewish community there, founded about one hundred years ago, especially by the Sephardic Jews of Sarajevo. It was the aid organization for the poor Jews of the city, it more or less disappeared under Tito, and now, before the war in the former Yugoslavia, it was reactivated. It has not only taken care of the needs of the Jewish community, but also, far beyond, it first of all took a neutral position, and then took care of the entire population around the Jewish community. The Jewish community by now is very small, just a couple hundred people.

For me, it began when I heard an interview on the radio, about Benevolencija, and through the radio station I established contact with a guy from Vienna who worked for them in Sarajevo for a while. So I really got involved, and we founded an association, friends of mine and I. We collected money and began to develop a support network. We are not the only ones doing this. The point is to support the Jewish community there and to ensure that Benevolencija can continue its work there. You realize this is all done outside the Jewish community in Germany. It does not have anything to do with the Jewish community, nothing at all. In fact, right from the start, we tried to establish contact with the Jewish community in H., but it never went further than visitors from Sarajevo being invited by them for lunch. So it went nowhere. Basically, there is no support at all. I also have the feeling that the German Jewish communities are very much preoccupied with themselves. In fact, I really asked myself, why are we so preoccupied with ourselves. A lot of money is being spent here, but it is all concentrated on Israel, and the typical reaction there is, why don't they simply all move to Israel.

In our work on behalf of Benevolencija, what is interesting to me is that very intentionally, we did not represent it as a Jewish organization that is only working for Jews. That is what is so exciting, and Ed Serotta, who is involved with it, always stresses that. He says it is a reversal of history because this time it is the Jews who are helping Christians and Moslems to survive. So I was saying earlier that families distribute roles among members. You have my brother's Zionism, my sister's continuation of my parents' life, and perhaps my insistence on the legitimacy of Jewish Diaspora life.

THE KALMANS

Whoever survived this has great difficulties in resolving conflicts

You are asking me about the Kalman side of my family, but you have to realize that in our family, the ties to my mother's family, the Zysmans, are far more important to us. On my mother's side, I have a real family, and with various forms of contact, basically with the generation of the cousins of my mother. All of them are considerably younger than my mother, as much as thirty years younger. In my grandfather's generation, there was an older sister who lived in Israel, and I am in touch with her daughter — not that intensively anymore, but we always got along very well, and am in close contact both with Lily in Israel and with Elise in Paris. Here in H. there are three children of the youngest brother of my grandfather. These kids all studied at Brandeis University in the U.S., but now, the eldest has taken over his father's business. It was sporting goods and clothes. The second son is involved with real estate, buying and renovating houses, selling or renting them.

As far as the Kalman side is concerned, that is a totally sad story, having survived together, and now this. I have thought about that again. I believe the three brothers were not in a position to resolve conflicts. Now this sounds very general. I don't know, but I believe whoever survived this has great difficulties in resolving conflicts. For a few years, the brothers were able to work together, because the roles among them were defined in that Albert was a kind of ersatz father. At least he was for my father because he was considerably older. He was also the main initiator. But if you really want a good picture of this family, you must interview my aunt Gertrud in Brooklyn. In my view it would be interesting because that part of the family was principled and left Germany.

For some time, my most important relationship with any of my Kalman cousins was with Dina. Since we both moved to H., we got in touch with each other after about fifteen years, and I think in terms of mentality, of all the cousins, I am closest to Dina. This concerns the question of living in Germany and also because we both share artistic and intellectual interests. For some time now, we are no longer in contact, I don't know why, but I believe Dina cannot separate me and our family history. All the grudges and reproaches that exist cannot be separated from me. There were again and again accusations on different grounds directed against me, not related so much to the family history as to the way I relate to her. That I don't do this when I do that, that I am too distant or too close. Most of all, somehow I had become an ersatz brother to Dina, and this is something I did not provide for her. I cannot provide that for her, that is not me. In the fall of 1999, I ran into Dina near a lake with her new baby and Johannes. But she immediately started accusing me of all sorts of things and I just left.

As far as the other cousins are concerned, Berthold, Ronnie, and Gabriel, I have no particular relation to them, I can't do much with them. Those three and Salek I met last on my father's birthday, but nothing ever comes of it. Being together once in ten years does not bring anything, nothing where one could pick up from and from which to continue or so. I really like Salek, though. Cornelia feels the same way. He is simply a character somehow. A very special, very original type, and I like that about him. Of all the cousins, Salek and I are the exact opposite of one another: Salek is the total externalizer, who throws all his aggression to the outside, whereas I direct all my aggression onto myself. With Esther, on the other hand, I always feel she presents herself as someone who she really is not. Although my brother Jonny and my cousin Esther both grew up in F., both made aliyah, both live in Israel, there is minimal contact between them. I believe they are really strangers to each other, and Israel has not brought them together, quite the contrary.

Here in Germany, my situation is not much different from that of my other cousins. The Jewish community is not differentiated enough, not culturally diverse enough to offer different paths for living one's Jewishness, or of starting and having a family outside the traditional structures. It is a kind of unfreedom, or that is how I find it. If you do not live here as a Jew in a relatively traditional manner and at peace with the Jewish environment, if you don't do that, you find yourself pretty quickly at the margins. I believe the Kalmans here in Germany all fail on that point, that is, Berthold, Ronnie, Gaby, and I. We are faced with these conflictual structures. Or we are failing, but what does that really mean?

Personally, I am trying to grapple with these conflictual situations in my own way. In my case it means that for over eight years now I have been involved in psychoanalysis and that I am trying, slowly, to understand things. It is an important part of my dealing with my own self. It means I am trying to deal with this actively and to get it under control.

IDENTITY IN GERMANY

This is a life that is here for me, and I am
trying to find out why I am here

I think from everything that I have told you so far it should be clear that I do not live without conflict and ambivalences here in Germany. I can illustrate that with how I experienced the Wende, the fall of the Wall. I was in Zurich at the time. Well, I did like the fact that Berlin was open all of a sudden. I did not like the situation of the closed city. Somehow, I think that the division of Germany was a piece of historical punishment that has now been canceled. You could say it is almost like a stigma that has been effaced. When it happened, I could not say that I did not begrudge the Germans their unification. I do not say it with joy, I could not say, great, Germany is once again a big country. It is a general fear, not only a Jewish fear in the face of an overly strong Germany, but on the other hand one also should not exaggerate that fear.

Given my ambivalences about Germany, you might ask, why did I not emigrate to Israel? How do you explain that? I think I am more tied to Germany than my brother. Psychologically, I have always been here more than my brother. I have always had more contact here and something within me is at home here. That's it. Some of these issues arise when I am looking at my own future, marrying, having children, and so on. There is that wish. And that is more difficult in the moment where you live together with a non-Jewish woman; you have to reconcile that with the claims of the family and also with your own needs; that is more difficult. Especially the question how you bring up the children, how do you give the children a Jewish education. In 1999, we were in the U.S. on a photography project, and I think in America, this is a lot easier; it is not that unusual there that the woman is not Jewish, and the husband is Jewish and the children are being raised as Jews. Within the spectrum of American Jewry, this is certainly more common there than here. Here, the woman normally must convert at least, and my partner would not do that. She would not be opposed to bringing the kids up Jewish, though, and we'll have to find a format for that, it is not that easy. I find it difficult; I can no longer simply do what I want. At the latest, the conflict arises when one has to decide, shall one go home for Pessach or not.

LILIAN: For Motti, marrying a non-Jewish woman . . . The other day, when Mom returned from a visit with Motti in H., we talked about that issue. I actually do believe it does not matter to my parents. They say, if he finds someone with whom he is happy, then that is okay. In earlier years that might have been different. It will be a real issue when they want to have children, and I think this is most important to him. I mean, if it is a non-Jewish woman, he will have non-Jewish children, and it begins with the birth, with bar mitzvah, that is very difficult.

MOTTI: In contrast to what I have seen in America, I believe that the form of Jewish life in Germany is very much determined and defined by the Holocaust. In Germany, you have to find a way within this particular constraint. You have to find a way where you can say, okay, I am a Jew, that is how it is. It is defined by and coming from my history, but I am living my Jewishness for myself, in a form in which I want to live it. That form should not be defined by the traumas suffered by my parents and by the assumption that in Germany you can be Jewish only in one very particular manner.

Q: *So at the same time then, you live here, as a Jew in Germany — is that or is that not a problem for you? I am also thinking of Ezer Weizman's speech, on his visit to Germany, that Jews should not live in Germany.*

Of course it is a problem for me. But I don't have the feeling that someone can dictate whether I am allowed to live here or not. It is my decision to live or not to live here, and I also don't believe Germany should generally be "judenfrei," without Jews. The question of Jewish life in Germany or not is a hypothetical question, because in fact it exists, and it exists more and more. There were attempts to stop this life from developing, and the idea of the packed suitcases was maintained as a pseudo-ideology, but I myself don't have a packed suitcase under my bed. As far as my family goes, it was often hinted that one could leave Germany at any time in case it would get more difficult here, but it never turned into a concrete plan. Much of it depended on what the children would do. It is possible that if we had all gone to Israel, my parents would have followed. At the point where none of us had set out on their own career path, there was in fact no time where we would have said, okay the family is going to move. In this respect, our story is probably not that different from that of most Eastern European Jews who were stranded here after the war.

This is a life that is here for me, and I am trying to find out why I am here and also perhaps, what sense it makes for me to be here. There is this talk about Jews in Germany being "foreign in their own land." I would turn this totally the other way: "at home in a foreign land." This in turn relates to the debate, are we German Jews or Jews in Germany? For me, "German Jews" still has the connotation of this strong cultural connectedness to Germany. I have that connection only in a limited manner. With me, it is not based on some tradition; I am not descended from a German Jewish family, but from Eastern European Jews. On the other hand, I am also more, in fact, than just a "Jew in Germany." This has not all been settled yet.

A VISIT TO AUSCHWITZ

In the family, I am the one who knows the most

Q: *Have there been any experiences, broadly speaking, in the background of the families of your parents and grandparents that have shaped you in any way?*

Experiences that have put a stamp on me, that is how I would put the question. My father survived labor camps and the concentration camp, my mother was liberated in Auschwitz. That experience has put a stamp on my parents and it is there in me. Much in my thinking and in my actions circles around that and is one of the reasons why I am in Germany. Something in me is attempting to grasp that and to come to terms with it. It is good to be in Germany for that, because you have to do it here more often. It is made less easy here not to be doing that.

In our family, I have the task, whatever the grounds of these psychological functions might be, I am the one. I have to take account and rework, I have to carry the memory. Three years ago, on the fiftieth anniversary of the liberation of Auschwitz, my mother, together with my father, took a trip to Poland. I was the one who went with them. I'd say this is symptomatic. We were in Auschwitz and Cracow and in Slawkusz, in the places where our family is from. Astonishingly, going there was easier in a way than I had thought. My parents felt surprisingly comfortable in Poland. They talked to people, they communicated incredibly often and must have had many childhood memories. There were no old acquaintances or families. Nobody. And I believe my father did not even want to meet anybody. The entire thing was a little like being drunk. Everything went by very quickly; we were in Slawkusz for no more than one hour or maybe two, the point simply was to see that again and to see the parental house once again, to describe to me how it had once been, and to leave.

As far as our trip to Auschwitz is concerned, my mother and I had very different reactions. For my mother, the fear of going there was greater than being there, the pain of being there. I don't know exactly what she has gone through there. At any rate, they returned from Poland and resumed their normal life. For me, this was not possible. It must have taken me at least four or five months until I found my way back to my normal life again. To have seen that and to continue, to get busy again with normal everyday life, to put that back together. I find that difficult.

Q: *In earlier years, in your family, was there much talk about that experience?*

Not really, at least until the Holocaust TV series was broadcast here in Germany, in 1979. This goes not just for the Germans, but for the Jews as well in general, I think. In my family, there was relatively little, and what's being talked about is always the history of survival, not a description of suffering. It is always the history of surviving. Of course it was talked about at some length, not merely in asides. And more intuitively, I have always done that, and have also spoken a lot with my grandmother. I always wanted to know about it, and in the family, I am the one who knows the most. I myself have data and also images and pictures somehow, nothing that is whole, just fragments of memory.

THE BERLIN HOLOCAUST MEMORIAL PROJECT

I was interested in the oral tradition, and the attempt
to continue to live with it

Q: *Toward the end of my first interview with you, we drifted into questions of two Jewish architectural projects, the Jewish Museum and Daniel Libeskind, its architect, and the National Holocaust Memorial in Berlin. At the time, in 1996, of all of the 450 proposals that had come in for the memorial, the German jurors originally had awarded the first prize to the giant, sliding concrete slab alluding to a tombstone, covering an area of almost two soccer fields, to be built adjacent to the Brandenburg Gate in Berlin.*

I found that concrete slab terrible. That was a totally horrendous idea, totally horrendous. I feel very strongly about the memorial, and though you may not know it, I had submitted a proposal myself. I'll show it to you, let's go to the other room.

My initial idea was the annihilation of European Jewry; how can you represent that? And then I hit on the idea of the different languages. European Jewry had spoken all those different languages, Hebrew, Yiddish, Ladino, all these were languages of the Jews in Europe. Then my idea was to create, in an abstract form, a railroad platform. And on the girders, I proposed to mount loudspeakers from where you would hear peoples' reports of what they had experienced, in all European languages plus Hebrew plus Yiddish plus Ladino, chaotically, all mingled together. The girders would lead you in here, into a very dark room, and to have a documentation center there. A room where you would always have a new debate with this topic, an artistic debate, and in a room that would always be used differently. In short, I was interested in the oral tradition, the attempt to understand that rationally, and the attempt to continue to live with it. So I wanted to return the diverse voices to the silent victims. It is the total opposite of a tombstone.

Glossary

Abitur graduation from Gymnasium

aliyah Hebrew: "ascent"; immigration to Israel

Arbeitslager (Nazi) labor camp

Ashkenazim Jews of German-speaking origin

bar/bat mitzvah religious coming of age ceremony for boys/girls

Betar revisionist (right-wing) Zionist Youth organization in Poland

CDU Christian Democratic (conservative) Party in Germany

chevra kadisha Jewish burial society

cholent a dish eaten on shabbat

Einheitsgemeinde Orthodox and liberal streams of Judaism in one Gemeinde

Gemeinde here: local Jewish community in Germany

get divorce according to religious law

goy non-Jew

Gymnasium upper stream high school

hachshara Hebrew: "preparation," "training"; here, immigration to Israel

halacha Jewish religious law

Hanukkah festival of lights (in December)

Hassid, Hassidim orthodox mystical stream in Judaism

heimish at home, familiar

Jabotinski, Ze'ev leader of Revisionist Zionists

Judenrat Nazi-appointed Jewish community councils

Kapo concentration camp inmates appointed by SS to supervisory function

kashrut the system of Jewish dietary laws

Kinderlager children's camp within concentration camps

kippa religious head covering

kosher Hebrew: "suitable"; in conformity with kashrut

Kultusgemeinde synonymous with Gemeinde

Lubavitcher Rebbe religious leader in the Chabad Hassidic movement

machané, machanot (Jewish Youth) camps

madrich Hebrew: "instructor," "leader"; here, leaders in youth
  movement

mezuza encased Hebrew inscription placed on door post

Nachmann, Werner former leader of Jewish community in Germany,
  accused of corruption

olim (chadashim) new immigrants to Israel

Ostjuden East European Jews

Pessach Jewish holiday

peula meeting; here, in youth group

peyes Hebrew: *pe'ot;* side locks

RAB camp camp for construction of Reichsautobahn (highways during
  Nazism)

Sephardim Jews of Spanish origin

Selektion here, sending inmates to their deaths

shechita ritual slaughter

shiva seven-day mourning period

shaliach (pl. shlichim) Hebr. "messenger" sent from Israel to Jewish
  communities abroad

shoichet, shokhet Jewish slaughterer

shul synagogue

siddur prayer book

tallit prayer shawl

tikkun to mend, correct, improve

treife non-kosher

ulpan Hebrew: "school"; Hebrew language course

Unterscharführer, Oberscharführer military ranks in ss

WIZO Women's International Zionist Organization

yahrzeit anniversary of death

Yiddishkait Jewishness

Yeckes German jews

ZJD Zionist Youth in Germany

Y. MICHAL BODEMANN is Professor of Sociology at the University of Toronto. He is the author of *In den Wogen der Erinnerung: Jüdische Existenz in Deutschland* (Deutscher Taschenbuch Verlag, 2002); *Out of the Ashes: The Vicissitudes of the New German Jewry* (Institute of the World Jewish Congress, 1997), and *Gedächtnistheater: Die jüdische Gemeinschaft und ihre deutsche Erfindung* (Rotbuch, 1996). He is the editor of *Jews, Germans, Memory: Reconstructions of Jewish Life in Germany* (University of Michigan, 1996).

Library of Congress Cataloging-in-Publication Data

Bodemann, Y. Michal,
A Jewish family in Germany today : an intimate portrait /
Y. Michal Bodemann.
p. cm.
Includes bibliographical references.
ISBN 0-8223-3410-0 (cloth : alk. paper)
ISBN 0-8223-3421-6 (pbk. : alk. paper)
1. Kalman family. 2. Jews — Germany — Biography. 3. Jews — Germany — History — 20th century. 4. Holocaust survivors — Germany — Biography. 5. Children of Holocaust survivors — Germany — Biography. I. Title.
DS135G5K353 2005
305.892'4043'0922 — dc22   2004011845